D0416857

NB

Young Irelands: Studies in Children's Literature

Also in this series:

Young Irelands

Studies in Children's Literature

Mary Shine Thompson

EDITOR

FOUR COURTS PRESS

Set in 10.5 on 12.5 Ehrhardt for
FOUR COURTS PRESS
7 Malpas Street, Dublin 8, Ireland
www.fourcourtspress.ie
and in North America for
FOUR COURTS PRESS
c/o ISBS, 920 N.E. 58th Avenue, Suite 300, Portland, OR 97213.

ISBN 978-1-84682-141-7

Printed in England by
Antony Rowe Ltd, Chippenham, Wilts.

Contents

6   *Contents*

Preface

This book was undertaken with the support of the Irish Society for the Study of Children's Literature and especially with the support of the members of its board. St Patrick's College, Drumcondra provided financial aid towards its publication. The editor of the volume wishes to thank Four Courts Press, the contributors to this volume and the readers of the essays, and in particular A.J. Piesse.

Introduction: childhood and the nation

MARY SHINE THOMPSON

This is the fourth collection in the Studies in Children's Literature series, a series that has been a vehicle for progressing scholarly debate on children's literature studies. The first book in the series[1] was also the first collection of critical essays in Ireland on children's literature addressed primarily to the academy, and subsequent volumes have gone on to identify some central preoccupations of its scholarship, as well as offering an opportunity for emerging critics to find a readership. By including essays from established and prestigious international scholars, the series proclaimed its intention that children's literature studies, a latecomer to critical forums in Ireland, should have a voice in Irish Studies. Significantly, this series also underlined its international context right from the beginning.

Previous collections of essays explored the influential concepts of the Irish nation and of childhood that evolved rapidly in the nineteenth century and that took forms during that century that are still recognizable and that continue to inform approaches to attitudes to the formation of the young. This book returns to the enduring and evolving issues of nation and childhood, hence its title, *Young Irelands*. The book examines how various texts read by children since the eighteenth century reflect concepts of Irish national and/or imperial identity, how they resist the empire and the nation's normative concepts; it also explores how non-Irish readers receive Irish children's books.

Certain common factors have influenced the evolution of the concepts of childhood and the nation, and a relationship has developed between them that is complex, contradictory, and suffused with anxiety. Both have attracted considerable attention independently of each other. Both have been idealized, yet are also perceived sites of negativity, lack, and inadequacy. In both instances, complexities have been elided. Each in its own way embodies a past to be remembered, a future intended to commemorate and retain an organic link with that past, and a present containing the essence of the past and the hope of a better future, but shaped in its likeness. Childhood provided nineteenth-century nationalist Ireland with a ready suite of metaphors and with an important vehicle for promoting and embedding its ideals.

---

1 Celia Keenan and Mary Shine Thompson (eds), *Studies in Children's Literature, 1500–2000*; Shine Thompson and Keenan (eds), *Treasure Islands: studies in children's literature*; Shine Thompson and Valerie Coghlan (eds), *Divided Worlds: studies in children's literature* (Dublin: Four Courts Press, 2004, 2006, 2007 respectively).

The ideology of sovereign, independent nationhood was widespread throughout Europe, including Ireland, in the nineteenth century, and culture – legend and myth, art, language and literature – was a key instrument in promoting and popularizing it. The Young Ireland movement, which has given us the title for this collection of essays, played a key role in disseminating cultural nationalism in Ireland, and it embodies attitudes to Irish culture, especially literature, that came to wield considerable influence on young people's educational experience. The Young Ireland movement – which was short-lived – had its roots in the Repeal Association founded by Daniel O'Connell in 1840 that campaigned for the repeal of the Union between Great Britain and Ireland, and it disbanded after an unsuccessful rising in 1848, in the aftermath of Ireland's debilitating and traumatizing famine of 1845–8. Whereas O'Connell believed in constitutional nationalism, the Young Irelanders were more influenced by romantic nationalism, and most notably German nationalists such as J.G. Fichte and J.G. Von Herder. The movement was informed by a broad cultural agenda, and to this end created a body of literature, especially verse in English, which enjoyed huge popularity and which became embedded in school curricula until the second half of the twentieth century. Its chief vehicle was a newspaper, *The Nation*, which began publication in 1842. Among the movement's leading figures were educationalists, intellectuals and writers, including Thomas Davis, John Blake Dillon, Charles Gavan Duffy, William Smith O'Brien, poet James Clarence Mangan, and Speranza (Lady Wilde, mother of Oscar Wilde, whose fairy tales are explored in this volume). Its membership was predominantly bourgeois and male and its economic policies generally conservative: its tenets included property ownership, for example.

Young Ireland set about overcoming the suffering of Ireland's recent colonial past by positing the hope of a glorious future in which the people of a sectarian, poverty-ridden Ireland would be united. In the process it elevated the role of educated intellectuals, such as the movement's leaders, in assimilating the various and contradictory elements of that past. Differentiating Ireland's political, ethical and cultural agenda from that of its imperial neighbour, Britain, was central to its plan. Cultural nationalism was concerned with countering actual geographic possession of the land (the imperial process), with psychic possession (the nationalist process).[2] The treasures of Gaelic medieval scholarship, for example, were seen as evidence of a glorious tradition of learning stretching into pre-history that illustrated Ireland's superiority to its imperial ruler. By managing culture, and in particular print culture, ideas could be firmly embedded and power centralized – and so ideological and political change could be generated. For conservative radicals such as the Young Irelanders, print both defined and resisted the secular rule of law, and played a significant role in

2 See Edward Said, *Culture and Imperialism* (London: Vintage, 1994), pp 62–97. 'The actual geographical possession of land is what empire in the final analysis is all about', p. 78.

disseminating their radical politics. They recognized – as did imperial and religious groups and communities – that formal education was a key means whereby their power could be dispersed. It is little wonder therefore that education became a battleground for control of values in the nineteenth century and for constructing concepts of childhood.

The growth in print media and the formalization of education especially through the establishment the national schools system in 1831 and the increased influence of religious communities such as the Irish Christian Brothers as education providers created a new role for children as transmitters of culture, whether nationalist or imperial. Education was no longer the haphazard affair of the hedge school, or the prerogative of the more affluent, but a formal, formative process. Thomas Davis put the case for education bluntly: 'The cheapness of books is now such, that even Irish poverty is no excuse for Irish ignorance – that ignorance which prostrates us before England. We must help ourselves, and therefore we must educate ourselves.'3 While poverty, emigration and illiteracy were the reality of many Irish children, a literate Irish child was a model of both modernizing nationalism and of imperialism, an aspiration if not an expectation for youth from the 1830s onwards. Literacy therefore became an important instrument in shaping young people's identity, and at the same time childhood was a metaphor for the emerging nation.

Given Young Ireland's middle-class respect for cultural capital, it is predictable that literacy and the education of the young were integral to its agenda, and that it recognized that youth could be rallied to its cause; they saw a new role for the young as transmitters of nationalist ideology. 'Educate that you may be free', was Thomas Davis' dictum, repeated passionately throughout his writings, which were widely disseminated especially through the periodical *The Nation,* and through a system of community reading (whereby the literate read the penny paper to their neighbours). From the point of view of cultural nationalists, a people who could read and transmit to their young versions of their literary heritage – in ballad form and otherwise – had bridged the gap between their glorious literary past and the future. Their devotion to their literary legacy was living proof of its superiority and its right to nationhood that transcended time.

Literacy served the interests of the British empire equally, in that it was essential to an industrialized economy and to economic expansion. Writers such as Maria Edgeworth for example, writing for children a half-century before Young Ireland *floriat*, articulated clear pedagogies for shaping an imperial-Irish child-identity that privileged values shared by the growing Catholic and liberal bourgeoisie. Davis might have adapted his maxim, 'educate

---

3 Thomas Osborne Davis, 'Influences of education', in T.W. Rolleston (ed.), *Thomas Davis: selections from his prose and poetry* (Dublin and London: Talbot Press, [1910]), pp 232–6, p. 236.

that you may be free', to read: 'educate that you may be free and also socially mobile'. Literacy was necessary to Britain in order to maintain and manage the furthest corners of its empire; in Ireland, the right kind of imperial education was seen as a means of containing and defusing resistance, and of moulding loyal children. So from the 1840s the Commissioners for National Education's textbooks, which contained prescribed curricula, extolled Britain's literary greatness. However, as the century progressed, the influential teaching community of the Christian Brothers, for example (which distanced itself from the non-denominational national school system and provided a strongly nation-alistic Catholic education for their boys, mostly drawn from among the poor), set itself the task of shaping a Catholic middle class with unequivocal nationalist leanings, modifying the Young Ireland nondenominational philosophy but drawing on its writings. Literacy was a necessary if insufficient condition of progress and modernization, and of the vision of a future independent Irish nation.

CHILDHOOD AND THE NATION

The nationalist child then, was one construct that was central to a new kind of future and that interacted with other prevalent concepts of childhood. To the socially mobile middle classes, both nationalists and imperial, children were the key to production of future wealth and capital culture, empty vessels to be filled, consumers of cultural, educational and material goods and vehicles of social mobility. As objects of affection, they provided adults with sites for the explo-ration of sentiment and nostalgia – and Young Ireland's nationalism was grounded in sentiment and nostalgia. Childhood is therefore a conflicted site, in which communal and individual adult hopes and expectations vie with their disappointment and perceived failure. However, childhood played another role in the nationalist agenda, in that it provided a cluster of metaphors for the emerging nation, and an instrument whereby nationalism might be transmitted. Many of these metaphors underlined anxieties at the core of nation creation. For example, the ever-changing complexities and contradictions of modernity, embodied in the changing individual, are more pronounced in children: every child embodies the growth of individual subjectivity and autonomy. In every child is evident the possibility of improvement, growth and change; as such he or she is a ready symbol of progress and possibility, but also an affirmation of present inadequacy and imperfection. Children are weak, vulnerable, in need of care and attention, and the low status of childhood exists in an uneasy asymmet-rical relationship to adulthood, thereby providing a ready symbol of inferiority. However, expressed in Romantic terms, childhood is the idealized past, a state of innocence and Edenic wildness. It is the 'natural' that is at odds with the excesses of industrialized modernity, and precedes current structures of socialization, exemplifying the point of origin to which a people might return if they are to divest themselves of malign imperial influence. The manner in which childhood constantly replenishes itself with a continuing tide of new births is comparable to the enduring quality of a nation, whose citizenry too is continually renewed. The tropes of nineteenth-century European nationhood – seen as elemental, natural and untainted by enlightenment ideology – are also the tropes of evolving Romantic concepts of childhood.

The construct of childhood was invaluable in other ways to emerging nationalist ideologies. Children embody the historicization of the nation, reinvented as enduring truths that its citizens hold, but also as a modernizing, acutely temporal entity. Children also exemplify various manifestations of collectivity: from an imperial perspective the colonized nation is like a child, in need of a steadying hand; on the other hand, the emerging nation is likely to see itself as the personification of youthful strength and as architect of the future. In such situations, imperial power becomes less a guiding hand than a heavy boot.

THE DILEMMAS

Of course childhood construed as a supporting pillar of nationalism is not without its problems for an emerging nation intent on forging its separate identity, as the contradictions and paradoxes already described suggest. Childhood is time-bound and timeless, temporal and provisional, and as such responds to the double dilemma of nationhood as articulated by Homi Bhabha. He observes that the past can be encountered as an anteriority that continually introduces an otherness or alterity into the present. He then poses the question, how does one narrate the present as a form of contemporaneity that is neither punctual nor synchronous?[4] Bhabha's question foments anxiety about the otherness of the children of an emerging nation: their education was intended to prepare them for the role of shaping the nation, yet they are regularly identified as other, lacking, continually changing, the embodiment of adults' past, an image of its early history. Joy Alexander's essays illustrates this point in that it shows how Arthur Mee, whose encyclopedic publications were intended to educate children on the greatness of the British empire, regards children as a race apart, at a remove from adult concerns; his instructive manuals were intended to limit the disruption that their otherness might create. What is clearly articulated by Mee is implicit in the work of many other writers considered in this collection of essays, Edgeworth and C.S. Lewis among them. So how could they be

---

4 Homi Bhabba, *The Location of Culture* (London, New York: Routledge, 2004, 1st pub. 1994), p. 226.

absorbed into the project of nationalism without punctuating it or underlining its contradictions? Childhood underlined certain dilemmas that creating a unified identity for the nation posed. As inadequate latecomers, children are characterized by the signs of Jacques Derrida's arrivant: the arrivant calls 'into question, to the point of annihilating or rendering indeterminate, all the distinctive signs of a prior identity, beginning with the very border that delineated a legitimate home and assured lineage, names and languages, nations, families and genealogies'.[5] As a shifting minority that history has tended to denigrate or marginalize, children antagonize 'the implicit power to generalize, to produce the sociological solidity'.[6] When they enter the realm of discourse they do so by a process that Bhabha calls supplementation, that is, not what will 'add up' but what might 'disturb the calculation'.

Power operated through the process of managing children's otherness and channelling it into the nationalist and imperial discourses of Ireland; as Bhabha noted, supplementation may renegotiate the 'times, terms and traditions through which we turn our uncertain, passing contemporaneity into the signs of history'.[7] As latecomers, as those inhabiting the limit, children perform an important role. The nation needs to 'perform' the unity of its people, to interpellate or address the 'contentious, unequal interest and identities within the population'.[8] Children embody both this inequality and an opportunity to 'perform' unity. They also provide the means, as Carolyn Steedman has observed. Developments in scientific thought in the nineteenth century showed that childhood was a stage of growth and development common to all of us, abandoned and left behind, but at the same time a core of the individual's psychic life, always immanent, waiting there to be drawn on in various ways.[9]

To prepare them to adopt responsibility for the nation's future, children had to be moulded in the image of the nation's proud heritage. This presented nationalists with at least two practical challenges. It meant that the nation had to simplify its cultural capital in order to make it amenable to the limited capabilities of the young, but at the same time, it meant that cultural capital had to retain those elements that made it desirable and unique, powerful and unchanging. It had to be simple, but not over-simplified. Second, that cultural capital had to be made available in the English language. Young Ireland and other cultural revivalists realized that the 'great gaps in Irish song' that it perceived were owed to the fact that the emerging nation's cultural capital was in Irish language, and therefore inaccessible to many among its ranks, especially in the modernizing middle classes. Translation was integral, therefore, to the shaping of the nation and to the transmission of its cultural capital to younger citizens. That process

5 Jacques Derrida, *Aporias*, tr. Thomas Dutoit (Stanford, CA: Stanford UP, 1993), p. 34. 6 Bhabha, *Location*, p. 223. 7 Ibid. 8 Ibid., p. 146. 9 Carolyn Steedman, *Childhood, Culture, and Class in Britain: Margaret McMillan, 1860–1931* (Rutgers NJ: Rutgers UP, 1990), p. 64.

created dilemmas, of which one is captured by Derrida in a discussion on the translation of texts: 'A text lives only if it lives *on* [*sur-vit*] and lives *on* if it is at once translatable and untranslatable ... Totally translatable, it disappears as a text, as a writing, as a body of language [*langue*]. Totally untranslatable, even within what is believed to be one language, it dies immediately.'[10] The problem of 'translating' heritage to make it amenable to children added a further layer of complexity. In this book Ciara Ní Bhroin's essay on the translations of *Táin Bó Cuailgne* (Cattle Raid of Cooley), the oldest Irish epic, Emer O'Sullivan's on the process of translation of contemporary Irish children's novels for a German readership, Coralline Dupuy's on translation into French, Aedín Clements on the circulation of Padraic Colum's folktales and myths in the United States and Mary Shine Thompson's on the history of *Gulliver's Travels* as a children's book, all offer insight into the challenges that making over iconic literature for the young creates.

Because an expectation of the children of a new nation is that they act as conduits of the spirit of the nation that is anterior to themselves, they need to develop dispositions that enable them to undertake that role. This in turn requires that they be taught to adopt certain modes of citizenship and types of subjectivity. In short, they have to be both compliant (to accept the nation's norms) but, paradoxically, also to be leaders, to lead the nation out of subjugation into the future, along clearly defined paths; to be leaders a capacity for independent thought and initiative is a necessary trait. So nationalists and imperialists intending to shape young minds ought defuse these antinomies, and in a form amenable to the young.

If the concept of Ireland as a nation was to be seen as natural and inevitable in the nineteenth and early twentieth centuries, then the means by which that unity was manifest ought appear 'natural' also. It ought not be perceived in terms of Enlightenment culture, that recent and acutely impartial form of rationality, but rather residing in the people who are awoken like fairy-tale characters from the sleep of centuries by handsome princes that were the latterday nationalists. The 'naturalness' of the romantic construct of childhood, which saw it as wild, untamed, at one with nature, held considerable appeal for nationalists. One problem, however, was that formal education – approved by the state in the form of the National School system and by religious orders such as the Irish Christian Brothers – contravened Rousseauesque principles of child formation. Jean-Jacques Rousseau disapproved of formal education and specifically of literacy,[11] and the Young Irelanders and like-minded bourgeois and upwardly mobile parents were inveterate educators. A means had to be found to square this circle.

---

10 Jacques Derrida, *Living on Border Lines Deconstuction and Criticism*, ed. Harold Bloom (New York: Seabury, 1979), p. 102. 11 See for example Jean Jacques, *Émile; or, On Education*, 1st pub. 1762, intro., tr. and notes by Allan Bloom (London: Penguin, 1991).

A strategy adopted was to admit no disjunction between literacy and oracy, and to appear to put literacy at the service of oracy. Daniel O'Connell was the exemplary nineteenth-century orator who showed how the spoken word could be a great political force and whip up nationalist fervour at mass meetings. Rhetoric was an essential skill of a would-be leader. Young men were schooled in it as part of their broader education. As the century progressed, much of the literature that was absorbed into school and university curricula was rhetorical in nature, intended to be declaimed at *feiseanna* (traditional Gaelic art and culture festivals) and elsewhere, by the young learning to be nationalists. From a romantic perspective, children embodied the spirit of oracy, of the spoken word, so oracy was a 'natural' starting point for their education. A challenge, however, was how to enable them to be 'oral' through their encounters with the written texts of the literary revival.

This emphasis on oracy was evident in the appeal of the storyteller who mirrors at local and domestic level the charisma of the national leader, in that both could deploy the power of the spoken word. Yet the Young Ireland movement astutely used print media to spread its message; its leaders saw newspapers as the stimulating power in Ireland. It often reported nationalist speeches in its pages. 'Speeches are more effective', Thomas Davis declared, and immediately combined the power of speech with the circulatory strength of the journal: 'we include them among the materials of journalism'. The movement's newspaper, *The Nation*, founded in 1842, which contained newly written songs and stories in English intended to serve the movement's nationalist purpose, was hugely successful, having an estimated readership at one point of a quarter of a million, young and old.[12] The articles in this book – on writers as disparate as Oscar Wilde, James Joyce, Padraic Colum, and on contemporary writers such as Morgan Llywelyn and Kate Thompson, whom children encounter on the written page – draw on the distinctively oral tradition that was embodied in the Young Irelanders' nationalism.

THE SOLUTION

The Nation was one vehicle for establishing norms of behaviour and of valuable cultural capital that citizens themselves should internalize, but the value of reading matter specifically for children was also recognized. In this collection of essays, Marnie Hay's exploration of the propaganda of the Fianna, Ciara Ní Bhroin's examination of retellings of the *Táin*, and Aedín Clements on the writings of Ella Young and Padraic Colum underline how literature was

---

12 D. George Boyce, *Nationalism in Ireland* (London: Croom Helm; Dublin: Gill and Macmillan, 1982), pp 158-9.

deployed to promote nationalist principles in the late nineteenth and through the twentieth century. Anne Marie Herron's thesis, that Kate Thompson's fiction draws on a rich oral and literary tradition that unifies citizens, exemplifies how oracy within written texts continues to be a marker of nationalism. Reading matter intended specifically for the young is a visible and clearly identifiable means of establishing normative frameworks for promoting cultural nationalism, since a book is 'a node within a network'.[13] The discipline of children's literature has a further advantage. As D.A. Miller has pointed out: 'discipline attenuates the role of actual supervisors by enlisting the consciousness of its subjects in the work of supervision.'[14] This process of enlisting children's consciousness in the task of supervising the spread of nationalist feeling through the written word takes numerous forms, from pedagogic discourses through leisure reading to the crystallization of a canon of children's classics in the nineteenth and the early twentieth century. A canon was evidence of literary greatness, and it implied a norm of childhood that dialogued with the opposing and interlinked norms of nation and empire. Sharon Murphy shows how Maria Edgeworth's writings, for example, insist that by raising their sons and daughters properly Britain's (including Ireland's) parents perform a vital national and imperial duty, shaping the characters of the men and women upon whom the future of Britain and her empire depend.

The essays in this volume fall into three broad categories whose boundaries are permeable, and many of the texts analyzed could be comfortably accommodated by all three categories. The first is concerned with texts that promote the norms of empire and/or nation, and shows literature deployed as a tool of social management. The second contains essays that explore how certain texts for young people resist, subvert (to varying degrees) or ignore the pieties of nationalism and imperialism. The final category explores the ways in which modes of Irish childhood and children's books are interpreted, or translated, for non-Irish readerships.

NURTURING EMPIRE AND/OR NATION

Within the first category are two essays that examine how children's allegiance to the British empire is nurtured, one on the work of Maria Edgeworth, another on Arthur Mee. Sharon Murphy's essay focuses on Edgeworth's perception that the fate of the British empire pivots on the education of its youth, and on how her writings for children address this issue. Arthur Mee is the 'happy wonderer' intent on depositing useful facts in young imperial minds.

13 Michel Foucault, *The Archeology of Knowledge* (London: Tavistock, 1974), p. 23. 14 D.A. Miller, *The Novel and the Police* (Berkeley and Los Angeles: U California P, 1988), p. 18.

For Edgeworth and Mee, Ireland is integral to the empire, whereas four other articles, by Marnie Hay, Michael Flanagan, Ciara Ní Bhroin and Anne Marie Herron, address the nationalist agenda as it affects children's reading matter. Marnie Hay shows how the propaganda of the Irish National Boy Scout Movement, founded in 1909, and better known as Na Fianna, reflected many of the values of other pseudo-military youth groups across Europe at a time when war threatened. While Na Fianna drew on the cult of discipline, training and manliness that prevailed in these groups, it sought to create a movement that would play its part in liberating Ireland. Propaganda written for Na Fianna encouraged members to nurture the bourgeois values of thrift and cleanliness, and to disdain 'degenerate' Britain and Britons. Patriotism and morality were inextricably linked with middle-class values.

Ciara Ní Bhroin shows how the *Táin* is retold for children with a view to recovering a heroic past. Michael Flanagan links the representation of Gaelic 'authenticity' in the Christian Brothers' popular culture and educational periodical, *Our Boys*, with other popular visual representations of an idealized Gaelic Ireland. He shows how the highly defined sense of place in 'Tales Told in the Turflight' series of stories may be viewed in the light of independent Ireland's pursuit of an image by which the state could define itself despite the absence of overt political references in these stories.

Anne Marie Herron's analysis of the work of Kate Thompson, a novelist who grew up in Britain but whose home is in the west of Ireland, identifies Thompson as a literary descendant of the revivialist James Stephens, in that her fiction inserts itself into his tradition of fantasy and draws on similar mytho-logical figures and landscapes. Herron shows how Thompson's emphasis is didactic, in that Thompson sees fantasy and myth as providing young readers with 'psychological maps' of what it is to be human, and thereby helping them to cope with moral choice. While Thompson does not focus primarily on shaping national identity, and while her fiction enjoys considerable success interna-tionally, her emphasis on character formation and her privileging of distinctively Irish iconography go towards needs to 'perform' the unity of the people of Ireland in an increasingly multicultural context.

RESISTING NATIONALIST AND IMPERIALIST AGENDA

While some resistance to orthodoxies is a feature of many works of literature, certain texts consciously refuse to be assimilated into either a nationalist or imperialist agenda, and this book explores the work of four writers of such works. The works that they discuss disrupt to varying degrees and in diverse ways, processes of homogenization and thereby liberate and privilege the 'other'. Among these are Oscar Wilde's fairy tales, and Anne Markey explores their Irish and European echoes. She shows how the tales are cultural hybrids whose combination of Irish folkloric and international literary echoes creates an aesthetic complexity that enriches their exploration of selflessness and self-absorption. In the process, the tales treat of issues central to young Irelanders (in the broad sense endorsed in this book), since the late Victorian era, issues such as the use and abuse of power, the purpose of education, and the function of art. As such they do not facilitate simplistic forms of nationalist or imperialist sentiment, but rather educate readers in methods of interrogating it. Their affirmation of childlike innocence, and of charity and generosity divinely rewarded, stands in sharp contrast to the values overtly expressed in C.S. Lewis' Chronicles of Narnia, for example.

Lewis' use of allegory and his commitment to a kind of muscular Christianity associated with the courage and bravery valued in the British empire, leads to certain stridencies of tone and limits the success of the tales, as another essayist, Jane O'Hanlon, shows. As such, his fiction might have been considered within the first category outlined here, works that promote imperial or nationalist cause. However, O'Hanlon also argues that the genre that Lewis adopts, the fantasy novel, together with his humour and the traits and roles of some of his minor characters, facilitate resistant readings in which alternative models of selfhood are valorized and readers are invited to question the values that govern its society.

James Joyce's resistance to the pieties of nationalism and empire are well documented, but Valerie Coghlan's essay focuses on three picture-book editions of a little known and posthumously published children's story penned by Joyce, *The Cat and the Devil*, which draws on an international folk tale and had its origins in a letter from the writer to his grandson. Her exploration touches on its cosmopolitanism as well as its distinctively Irish features. It has the inhabitants of the French town of Beaugency duelling with the devil – and outwitting him. It touches on, inter alia, three illustrators' interpretations of the book and of the bridge motif that it shares with *Finnegans Wake*, showing how a simple tale can prompt numerous constructions of meaning, visual and writerly. The humour and irreverence of the story and of the illustrations playfully resist any attempt to see the tale as the site of formal learning. Although folk tales form part of the social discipline of modernizing nationalism, Joyce and Wilde refuse to allow them to serve nationalist or educational agenda, to be limited to stereotypes.

TRANSLATING IRISH IDENTITY

The process of translation carries additional resonances to the task of transforming culture. On the one hand it plays an important role in making it amenable to young people while not over-diluting it and ensuring continuity and respect for that culture. Seen in another way, translation interprets culture and identity. Two writers, Coralline Dupuy and Emer O'Sullivan, consider the consequences of the translation into French and German respectively of contemporary Irish fiction for young people, while Aedín Clements and Mary Shine Thompson examine the international reception of other key texts. Clements' focus is on the work of two writers of the Irish revival, Padraic Colum, and, to a lesser extent, Ella Young, as children's writers in the United States, while Shine Thompson documents the historical process whereby Jonathan Swift's *Gulliver's Travels*, acquires a double identity: it is an adult satirical text transformed into a children's classic: another form of cultural translation.

Emer O'Sullivan shows that the dominant strategy of translators into German of Siobhán Parkinson, Eoin Colfer and Roddy Doyle's fiction is to perform what she terms a linguistic colonialization, eliding the nuances that arise from playful, contemporary Hiberno-English vernacular in favour of a standard form of fluent, idiomatic German. The result is that certain German translations of these texts avoid challenging readers' expectations of how language is used, and instead opt to 'domesticate' the idiom of youth culture, an idiom that resists domestication in the original Hiberno-English. She also analyzes examples of successful divergences from this approach. When translators deploy techniques such as phonetic deviation and slang expressions to mark specifically Hiberno-English equivalents, when they intralingually translate interlingual translations, and when they provide metalinguistic commentaries, for example, they are accepting the otherness of the original and communicating it as a value to their readers.

Dupuy analyzes a translation of Llywelyn's novel *Cold Places* for a French young adult readership. She underlines the importance of location in the process of developing selfhood, and notes how French readers not only derive entertainment from her novel, but also *dépaysement*; an experience of being thrown into an alien world; the feeling of leaving one's country ('pays' in French) and of finding oneself 'sans pays', and immersing oneself into the universal themes dealt with by the author.

Clements draws on a wide range of reviews of Colum's work for children in the prestigious *Horn Book Magazine*, which promoted only what it considered 'good books', in order to assess their impact in the United State and also gives an insight into American reviewers' expectations of Irish literature for children. Padraic Colum was writing for children in the United States at a time when the Irish communities were socially mobile, but also when there were few representations of Irish characters in American children's fiction. Significantly, he underlines the oral quality of his tales with various devices, thereby highlighting their suitability for young readers. Clements shows how his work raised the status of the Irish communities in the United States by countering prevalent negative stereotypes, and she also credits his work with elevating the standing of Irish folklore. Colum's task is an example of a translation process, whereby he transmits Irish nationalist cultural capital to an increasingly influential diasporic community, at once making it amenable and attractive to new readerships and retaining its nationalist integrity.

Gulliver's Travels refuses to allow itself to be the normative literary event of a political, cultural or literary elite or a means of instruction for children, despite having been designated a sanctioned text in school curricula of both nationalists and imperialists. Its extraordinary success internationally is evidence of its plasticity, its readiness to take on local colour. The essay in this book shows how children both can absorb its authorized and transgressive meanings. It also suggests that the book interrogates the power imbalance between children and adults through its thematic emphasis on proportion. It reveals a widespread dismissive attitude towards children, but also shows that, with the alternative perspective of the young and less powerful readers come alternative proportions, since it is in the eye of the beholder that the proportion is perceived. So put in the hands of the young, *Gulliver's Travels'* satirical exposé of the limitations of Enlightenment rationality is carried a step further.

Taken together, these essays attest to the complexity and the contradictions of Ireland's identity as constructed for the young. They emphasize the challenge implicit in presenting concepts of national identity in forms amenable to children: these concepts needs must be simplified, edited, abridged, narra-tivized/re-narrativized, domesticated and yet retain their essential complex richness. In the process of exploring these issues that underlie the creation of national literature for the young, what also emerge from the essays are the diverse roles that children play in Ireland's evolution.

'The fate of empires depends on the education of youth': Maria Edgeworth's writing for children

SHARON MURPHY

There was once a writer called Maria Edgeworth (1768–1849), who enthralled readers, young and old alike, with her stories for children. This was because the heroes and heroines of these stories were appealing, and Edgeworth described their adventures in a way that was particularly exciting and vivid; it was also because Edgeworth and her father stressed the essential veracity of the stories, emphasizing that they were based upon the observation of children in the real world.[1] The popularity of Edgeworth's works for children can also be attributed to another factor, however, and this is that they both addressed and appeared to offer solutions to the socio-political problems of their era. When Edgeworth published her first work for children, *The Parent's Assistant*, in 1796, for instance, Britain was already at war with Revolutionary France, engaged in a conflict that would not be resolved without a further nine years of struggle. During these years, contemporaries keenly felt the threat of invasion by France, and were by no means certain it would prove possible to confine the French to their side of the English Channel. Like so many writers of the period, Edgeworth engaged with the issues that were raised by the spectre of Revolutionary France, in her case reassuring anxious readers that the proper education of Britons would produce that security upon which the good governance and prosperity of both the British nation and its Empire depended. 'All who have meditated on the art of governing mankind have been convinced, that the fate of empires depends on the education of youth', as Richard Lovell Edgeworth observed in his preface to *The Parent's Assistant*, quoting Aristotle, and his clear implication is that the truth of this would be proved by the tales that follow.[2]

This essay will consider a selection of Edgeworth's writing for children, exploring in particular the ways in which her little heroes and heroines – and their readers – are made to understand that there is always a national and imperial imperative to their education and subsequent behaviour. In works such

---

1 For my more detailed treatment of the Edgeworths' efforts in this regard, see S. Murphy, *Maria Edgeworth and Romance* (Dublin: Four Courts, 2004), especially pp 35–7 and 47–52.
2 R.L. Edgeworth, preface, *The Parent's Assistant* (1800) in E. Eger and C. Ó Gallchoir (eds), *The Novels and Selected Works of Maria Edgeworth*, 12 vols (London: Pickering & Chatto, 2003), x, p. 1. With two exceptions, noted below, further references to tales in *The Parent's Assistant* are to this Pickering & Chatto edition and are cited parenthetically in the text.

as *The Parent's Assistant* or *Harry and Lucy Concluded; being the last part of Early Lessons* (1825), as we shall see, children discover that there are inevitably public consequences to private actions, and that the decisions of individuals always affect their wider community. In impressing this point upon her readers, moreover, Edgeworth keeps a careful eye on her adult as well as her child audience, emphasizing that it is essential they recognize the true extent of their responsibilities as parents. By raising their sons and daughters properly, she insists, Britain's parents perform a vital national and imperial duty, shaping the characters of the men and women upon whom the future of Britain and her empire depends.

Edgeworth's works for children can be situated in that great outpouring of children's literature that took place from the mid-eighteenth century, and which was imbued with such a particular ideological importance during the Revolutionary period.³ In the years between 1750 and 1814, 'some twenty professional writers of children's books produced some 2,400 different titles', and these works played a crucial role in constructing the notions of childhood *and* adulthood that were emerging at this period.⁴ By 'project[ing] an image of those virtues which parents wished to inculcate in their offspring',⁵ these works were intended to attract adults as well as children, and to inculcate in both sets of readers very particular attitudes to issues such as gender, race, or class. The final aim of such literature was therefore didactic; its ambition was to 'manage' the child *and* the parent inside and outside of the text that was produced.⁶

In the interests of 'managing' the textual and extra-textual child and parent, *The Parent's Assistant* keeps an eye on its adult as well as its child audience, with stories such as 'Lazy Lawrence', 'Simple Susan', or 'The Little Merchants' impressing upon parental readers that they will inevitably suffer if their children's education is inappropriate or neglected.⁷ In each of these stories,

---

3 Edgeworth's works were influenced by, as well as part of, this tradition, of course. As Marilyn Butler points out, Edgeworth read not only 'the broad corpus of early modern works on education', but also the works of writers such as 'de Genlis, Armand Berquin ... La Fontaine ... [and] Marmontel': M. Butler, general introduction to J. Desmarais, Tim McLoughlin and M. Butler (eds), *The Novels and Selected Works of Maria Edgeworth*, 12 vols (London: Pickering & Chatto, 1999), i, pp xii, xxi. Edgeworth's debts to other writers for children is also sometimes made peculiarly apparent in her stories. She particularly admired Anna Laetitia Barbauld's works, for instance, and Harry and Lucy read aloud one of that writer's *Hymns in Prose for Children* (1781) in *Continuation of Early Lessons* (1814): M. Edgeworth, *Continuation of Early Lessons*, 2 vols, 3rd ed. (London: R. Hunter, 1816), ii, pp 148-9. 4 L. Stone, *The Family, Sex, and Marriage in England, 1500-1800*, abridged ed. (London: Penguin, 1979), p. 258. 5 J.H. Plumb, 'The new world of children in eighteenth-century England', *Past and Present*, 67 (1975), 81. 6 I am drawing here upon Alan Richardson's reading of children's literature during the Romantic period. The ambition of this literature, he suggests, 'was one of reforming the child in every sense – capitalizing on the alleged textual quality of the child's mind to make word become flesh and flesh become word': A. Richardson, *Literature, Education, and Romanticism: reading as social practice, 1780-1832* (Cambridge: Cambridge UP, 1994), p. 141. 7 Edgeworth revised the

Edgeworth contrasts good and bad children, and the latter *and* their parents are
punished at the story's end. Edgeworth's point is that parents inevitably reap
what they sow, and so bad parents should not be surprised when their children's
laziness, deceit, avarice, or malice rebounds on them.[8] As Richard Lovell
Edgeworth's preface to *The Parent's Assistant* makes clear, though, there are
national and imperial connotations to such a realization, and no less than the
future security and prosperity of the British nation itself is at stake in an apparently 'simple' story like 'Lazy Lawrence'. The first object of this tale may be to
inculcate 'a spirit of industry' in young children, he observes, but it is also
intended to persuade adult readers that, for their nation's good, *all* late
eighteenth-century Britons must learn to be honest as well as industrious (x: 3).
'In a commercial nation', he remarks, 'it is especially necessary to separate, as
much as possible, the spirit of industry and avarice; and to beware lest we
introduce Vice under the form of Virtue' (x: 3). The very particular 'commercial
nation' with which Edgeworth's father is concerned here is late-eighteenth-
century Britain, of course, and his ambition is to convince all Britons that they
must be virtuous as well as industrious if their nation is to reap the rewards of
the unparalleled mercantile – and territorial – expansion in which it is engaged.[9]

This theme of the need to separate industry from avarice in late eighteenth-
and early nineteenth-century Britain is important to Edgeworth, and so she
returns to it repeatedly in her stories for children and, indeed, in her works for
adults and adolescents. Her point is that, while the prospect of pecuniary – or
territorial – reward is always exciting and attractive, it is important to ensure that
its pursuit does not mean that Britain's essential honour is debased. In 'Lame
Jervas' in *Popular Tales* (1804), for example, she traces not only how her hero
amasses a fabulous fortune for himself in India, but also stresses that he remains
faithful to 'British' notions of generosity, compassion and justice while accumu-
lating his riches.[10] It is these virtues that underpin British superiority, Edgeworth

selection of tales in *The Parent's Assistant* for the third edition of 1800, and 'Simple Susan' and
'The Little Merchants' were two of the stories that were first introduced to the collection at this
time. For the complex compositional and publication history of Edgeworth's writing for children,
see M. Butler, *Maria Edgeworth: a literary biography* (Oxford: Clarendon Press, 1972), pp 146–
74. **8** Lawrence's father is publicly shamed when his son is led away as a thief at the end of
'Lazy Lawrence', while Piedro's father in 'The Little Merchants' becomes the victim of his son's
avarice and cunning. I return below to the fate of Barbara Case's father in 'Simple Susan'. **9** In
eighteenth- and nineteenth-century Britain, trade and territorial expansion effectively went hand
in hand. 'By the early 1700s', as Linda Colley puts it, 'the British state and the major trading
companies associated with it, claimed authority over more than half a million white settlers, as
well as hundreds of thousands of free and enslaved non-whites scattered over four of the five
continents of the world. By the 1820s, British dominion had dramatically expanded to encompass
a fifth of the population of the globe': L. Colley, *Captives* (New York: Pantheon Books, 2002), p.
4. **10** *Popular Tales* was intended for lower-class readers and, as such, miners, haberdashers,
glove-makers, farmers, and merchants feature in the stories that make up the collection.

intimates, and, if Britons forget this, the very security of the British nation will be imperilled. While this theme is everywhere implicit in Edgeworth's writing, it is made particularly explicit in *Essays on Professional Education* (1809), where she insists that pecuniary rewards alone should not be the motivation of young men in Britain's naval academies or military schools. 'In a commercial nation like this', she writes,

> it is peculiarly necessary to guard against that mercenary spirit, which is incompatible with the generous martial character. When every thing is reduced to a monied rate, honorary distinctions lose their value and power over the human mind; and, instead of noble enthusiasm in the course of virtue and freedom, a calculating, selfish temper prevails; the people are debased and enslaved; mercenary troops fight their battles without the ardour of freemen, and at last a nation, incapable of defending even its darling wealth, falls an easy prey to the bold invader.[11]

The little heroes of the tales in *The Parent's Assistant* are not destined for careers in the army or navy, of course, but they, their female counterparts, *and* their readers, all learn that there is a vital link between personal and public honour, and that it is of acute concern to their community and nation whether or not they develop personal qualities such as industriousness, generosity, honesty, resourcefulness, compassion and courage.[12] In 'Simple Susan', for instance, Edgeworth traces how the harmony of a retired English hamlet is disturbed not only by a visit from a recruiting party for the militia, but also by the calculating and selfish behaviour of Barbara Case and her father, an attorney. When Susan's father is drawn for a militia-man, the Cases try to profit from the circumstance; in Barbara's case, by trying to extort money that Susan and her friends have raised to pay for a substitute to take Mr Price's place; in that of the

11 R.L. Edgeworth, *Essays on Professional Education*, 2nd ed. (London: J. Johnson, 1812), pp 175–6. Although this work was originally published under her father's name alone, it is clear from Edgeworth's correspondence that she was the effective author of this text. She wrote to her cousin, Sophy Ruxton, in 1805, for instance, that 'father has excited my ambition to write a useful essay upon professional education ... I have thrown aside all thoughts of pretty stories, & put myself into a course of solid reading'. Three years later, Edgeworth expressed to Sophy her anxiety at the thought of the work's impending publication: 'I cannot help however looking forward to its publication, & fate with an anxiety & an apprehension I never felt before in the same degree – for consider my father's credit is entirely at stake!' See Maria Edgeworth to Sophy Ruxton, 26 February 1805, letter 451, and Maria Edgeworth to Sophy Ruxton, 23 [?] January 1808, letter 612 in part 2 of *Women, Education and Literature: the papers of Maria Edgeworth, 1768–1849*, microfilm edition (Marlborough, Wilts., 1994). 12 In one of Edgeworth's later works for children, the parents of the young hero actually observe they 'do not want to make a soldier' of their son, but remark that it is it is their desire 'to make him a brave man, and then he will be whatever his duty requires': M. Edgeworth, *Frank: a sequel to Frank in Early Lessons*, 3 vols, 2nd ed. (London: R. Hunter, 1822), ii, pp 21–2.

attorney, by attempting to use Mr Price's situation to silence his opposition to plans to enclose some village land.[13] The point that Edgeworth is concerned to make in the story is that the mercenary behaviour of the Cases threatens the security of their village, and more immediately than the war with France that causes the visit by the recruiting party for the militia. It is in this context that the conclusion of Edgeworth's narrative includes a scene that underlines both the community's reaction to the news that the Cases have been banished from the parish, and how the virtues of Susan and her parents have caused their little community to be restored: 'The good news, that farmer Price was to be employed to collect the rents, and that Attorney Case was to leave the parish in a month, soon spread over the village. Many came out of their houses to have the pleasure of hearing the joyful tidings confirmed by Susan herself; the crowd on the play-green increased every minute.' (x: 105)

'Simple Susan' is much more complex a tale than this brief summary suggests, of course, and Edgeworth raises significant issues relating to both gender and class in her description of the adventures of her little heroine.[14] In doing this, however, she at the same time reveals a concern with a theme that is finally central to *The Parent's Assistant* and, indeed, to all of her writing: namely, the idea that there is such a thing as the '*spirit* of a true-born' English, or British, man or woman, and that, for the good of all, every individual must learn what this spirit is (x: 52). In tales such as 'Forgive and Forget', from which the latter quotation comes, Edgeworth indicates that this spirit has nothing to do with the proverb 'Better live in spite than in pity' and, in others such as 'Waste Not, Want Not' or 'The Mimic', insists that it has everything to do with a willingness to perceive and ameliorate the poverty and suffering of others (x: 49).[15] In 'The Little Merchants', she demonstrates that the spirit of true-born Britons is inextricably linked to their innate sense of generosity and justice, and uses a

13 Militias were raised from the civilian population, purportedly only in times of emergency, and were intended to supplement the regular forces. Some men volunteered for militias, but most joined as a result of having their names drawn by ballot from a list of the eligible individuals within their community. 'Simple Susan' reflects the fact that there were ways in which balloted men could avoid serving in militias, either by producing substitutes to take their place, or by paying a fine of £10 which exempted them from service for four years. On the formation of militias in late eighteenth- and early nineteenth-century Ireland, see Ivan. F. Nelson, *The Irish Militia, 1793–1802: Ireland's forgotten army* (Dublin: Four Courts, 2007), pp 48–9.   14 She stresses that Susan's exemplary mother taught the little girl 'to wish to be like her', for instance, and intimates how Sir Arthur Somers' enlightened attitudes to landowning ameliorates the situation of his tenants (x: 66).   15 Hal is brought face to face with the reality of poverty by his uncle in 'Waste Not, Want Not': 'I've often seen terrible-looking, tumble-down places, as we drove through the town in mamma's carriage; but then I did not know who lived in them; and I never saw the inside of any of them' (x: 34); Marianne and Frederick Montague are upset by Theresa Tattle's casual dismissal of the dangers faced by child chimney sweepers in 'The Mimic': 'Chimney-sweepers get wedged in chimnies [*sic*] every day, it's part of their trade, and it's a happy thing when they come off with a few bruises' (x: 120–1).

Neapolitan setting to show that the spread of British influence will inevitably benefit other nations and races.[16]

Edgeworth returns to these several themes repeatedly in her stories for children, elaborating upon them as her little characters *and* their readers achieve greater maturity. In *Harry and Lucy Concluded: being the last part of Early Lessons* (1825), for example, she once more stresses the importance of proper education for children, but this time directly links this education to the advances that Britain has made in science and to her growing dominance of the world's markets.[17] Observing that the 'essential point' of her work 'is to excite a thirst for knowledge' in readers, Edgeworth intimates that it has been the inculcation and satisfaction of such a thirst in children like Harry and Lucy that has facilitated Britain's development of devices such as the air pump and steam engine and that, in their turn, these have enabled the nation to secure a firm hold upon foreign markets and lands.[18] During a visit to a manufactory, the children consequently discover that, while 'muslins were formerly all made in India', an immense quality and value of the fabric is now made in England and Scotland; 'All this we owe to our using ingenious machinery, in these countries', the proprietor significantly remarks to the children, 'instead of doing all by the labour of men's hands, as in India' (i: 232–3).

In celebrating Britain's scientific and industrial advances in this way in her narrative, Edgeworth reveals a continuing anxiety to impress two very particular points upon her readers: firstly, that these advances are the inevitable result of Britain's enlightened approach to education and, secondly, that they go hand-in-hand with a moral and cultural superiority that is inevitably recognized by other races. Upon a visit to family friends, the Franklands, Harry and Lucy therefore learn how England inevitably impresses foreign visitors. I quote the following passage at length because of its significance:

> They [that is, some French and Italian gentlemen] had paid visits to several of our country gentlemen, and liked their mode of living so much, that even the Frenchman protested, that if he had not had the honour of being born a Parisian, he should prefer the lot of an English country gentleman to that of any other being in the universe.[19] The Italian was further struck by the

16 Edgeworth's little Neapolitan heroes and heroines learn from Arthur, an English servant, that 'an Englishman never [forgets] a good turn, be it from a countryman or foreigner', for example, and that England's brand of 'cool justice' is dependent upon 'the excellence' of its trial-by-jury system: M. Edgeworth, *The Parent's Assistant*, 3 vols, 1800 ed. (London: Longman and Company, 1845), ii, pp 64, 93.   17 Harry and Lucy first appeared in 1801 in *Early Lessons*, a work that was aimed at very young children. The conclusion of their adventures, however, was intended for children aged between 10 and 14 years old.   18 M. Edgeworth, *Harry and Lucy Concluded; being the last part of Early Lessons*, 3 vols, 5th ed. (London: Washbourne, 1853), i, p. x. Further references to this edition are cited parenthetically in the text.   19 Edgeworth devotes a chapter of

liberty enjoyed, and the equal justice done to all, as far as he could see, in England. He found, that many of our most distinguished men have made their own fortunes, many risen by their own talents and exertions, from the lower ranks of life. He found, that in this country, though birth has great advantages, education does more; and industry and genius have the road to fame, and wealth, and honours, open to them; he would therefore, as he declared, rather have been born in England, even in a lower rank, than in the highest class in any country, where such equal laws and liberty, and such strong motives for exertion, are not to be found. (ii: 77)

The emphasis that many of Britain's 'most distinguished men have ... risen by their own talents and exertions' is a theme that is central to all of Edgeworth's writing; in particular, to her insistence that many of Britain's achievements can be directly linked to the fact that the nation extends educational opportunities even to the lower classes. As the hero of 'Lame Jervas' puts it, 'obscure individual[s], in a country like England, where arts, sciences, and literature are open to all ranks, may obtain a degree of knowledge which an eastern despot, in all his pride, would gladly purchase with ingots of his purest gold'.[20] The heroes and heroines of Edgeworth's stories for children variously demonstrate the wider national and imperial implications of Britain's enlightened approach to education, revealing, for instance, that the possible effects of this policy upon the lower classes have to be carefully managed. In 'Lame Jervas', the benevolent master of the young hero thus rewards his honesty by giving him an education, but the tale at the same time makes clear that the boy's (inappropriate) dream of earning his living through writing is positively discouraged.[21] In a similar fashion, tales such as 'Simple Susan' or 'The White Pigeon' in *The Parent's Assistant* also stress the importance of lower-class education, while simultaneously emphasizing that the results of this education need not be feared by the upper orders. Rather, they insist, the continued wellbeing of admirable lower-class children like Susan or Brian is demonstrably bound up with the ongoing prosperity and security of benevolent masters like Mr Somerville or Sir Arthur Somers; these alone can properly regulate society, the tales aver, punishing the dishonest and lazy, and seeing to it that the honest and hardworking are rewarded and encouraged.[22]

Essays on Professional Education to the English country gentleman (278–317). **20** M. Edgeworth, 'Lame Jervas', *Popular Tales* (1804) in E. Eger, C. Ó Gallchoir and M. Butler (eds), *The Novels and Selected Works of Maria Edgeworth*, 12 vols (London, Pickering & Chatto, 2003), xii, p. 35. Further references to this tale are cited parenthetically in the text. **21** Jervas is taken from the tin mines of his Cornish master when he prevents a robbery, and is put into the care of Dr Y – as a reward. This gentleman facilitates Jervas' education, but discourages the boy's ambition to write verses, pointing out it was 'not likely, ... [he] should ever either earn [his] bread or equal those who had enjoyed greater advantages of leisure and education' (xii: 17). **22** Sir Arthur, as we have seen, appoints Susan's father as his agent and gives the children a playground

The emphasis that the Italian gentleman places upon the fact that 'liberty' and 'equal justice' are extended to all in 'dear Old England' is somewhat problematic for Edgeworth given that nation's relationship to slavery, and her writing for both children and adults consequently manifests an acute awareness of the need to account for, or disguise, the fact that much of Britain's late eighteenth- and early nineteenth-century prosperity actually depended upon slave labour (ii: 77). As in earlier works such as 'The Grateful Negro',[23] she tries to do this in *Harry and Lucy Concluded* by suggesting that British superiority inevitably results in the amelioration of the condition of the enslaved, in this case insisting that moral, industrial and scientific advancement *and* social improvement necessarily go hand in hand. Harry and Lucy are thus delighted to learn that Josiah Wedgwood's efforts were not motivated purely by a desire for pecuniary reward, for instance, and that there was a distinctly philanthropic dimension to all of this industrialist's achievements. As well as making a fortune for himself and his family, they are informed, Wedgwood 'increased amazingly the industry, wealth, and comforts, of the poor in his Neighbourhood; multiplied the conveniences, elegancies, and luxuries of life for the rich; raised, at home and abroad, the fame of the arts and manufactures of his own country; extended her commerce, and spread his own name with his productions, to the most remote regions of the civilized world' (ii: 19). Pointedly, though, the fact that even the slaves that labour upon Britain's colonial plantations should be numbered among those who have benefited from Wedgwood's efforts is impressed upon the children – and the reader – several pages later, when Mrs Frankland presents each of them with one of his anti-slavery cameos: 'Lucy's, which was black on a white ground, represented a negro in chains, kneeling with his hands raised, in a supplicating manner, with this motto engraved; "Am I not a man and a brother?"' (ii: 40). Wedgwood distributed hundreds of these, Mrs Frankland tells the children, 'And no doubt considerable effect was produced by – "the poor fettered slave, on bended knee, From Britain's sons imploring to be free"' (ii: 40).[24]

As twenty-first-century readers, we are all too aware of how long it took before abolitionists finally secured the liberty of all of Britain's slaves, and we know, too, that not every British slave-owner was as enlightened as Edgeworth's Mr Edwards, St Albans, or Mrs Howard.[25] For these reasons, the conflicting nature

at the end of 'Simple Susan'; Mr Somerville rewards Brian's honesty in 'The White Pigeon' by making his father the master of a new inn, observing: 'Those who bring up their children well will certainly be rewarded for it, be they poor or rich': M. Edgeworth, *The Parent's Assistant*, 3 vols, 1800 ed. (London: Longman and Company, 1845), iii, p. 41.   **23** 'The Grateful Negro' is another of Edgeworth's *Popular Tales*, and a central concern of the story is to prove how the benevolence of the enlightened Mr Edwards immeasurably improves the conditions of his slaves. **24** To view an image of Wedgwood's cameo, go to http://www.wwnorton.com/nto and follow links.   **25** St Alban features in 'The Two Guardians', in *Comic Dramas, in Three Acts* (1817); he frees his slave, Quaco, the moment he arrives in England. Mrs Howard appears in 'The Good Aunt', in *Moral Tales*; she sells her property in the West Indies, ordering that the oldest slaves of Edgeworth's treatment of slavery in her works is particularly apparent to us, and we perceive that it was informed by not only moral concerns, but also a desire to ensure the ongoing security of the imperial process in which Britain was engaged.[26] While this may be an uncomfortable realization for us, it was no doubt hugely attractive to late eighteenth- and early nineteenth-century Britons, for it apparently offered a solution to one of the most pressing ideological debates of their era. As Edgeworth had it in her children's works and, indeed, throughout her writing, the hugely divisive issue of Britain's relationship to slavery was something that should not be feared by contemporaries; the superior nature of Britain – of her system of education, and of her scientific and industrial progress – meant that its resolution is assured.

Through their reading of Edgeworth's writing for children, we can see, then, late eighteenth- and early nineteenth-century readers found comfort, because they discovered that education was the solution to all of the socio-political problems of their era. The proper education of each and every child would inevitably enable Britain to see off the threat of the Revolutionary French, Edgeworth implied, for instance, or to resolve the complex issues surrounding that nation's relationship to slavery; this was because that education would produce men and woman whose moral and, hence, cultural, political, commercial and scientific superiority was assured. For this reason, it is hardly surprising that Edgeworth's tales for children were so hugely popular with their adult as well as their child audiences during the Revolutionary period, nor that they continued to be read and enjoyed long after her other works had passed out of fashion. In a nineteenth century that was increasingly preoccupied with both the opportunities and problems of empire, Edgeworth's writing for children reassured readers, promising them that the right education of youth alone would produce that security upon which both nation and empire could depend.

should be freed and provision made for them. For an excellent account of Britain's relationship to slavery in the late eighteenth and early nineteenth centuries, see Anne K. Mellor, '"Am I not a Woman, and a Sister?": slavery, romanticism, and gender', in Alan Richardson and Sonia Hofkosh (eds), *Romanticism, Race, and Imperial Culture, 1780–1834* (Bloomington and Indianapolis: Indiana UP, 1996), pp 311–29.   **26** I discuss Edgeworth's treatment of slavery at length in chapter 3 of *Maria Edgeworth and Romance*, pp 101–28.

Arthur Mee, the 'happy wonderer': instructing children and constructing knowledge in the *Children's Encyclopedia*

JOY ALEXANDER

'The Happy Wonderer' is the delightful yet apt title of the centenary article about Arthur Mee in the *Times Literary Supplement* of 11 July 1975.[1] Mee has an honoured place in the history of children's non-fiction, principally as editor of the *Children's Encyclopedia*, its significance for the history of children's books being that 'before the *Children's Encyclopedia* commenced publication in 1908, nothing on a similar scale had ever before been produced for young readers.'[2] This judgement is made in the introduction to the Australian schools textbook and the children's literature research collections in the Special Collection of Deakin University Library in Geelong, Australia, where it is noted that although the *Encyclopedia* is 'contained within the textbook collection, it crossed the boundaries of home and school and its popularity and unusual format make it of particular interest.'[3] Attention is drawn to the *Encyclopedia*'s international impact, as well as its historical importance:

> The *Encyclopedia* was immensely popular whilst it was being published; it is estimated that up until 1946, somewhere in the vicinity of 5,380,000 sets were sold; the serial version (which many subscribers had bound) would increase that figure by approximately 1,500,000. Australian readers had to order the *Encyclopedia* from England as it was not published in Australia. However it seems clear that it made its way into many households.[4]

Further information is given later about the *Children's Encyclopedia*'s penetration of the world-wide market; however, the central focus of this essay is on its continuing relevance to studies of the nature and development of non-fiction for children. The *Encyclopedia*'s representation of Ireland for the young was principally for child readers in countries other than Ireland and its depiction of Ireland is coloured by the imperial outlook of Edwardian England. However its method of instructing children through wonder and of constructing knowledge as story

---

1 Anthony Quinton, 'The Happy Wonderer', in *Times Literary Supplement*, 11 July 1975, pp 761–2. 2 www.deakin.edu.au/library/spc/exhibitions/meeencyclopaedia.php. Accessed 12 Nov. 2008. 3 Quinton, 'Wonderer'. 4 Ibid.

constituted an advance away from didacticism and towards more child-friendly ways of treating fact. In these particular respects it had a far-reaching, if unacknowledged, influence on how non-fiction for the young was conceptualized and practised.

ARTHUR MEE AND THE *CHILDREN'S ENCYCLOPEDIA*

Arthur Mee was born in 1875 and was very much formed by Victorian values. He embodied the qualities that have come to characterize the age; he was hard-working, earnest, charitable, moralizing and self-reliant. At the age of fourteen he entered into employment with the *Nottingham Evening Post*, moving on several years later to the larger world of journalism in London. In 1898 he joined the staff of the *Daily Mail*, becoming its literary editor in 1903. He was a prolific writer, especially of feature articles on a vast range of topics of interest. In later life he claimed to have written on average a million words a year for fifty years.[5] His friend and biographer, Sir John Hammerton, lists his chief characteristics as his Christian faith, his love for his native land, his belief in the beneficent legacy of the British Empire, his concern for the welfare of the young, his hero worship, and his deep joy in his life and work.[6] There is much here that could be commented on, but Hammerton is cited at this point simply to give a flavour of the kind of person Mee was. Mee's employer Lord Northcliffe described him - Hammerton says 'playfully' – as 'a narrow-minded little Nottingham Nonconformist'.[7] Mee died in 1943, mercifully before the facts of the Holocaust and Hiroshima could shatter his optimistic and ardent faith in the League of Nations and the brotherhood of mankind (the gendered terminology is used here deliberately).

Mee's brain-child, the *Children's Encyclopedia*, two years in the making, was issued in fifty fortnightly parts between March 1908 and February 1910, and proved a success with the Edwardian public almost from the start. By the final issue of the serial edition in 1910, 'the work had become a sensational success and its appearance an important landmark in the history of modern publishing. Nothing quite like it had been attempted before, but after its publication it had numerous imitators.'[8] Before the last part of the serialization appeared, it was already being issued in a set of eight volumes, which was further expanded and issued as a ten-volume set in 1923. It remained in print until the 1950s, going through almost thirty editions. By the time Hammerton was writing Mee's biography in 1946, the volumes sold were counted in millions, with French,

5 See Ian Sansom, 'Why Do I Cry?', *The Guardian*, 21 July 2007. 6 Sir John Hammerton, *Child of Wonder: an intimate biography of Arthur Mee* (London: Hodder & Stoughton, 1946), p. 139. 7 Hammerton, *Child of Wonder*, p. 105. 8 Brian Doyle (ed.), *The Who's Who of Children's Literature* (London: Hugh Evelyn, 1968), p. 196.

Italian, Chinese, Spanish and Portuguese versions also doing well.[9] In 1910, the Grolier Society secured the rights to produce the *Encyclopedia* in America and Canada, re-naming it *The Book of Knowledge* and using its English name as a sub-title. In the US it proved to be a runaway best-seller, so that Arthur Mee's name 'became almost as hallowed in the United States as that of Dr Johnson,'[10] although subsequently it was re-edited and thoroughly Americanized.[11] Hammerton's judgment that 'In the field of juvenile education it is the paramount publication of the century'[12] seems justifiable. There is a photograph of Mee[13] in which he looks suitably self-satisfied; he is at an imposing desk editing the first edition of the *Children's Encyclopedia*, with the current number propped in front of him and several bound volumes on top of his desk, watched over from the wall by photographs of his employer, Lord Northcliffe, and his daughter Marjorie Mee, who was supposedly one of the inspirations for the *Encyclopedia*.

Mee states in the introduction to the *Encyclopedia* that it is the 'first book that has ever tried to tell the whole sum of human knowledge so that a child may understand.'[14] The target audience is certainly the child-reader and the range is unquestionably encyclopedic, but in some respects the title is a misnomer, because the arrangement is not alphabetical, which renders it an unfriendly reference work. One of the first questions addressed in the 'Wonder' section is 'What does Encyclopedia Mean?'[15] Noting that 'the name of this book is longer than any word in it,' the definition appeals to etymology: an encyclopedia is 'a circle of teaching.'[16] The metaphor of the circle is appropriate for the *Encyclopedia*'s genuine attempt to embrace all knowledge, but a present-day reader might demur at the strong sense in which Mee means the word 'teaching'. He goes on to say that 'teaching suggests child and a child suggests teaching.'[17] The adult perspective is unmistakable. In the final volume the introduction to the index is explicit: 'It is an encyclopedia that educates. It is arranged with that end in view; it is a book to be widely read for its own sake.'[18] As a reference book, then, it is a double oddity: first, its mission is to educate, and secondly, it can be read for its own sake. Its coverage is more extensive than conventional encyclo-pedias and both in the style in which it is written and in the way in which it is structured it resembles a story-book more than a compilation of factual infor-mation.

A unique feature of the work is the compendious 350-page index, which is a complete reference work in itself. The index is sub-titled 'A Little Guide to

9 See entry on Mee in Doyle (ed.), *The Who's Who of Children's Literature*. 10 Humphrey Carpenter and Mari Pritchard, *The Oxford Companion to Children's Literature* (Oxford: OUP, 1984), p. 112. 11 Hammerton provides details of *The Book of Knowledge* in *Child of Wonder*, pp 129–30. 12 Ibid., p. 128. 13 Ibid., Plate V, facing p. 128. 14 Arthur Mee (ed.), *The Children's Encyclopedia* (London: Educational Book Co., various editions, 1910–54), vol. 1, p. 2. 15 Ibid., vol. 1, p. 60. 16 Ibid., vol. 1, p. 60. 17 Ibid., vol. 1, p. 60. 18 Ibid., vol. 10, p. 7055.

Knowledge'. It contains illustrations and brief summaries of many topics. Another interesting aspect of the ten volumes which has frequently invited comment is that they are not necessarily the type of book to which a child would immediately turn to look something up. Instead they are ideal for the browser, attracting the reader from one section to the next by their sheer variety. The *Children's Encyclopedia* is in fact a vast compendium of factual narrative, which Mee described as 'The Book of My Heart'. These then are the three most obvious features of this unconventional encyclopedia – its content is the circle of all knowledge; its purpose is to educate; its style is narrative. Mee the adult conceived of it in this way precisely because he was ever conscious of his responsibilities to the children for whom it was designed. He instinctively adopted the twin criteria for writers advanced by Sir Philip Sidney and, before him, by Horace: instruction and delight.[19]

Mee's taxonomy of knowledge breaks down into eighteen sections, with successive chapters on each topic in turn – Wonder, Art, Ourselves, Plant Life, Countries, Poetry, etc. Read originally in serial form, each issue must have seemed like a bumper edition. Put together in volumes, there is less coherence. Someone reading the History section, for example, has to flip forward over seventeen sections until History has its turn again. This, of course, suits the browser in opening up new areas of interest. On opening Volume 4, for example, the reader proceeds, with an engaging happenstance, from waterfalls of the world, to great doctors, then to animals that lay eggs, and on to Charlemagne. Only eight sections survive till the very last part of volume 10; the other ten sections gradually disappear once each has exhausted its topic. There is an emphasis on the arts rather than science, but coverage of knowledge is comprehensive, with sport being the topic most obviously neglected. There is overlap between some of the sections, which is hardly surprising given that they are catch-all groupings rather than strict classifications. The sub-headings to the various sections are worthy of note on three counts. First, eight of the eighteen sections are titled, 'The Story of ...'; the *Encyclopedia* is underpinned by a relentlessly narrative drive. Second, there is a repeated anthropomorphizing strain: 'Earth *and its neighbours*',[20] or the story of animals which starts off with 'Nature's thousands of children'.[21] Third, there is the recurrence of the words 'wondrous', 'wonderful'. The *TLS* centenary article claims that Mee's favourite words are 'wonderful, marvellous, immortal, imperishable, beautiful, great'.[22] Gillian Avery aptly writes of his style of 'radiant idealism'.[23] This is an encyclopedia with attitude; its vocabulary hints at an agenda to inspire as well as inform.

19 Horace, *On the Art of Poetry* in *Classical Literary Criticism* (London: Penguin, 1965), p. 90; Sir Philip Sidney, *An Apology for Poetry* (London: Nelson, 1965), p. 101.   20 This is the title of the recurring major section covering astronomy, geology, geography, chemistry and physics (my italics).   21 Mee, *Encyclopedia*, vol. 1, p. 37.   22 Anthony Quinton, 'The Happy Wonderer', *Times Literary Supplement*, 11 July, 1975, p. 761.   23 Gillian Avery, 'Popular education and big

The *Children's Encyclopedia* is genuinely compendious in its desire to include everything – every country, all aspects of the natural world, etc. A significant feature distinguishing it from other alphabetically-arranged encyclopedias is the way connections are always being made and everything is placed in a wider context. The general approach is for topics to be grouped together – Famous Monks;[24] animals that gnaw and burrow such as the squirrel, beaver and dormouse;[25] Creators of Liberty, which range over a wide variety of period and nation: Themistocles, Boadicea, Alfred the Great, William Wallace, Giuseppe Garibaldi, Simon Bolivar and F.-D. Toussaint l'Ouverture.[26] The illustrations are especially noteworthy. Some sections are solely in picture form. Eight pages[27] show the entire Bayeux tapestry, reproduced in colour, with the history recorded in the tapestry told in a single line below the relevant picture. There are numerous pictorial maps, of a style instantly recognizable as belonging to the *Encyclopedia*, such as those showing 'The Animals of Greenland and Iceland' and 'Plants and Industries of Greenland',[28] where the outline of the country is entirely filled in with tiny drawings and informative captions. Photo stories make links evident, as in the story of wool from sheep to garment, told in twenty-seven pictures.[29] Then there are picture-lists of, for example, different types of bridges – thirty in all.[30] Generally the pictures are imaginative and informative. A full-page picture is titled 'What a Light Year is'. Part of the caption underneath the picture reads:

> How far back in history would a car at fifty miles an hour have to go before it covered the distance covered by a ray of light in a year? The answer is amazing. The car would have to run through all the ages back to the first appearance of man on Earth, through the great periods of mastodons and saurians and flying dragons, back to the days of the iguanadon and the great coal forests.[31]

The picture shows a car at the bottom of the page starting from a city with sky-scrapers on a road which soon passes newly-built pyramids and then stone-age hunters before winding through primeval forest with dinosaurs up to the opposite top corner of the page. It is an original and appealing representation of a time-line. Another three-fold illustration shows pictorially different conceptions of the world, with the explanatory titles: 'one idea in the very long ago was that the earth was surrounded by water'; 'the Hindus used to think the earth was borne on the back of a tortoise'; 'an early Greek map of the world, thousands of

money: Mee, Hammerton and Northcliffe', in J. Briggs, D. Butts and M.O. Grenby (eds), *Popular Children's Fiction in Britain* (Aldershot: Ashgate, 2008), pp 229–50, p. 233. **24** Mee, *Encyclopedia*, vol. 2, pp 1385–90. **25** Ibid., vol. 2, pp 1029–36. **26** Ibid., vol. 2, pp 889–98. **27** Ibid., vol. 1, pp 709–16. **28** Ibid., vol. 10, pp 6976–7. **29** Ibid., vol. 2, p. 801. **30** Ibid., vol. 10, p. 7153. **31** Ibid., vol. 6, p. 3853.

years old'.[32] In this case each of the pictures attractively packages information which it would take several pages to explain verbally. Mee understood the appeal of visual representation for children and that it is helpful if knowledge can be pictorialized. The *TLS* centenary article, discussing pictures of fish in the *Encyclopedia*, points out that their Latin names are not given – 'a decision of magisterial good sense and non-pedantry, the creatures are for looking at, not naming'.[33] Pictures are used, not only to enhance the text, but to carry information in their own right. Everything early twentieth-century printing has to offer is exploited in the use made of photographs, illustrations, and diagrams to pioneer novel methods of conveying knowledge.

'HAPPY WONDERER'

Arthur Mee had good reason to feel satisfied that he had achieved his aim of arousing a sense of wonder in child-readers. Kieran Egan, professor of education at Simon Fraser University, Vancouver, Canada, has worked for a number of years to develop a theory of teaching and learning which captures the imagination. He lists what he calls the 'cognitive tools' that a literate child, from the age of about seven or eight, draws on to help him or her to think and understand, among which are: story; metaphor; binary opposites; rhyme, rhythm, and pattern; jokes and humour; mental imagery; play; mystery; extremes of experience and limits of reality; association with heroes; sense of wonder; collections and hobbies; narrative understanding; revolt and idealism.[34] Mee appeals to many of these qualities and thus catches the imagination and opens the mind of the child. He devotes a section to Wonder, asking and answering dozens of questions about which a child might wonder: Why is a snow-flake lighter than a raindrop? Do animals think? Why do the branches of trees grow sideways? Have things colour at night? Why does a mattress have leather buttons? What makes the heart beat? It might be objected that these are questions posed by adults rather than ones that a child might really ask, but the effect of looking through the Wonder section is to arouse a spirit of curiosity and enquiry. It is hard to think of someone consulting this section as a means of deliberately looking something up; as with so much of the *Children's Encyclopedia*, its knowledge is most readily disclosed to browsers, who leaf their way to some of the Wonder questions and are thereby encouraged to have an active and questioning mind.

32 Ibid., vol. 2, p. 915. 33 Anthony Quinton, 'Wonderer', p. 761. 34 Kieran Egan, *An Imaginative Approach to Teaching* (San Francisco: Jossey-Bass, 2005), chapters 1 and 2.

IRELAND IN THE *CHILDREN'S ENCYCLOPEDIA*

The coverage of the *Encyclopedia* can be gauged by looking at references to Ireland in its pages. These are spread through the ten volumes and are representative of the breadth, depth and serendipity of the other sections. There are about fifty photographs: ten pictures, for example, of 'Ancient Abbeys, Towers, and Strongholds',[35] or eight pictures of 'Irish Art a Thousand Years Ago'.[36] There are three pictorial maps: one of animal life,[37] one of industrial life,[38] and one of Irish history.[39] There are a number of poems by such Irish poets as Thomas Moore and William Allingham[40] and ten Irish stories, such as the tales of Cuchulain,[41] Oisin,[42] and the Children of Lir.[43] Besides these many scattered references, there is one chapter dedicated to 'Ireland and its story'.[44] A flavour of its content can be derived from its sub-headings:

> Why Ireland has never been a land at peace
> Messengers of Christ who came to Ireland in the long ago
> The lonely island retreats of the early pillars of the church
> The romantic story of the glorious Book of Kells
> The tragic failure of England to give Ireland peace
> The landmarks that stand out in the story of Ireland
> The wealth of natural beauty in a country that is poor
> Why the population of Ireland is steadily going down
> The great need of the Irish people for education

There is here a mix of geography and history in simplified form. The historical account would be vulnerable to critical analysis from a postcolonial standpoint; even more apparent is a belief in differing rates of racial evolution from barbarism to civilization. Overall the view taken of Irish history is of repeated attempts to reconcile differing groups of people. The 'imperial frame of reference'[45] was inherent in the British juvenile stories and magazines which were popular in Ireland in the early twentieth century. The autobiographies of

35 Mee, *Encyclopedia*, vol. 5, p. 3060. 36 Ibid., vol. 5, p. 3063. 37 Ibid., vol. 1, pp 726–7. 38 Ibid., vol. 1, p. 350. 39 Ibid., vol. 1, p. 600. 40 11 poems by Moore and 4 by Allingham are dispersed through the 10 volumes. 41 Mee, *Encyclopedia*, vol. 2, pp 1275–6; vol. 8, pp 5469–70; vol. 8, pp 5585–6. 42 Ibid., vol. 8, p. 5226. 43 Ibid., vol. 10, pp 6687–8. 44 Ibid., vol. 5, pp 3061–66. 45 Michael Flanagan, '"There is an isle in the western ocean": the Christian Brothers, *Our Boys* and Catholic nationalist ideology', pp 43–52, in Mary Shine Thompson and Celia Keenan (eds), *Treasure Islands: studies in children's literature* (Dublin: Four Courts, 2006), p. 46. In the same book, Marnie Hay in 'This treasured island: Irish nationalist propaganda aimed at children and youth, 1910–16', writing about the popularity of British boys' magazines, says that 'advanced nationalists were particularly scathing in their condemnation of the (ironically) Irish press baron Alfred Harmsworth (Lord Northcliffe).' (p. 41) Northcliffe was Mee's employer and friend.

Frank O'Connor and Sean O'Faoláin[46] make reference to the imperial complexion at this time of children's literary culture in Ireland; the *Children's Encyclopedia* reflects that same background but its representation of Ireland's story is principally directed at young readers outside the island of Ireland and aims to be simplified and readable. The *Encyclopedia*'s unthinking Anglocentrism results in a narrative that is sometimes tendentious or partisan and occasionally mythologized.

The chapter ends with a plea for education:

> One of the needs of Ireland is a really efficient system of national education that would give the poorest a chance … The Irish people need education fully to justify themselves.

This is extremely ironic, given that the national school system was established in Ireland long before it was provided on the British mainland, and also given that texts developed within the Irish national system were widely used throughout the empire. These words echo the *Encyclopedia*'s own sub-text, which is to enlighten and educate young people, but this can lead to a paternalistic and patronizing undertone and, in this instance, the text reveals its own ignorance. Undoubtedly the *Encyclopedia* is a product of its time, though the view of *The Oxford Companion to Children's Literature* is judicious, namely, that 'sheer information predominated over anything that could be called polemic'.[47] However it is ahead of its time in the somewhat informal, direct-address method of narration. Its uniqueness lies in its style rather than in its content; its place in the history of writing for children is merited as a prototype of the range of ways in which non-fiction could be handled.

NARRATIVE STYLE

The narrative cast of the *Children's Encyclopedia* has been emphasized. While this gets in the way of its usefulness as a work of reference, it makes it enormously readable. The style is that of a story teller addressing the reader. It was not only from his journalistic background that Mee learned this style. Since childhood he had been used to listening to Sunday-school stories and sermons. In his early teens he read the parliamentary news aloud each night to a local baker while he worked. His first two years of employment were as a copy-holder at the *Nottingham Evening Post*, reading out the copy while the proof-reader checked

---

46 See Frank O'Connor, *An Only Child* (Belfast: Blackstaff, 1993) and Sean O'Faoláin, *Vive Moi!* (London: R. Hart-Davis, 1965). **47** Humphrey Carpenter and Mari Prichard, *The Oxford Companion to Children's Literature* (Oxford: OUP 1984), p. 112.

it.[48] By such means he absorbed oral styles. Perhaps if Mee had set out from the beginning to write a reference book, the style would have been different, but the narrative style suited the serial issue, with each magazine made up, as it were, of a number of chapters or articles on different subjects. The desire to turn everything into a pleasant tale with which to entertain young people is carried to a ludicrous extreme in the School Lessons on Music, where learning to play the piano is taught with the doubtful aid of the story of the 'Magic Kingdom of Piano'. Mee was prone to imagine that fairies were necessary components of a child's world, so it is supposed that fairies and goblins inhabit the white and black notes on the piano, and from there the story rapidly becomes increasingly complex. For example, we are told:

> Do you not think that this magic kingdom of the piano is a very happy one? In the Treble Road we find fairies in their motor cars, E, G, B, D, F. In the Bass Road fairies are laughing in their coconuts. Their names, as you know, are G, B, D, F, A. Treble Clef again shows us fairies kissing the petals of the delicate flowers in which they have found so pretty a home – the Fairies F, A, C, E.[49]

Though all this talk of fairies, motor-cars, roads, shells, coconuts is worked out in story-form with the aid of illustrations of musical notation, it might be thought to complicate unnecessarily the task of learning to play the piano.

In an article on the *Children's Encyclopedia* in *Signal 58*, Hugh Crago writes that 'much of the Encyclopedia's factual material is heavily fictionalized'.[50] It would be more accurate to say that it is romanticized or dramatized; fact is presented in story-style. It has been said that 'to children, all knowledge is first of all a story.'[51] Here is a typical example of the *Encyclopedia*'s narrative style, selected at random. It is a passage about gannets in a chapter on 'Ducks and Geese':

A Living Aeroplane that can drop like a Dart to the Sea

> There can be no such doubt about the gannet or solan goose, the connecting link between the darters, cormorants, and pelicans. Of course the almost white plumage here suffices for distinction, but that is not conclusive at all times; it takes a gannet six years to grow to maturity, when first it gets the entirely white coat of feathers, varied only by the black flight feathers and the buff of head and neck.

48 For information on the young Mee, see 'As the twig is bent ...', chapter 3 of Sir John Hammerton, *Child of Wonder: an intimate biography of Arthur Mee* (London: Hodder & Stoughton, 1946), pp 29–39. 49 Mee, *Encyclopedia*, vol. 2, p. 880. 50 Hugh Crago, 'The Last Days in the Old Home', *Signal*, 58 (1989), 67. 51 C. Meigs, A.T. Eaton, E. Nesbitt and R.H. Viguers, *A Critical History of Children's Literature* (New York: Macmillan, 1964), p. 393.

The manner of the bird is, however, quite distinctive. We see it flying, thirty-four inches of it, high in the air, watching with keen, yellow eyes the wrinkled sea beneath. It espies its prey, a shoal of mackerel, herrings, sprats, or pilchards. Then a lovely living aeroplane is converted into a kind of projectile. Suddenly as you watch, the bird, changing from a level keel, seems to stand on its head in the air, then down, like a great white dart it flashes into the midst of the shoal.

Master of such grace and determination, the gannet seems to merit greater dignity of title than that of booby, which is an alternative name. But at home, teeming in thousands on the Bass Rock, or, in smaller numbers at less famous British stations, the bird loses some of its majestic attributes.

The Flight of the Gannets like a Snowstorm upside down

With the same intense devotion to its eggs which poultry show, this bird of the wild seashores will remain close to duty till a hand pushes it from its nest. Then it will fall over the cliffs into the air, and throw up a half-digested fish or two in the process. The ease with which the old birds return their food explains why, in warmer climes, they are so shamelessly victimized by the frigate birds.

In the young, however, the habit appears a defence. The young birds writhe, ugly, repulsive, in their filthy nests and, casting up their oily meals, make themselves so offensive that the habit seems like an impalpable armour.

Yet there is a wonder of loveliness as well as the objectionable in a gannet rookery. The birds nest so thickly together that their home, seen from afar, suggests a great white sail on the horizon. When timorous thousands rise from their roosting places into the air all together, then it is as if the island were snowing – *upwards!*[52]

Notice first of all the eye-catching captions which capture the attention of the browsing child. Mee's biographer Hammerton speaks of his 'aptitude for slogans';[53] the writer of the *TLS* article states that Mee the journalist was 'a natural caption-writer',[54] writing snappy picture captions and sub-headings. These headings divide the article into bite-sized chunks, while relating the gannet to other similar birds and setting it in its natural context. The style is personalized – 'we see it flying', etc. The gannets are humanized – 'devotion', 'shamelessly', 'timorous'. A surprising amount of information is conveyed in

---

52 Mee, *Encyclopedia*, vol. 6, p. 3750.   53 Sir John Hammerton, *Child of Wonder: an intimate biography of Arthur Mee* (London: Hodder & Stoughton 1946), p. 105.   54 Anthony Quinton, 'The Happy Wonderer', *Times Literary Supplement*, 11 July, 1975, p. 761.

generally child-friendly language, yet which at times can be poetic – 'down, like a great white dart it flashes ...' This attractive, leisurely style is characteristic of the *Encyclopedia*. It can be compared with the entry for the gannet in *The Observer's Book of Birds*, the book which launched the *Observer* series, popular with young people, in 1937, part of which reads:

HAUNT. The coast and sea, and at breeding time rocky isles and stacks, chiefly on the north and west of the British Isles.
NEST. Of seaweed and tufts of grass or thrift; on the rocky ledge of a stack or island in a great colony with others.
EGGS. 1, nearly white, chalky. March or April.
FOOD. Fish.
NOTES. Short and harsh.[55]

For ready reference, the annotated classifications are convenient but do not bring the gannet to life in the way that the *Encyclopedia*'s more expansive prose description does. The comparison of the two very clearly displays the distinctiveness of the latter's manner of presenting factual knowledge to children. It amounts to a house-style and is effectively applied to all kinds of subject-matter. Hugo Crago prefaces his *Signal* article with several quotations including one by an exasperated public librarian complaining that 'it's the worst encyclopedia ever published – it's impossible to look anything up in it!'[56] However others have found merit in the *Children's Encyclopedia*'s method of organization:

The sequencing and setting out of everything in time and space gave young readers a mental framework into which they could assimilate new knowledge, including their school learning. Because the *Encyclopedia* encouraged them to explore everything, they could restructure this mental schema as they learnt more – the ideal Piagetian route for intellectual development.[57]

The relentless grouping of topics subconsciously leads the reader to sub-divide information into logical and inter-related categories, thus proving not only a child-friendly classification system but also a subtly didactic one in that it is a training in how to organize thought. Although the intent to educate can lead to a tendency to moralize, the *Encyclopedia* does not talk down to young people. The objective, factual tone of a reference work is usually muted; in pointing out

55 S. Vere Benson, *The Observer's Book of Birds* (London: Frederick Warne, 1966). 56 Hugh Crago, 'The Last Days in the Old Home', *Signal*, 58 (1989), p. 51. 57 See 'Imagination in education – Arthur Mee's Children's Encyclopedia: an endangered achievement of twentieth-century art', accessible at http://home.vicnet.net.au/~ozideas/arthurmee.htm. Accessed 14 November 2008.

that the *Encyclopedia*'s style is not scholarly, Hammerton writes that 'it is far too lively, exuberant, humane for that'.[58]

Mee's predilection for narrative originates in his aim to entertain and give enjoyment to his young readers. However it related to a further more fundamental goal. In his introduction he says of his work that: 'Its purpose is to fascinate and educate. It teaches in story and in picture.'[59] He wanted not so much to inform as to teach. In an essay in the Ideas section on 'Knowledge' he states that 'education is not a cramming of the memory with facts. It is an energizer of the soul.'[60] The latter phrase is nebulous, but what is abundantly clear is that Mee was driven by a moral imperative. The design to instruct is most plainly evident in the section which runs through the first four volumes on 'School Lessons', covering Reading, Writing, Arithmetic, Music, Drawing and French. It could be argued that it is no part of an encyclopedia as conventionally conceived to teach how to count[61] or draw. Given that to use an encyclopedia at all entails a minimum level of attainment in reading, it seems odd to find space devoted to showing how to read and write letters. However, if I can be allowed a personal interjection, I discovered as, decades later, I studied again the *Children's Encyclopedia* which had once been a childhood companion, that the parts that seemed most familiar to me were the lessons on how to read and write. I can only speculate that to me as a child they provided the security of what was known as I explored so much that was new knowledge.

Mee, of course, hoped to inculcate much more than elementary literacy. It is easy to play the post-colonial game and deconstruct his white, Anglo-Saxon, protestant beliefs, so forthrightly declared. Sometimes these are trivial, as in his opinions on cosmetics: '... some foolish people make their eyebrows darker than they really are, but if you have a bright and healthy mind your eyes will look nice enough without any silly help of that kind.'[62] A pervasive bias for which he was well-known is revealed in the title of one section, 'Alcohol, the Enemy of Life'.[63] Prejudice becomes blatant in such sentences as 'the Spaniards, as a race, are unimaginative and a little cruel',[64] and in the naked prejudice in the question posed in a 'Wonder' section: 'Why is a White Man more Civilized than a Black Man?'[65] These views derive from a belief in evolution and in a liberal, non-doctrinal form of Christianity. We are told that 'religion ... is a progressive revelation, and life everywhere an unceasing evolution',[66] and that 'the day is surely coming when this mighty struggle of evolution will end at last in the universal brotherhood of man united in love and service under the Fatherhood

---

58 Sir John Hammerton, *Child of Wonder: an intimate biography of Arthur Mee* (London: Hodder & Stoughton 1946), p. 165. 59 Mee, *Encyclopedia*, vol. 1, p. 3. 60 Ibid., vol. 4, p. 2793. 61 For a study of maths in the *Encyclopedia*, see Alex Craik, 'Arthur Mee's *Children's Encyclopedia* revisited', *BSHM Bulletin: Journal of the British Society for the History of Mathematics*, 21(2) (2006), 122–6. 62 Mee, *Encyclopedia*, vol. 1, p. 183. 63 Ibid., vol. 4, p. 2679. 64 Ibid., vol. 2, p. 1308. 65 Ibid., vol. 10, p. 6729. 66 Ibid., vol. 3, p. 1586.

of God'.[67] Jesus is admired as a great Teacher, and God is a Power with a capital P. Mee's philosophy is especially on display in the 'Ideas' section, which consists of essays on abstractions such as Faith, Justice, Eternity, Providence. It seems unlikely to me that any browsing child ever stopped for long to read them. The *Encyclopedia*'s method of organization establishes the serendipitous habit of leafing over the pages until something engages your interest. Despite his didacticism, I have therefore some scepticism about the extent to which Mee's prejudices rubbed off on his young readers and so, rather than focus on specific beliefs, I want to consider more general thoughts and feelings that the reader may unconsciously pick up.

CONSTRUCTION OF CHILDHOOD

The putative reader is a child. An Edwardian child, comfortably middle-class, like the children in the happy family in the picture story in the French lessons, going off on holiday to a hotel in France, with a nanny to look after the baby.[68] A child who is addressed in a friendly but serious and earnest tone. A still young child, pre-sexual. Works of art are doctored so as not to cause distress to young readers or offence to their parents and so, for instance, Michelangelo's statue of David is minus genitalia.[69] In *The Cambridge Guide to Children's Books in English*,[70] the entry on 'Fairy fantasy' says of early twentieth-century female illustrators that they 'introduced fairies to point up the charming otherness of infancy.' Arthur Mee similarly seems to regard children as a race apart, at a remove from adult concerns. Writing about the stories of Mary Louise Molesworth, J.C. Sommerville in his book *The Rise and Fall of Childhood*[71] says that

> she describes an English nursery world in which adults ... have a rather shadowy existence ... The children are pictured as naturally sweet, frank, generous, spirited and devout ... Mrs Moleworth's favourite character type is 'the little friend of all the world'.

A 'nursery world' seems to me an apt term to apply to Mee also, not in the sense that it is babyish, but insofar as it is cocooned and controlled and demarcated, at the same time as it is expansive and benevolent. As regards the construction of knowledge and of the child in the *Children's Encyclopedia*, Mee believed that 'a child is largely its own teacher',[72] free to browse and pursue interests through the

67 Ibid., vol. 4, p. 2883. **68** Ibid., vol. 1, p. 136. **69** Ibid., vol. 1, p. 72. **70** Victor Watson (ed.), *Cambridge Guide to Children's Books in English* (Cambridge: Cambridge UP, 2001). **71** J.C. Sommerville, *The Rise and Fall of Childhood* (London: Sage, 1982), p. 174. **72** Mee, *Encyclopedia*, vol. 1, p. 2.

world of the *Encyclopedia* as his or her wonder and imagination are engaged. This adult-free zone where children can wander at will has of course been created for children by adults and Mee's name and reputation were the guarantor for parents that, in the happy phrase of the *TLS* centenary article, they were in 'safe and clean hands',[73] and that they would not be perplexed by perceived adult matters such as sexuality but would encounter only exhortations to love and harmony.

As I have argued, the *Encyclopedia* is remarkable for its narrative form. It is the story-book of the universe, a narrativized account of the real world. Any story locates a person in place and in time: 'once upon a time a king lived in a castle.' The style of the Encyclopedia seems to place the child in a story realm but in fact he or she is located in the whole universe in a time-frame that sweeps across recorded time. It is a world in which everything is organized and managed and tidy and orderly. It may be vast and expansive, but it is humanized and recognizable, so there is a friendly feel to it which draws in the youthful reader. The sections are constantly making connections as, for example, in the chapter on 'How Euclid helped to build the Forth Bridge and the steam engine'.[74] In this respect it is very different from a conventional encyclopedia which fragments knowledge into arbitrary divisions, often alphabetical. Nowadays reference books are designed to allow speed of use and quick location of specific information but Mee takes us back to a slower Edwardian pace; the browser can be relaxed and leisurely in this storied world. It is an appropriately sanitized environment, sanctioned by adults, but the consequence of this is that there is nothing that is likely to prove disturbing for a child. The net result of these features is that the *Children's Encyclopedia* offers the security, interest and trust of a story-book.

A picture on page seventeen of the first volume displays in summary form the *Encyclopedia*'s world-view and the manner in which Mee represents childhood. It shows two children sitting on a cloud in the bottom right-hand corner, with one of them pointing towards the solar system – the planets circling the sun, with stars, clouds and a comet scattered on the dark background. Still today nothing is so likely to evoke wonder as the universe of stars and planets, though in this illustration the earth is reassuringly dominant. One assumes that the watchers are a boy and a girl, though the male is feminized. Their posture, faintly reminiscent of cherubs in a Renaissance painting, is easy and comfortable. They are masters of all they survey. The world is framed and contained so that they can look and learn and enjoy. The earth appears to be the largest planet, with the British Isles visible almost at the mid-point of the whole picture. It is this commanding view of the world that the *Encyclopedia* offers children. Mee delivers the whole of human life deemed suitable for children in story form. In

---

73 Anthony Quinton, 'The Happy Wonderer', *Times Literary Supplement*, 11 July 1975, 762.
74 Mee, *Encyclopedia*, vol. 2, p. 986.

this respect the *Children's Encyclopedia* is admirable both in its conception and in its realization. It is a striking example of that fundamental fact: the power of narrative.

For someone who favoured the story-teller's style, Mee had surprisingly little interest in reading stories himself. Hammerton writes that:

> Fiction he viewed with contempt ... Arthur's reading was never gladdened by acquaintance with the masterpieces of creative fiction; indeed, he read astonishingly few novels throughout his career; to put the number at two score might be to exaggerate.[75]

However he was indefatigable in his efforts to provide young people with wholesome reading. He capitalized on the success of the *Children's Encyclopedia* to produce a large number of spin-off books, such as *The Children's Bible* (1924), *One Thousand Beautiful Things* (1925), *The Loveliest Stories in the World* (1929), *Heroes of Freedom* (1936), but the most notable venture to arise out of it was *The Children's Newspaper*, which appeared weekly from 1919 until 1965, with Mee as editor from its inception until he died in 1943. Hammerton states that it was started in order 'to make Goodness News'.[76] It was the factual counterpart to the weekly fiction of children's comics. It carried forward in a different genre Mee's project to make non-fiction interesting and attractive for children (though it included serialized fiction by such children's writers as Geoffrey Trease, Malcolm Saville and Anthony Buckeridge). Ultimately it metamorphosed into *Look and Learn*,[77] which was able to build confidently on the pattern established by the trail-blazer Mee. It is on this account that Hammerton commends Mee:

> To designate *The Children's Encyclopedia* as the wonder-book of the twentieth century in the history of book-publishing would be no exaggeration ... Its central idea, the arrangement of its contents, its methods of exposition and illustration, have all been copied by hundreds of editors in every country where books are made, but the original production was the finest creation of Arthur Mee's inventive genius. It is beyond all computation the modern classic of the children's world.[78]

The impact of the *Children's Encyclopedia* in its day is a matter of record. Its originality emanates from how it represents the world to the child, which is dependent on how it constructs the child. This essay has explored how Arthur Mee conceived the world which he encyclopedically portrays and how he created

---

75 Sir John Hammerton, *Child of Wonder*, p. 33.   76 Ibid., p. 14.   77 See www.lookand learn.com for the history of both publications and reproductions of *The Children's Newspaper*. 78 Hammerton, *Child of Wonder*, p. 121.

his child-reader. Key to the former is the idea of curriculum-as-narrative and paramount in the latter is imagination and Wordsworthian wonder. The idealized child in a sanitized world, imprinted by Mee on middle-class consciousness, populated much contemporaneous children's fiction until it was routed by a more downright, in-your-face realism. Sadly, unlike classic children's fiction, reference books date with the advance of knowledge and so the *Children's Encyclopedia* has irrevocably had its day. The twenty-first century is often described as an information age or a knowledge economy; from its standpoint it is interesting to look back at the paradigms and norms of non-fiction for young people in earlier times. Despite its 'Englishness', the *Encyclopedia*'s penetration of the global market means that it remains as an early bench-mark for non-fiction in many countries. It is remembered with nostalgic fondness by those who grew up with it, for whom it was a loved book and a significant source of knowledge about life. The Orbis Pictus Award for Outstanding Non-fiction for Children is presented annually in the US. It has four literary criteria: accuracy, organization, design and style. By each of these measures Arthur Mee's *Children's Encyclopedia* was in its time an innovative, singular and exceptional prototype of the genre.

The propaganda of Na Fianna Éireann, 1909–26[1]

MARNIE HAY

In 1909 two Irish Protestant nationalist activists, Countess Constance Markievicz (1868–1927) and Bulmer Hobson (1883–1969), established a nationalist youth organization called Na Fianna Éireann, or the Irish National Boy Scouts.[2] The foundation of the Fianna was an Irish nationalist manifestation of the proliferation of 'pseudo-military youth groups' that occurred in many western countries in the late nineteenth and early twentieth centuries. These groups were not only part of the cult of discipline, training and manliness that grew out of the menace of the coming war in Europe,[3] but also a reaction to a widely-perceived *fin-de-siècle* 'decadence'. For instance, the British Army's poor performance against a force of South African farmers during the Boer War (1899–1902) provoked much concern that British men were in a state of decline. Fearing that they were losing their competitive edge in industrial and military affairs and that their populations were deteriorating both physically and morally, western countries like Britain began 'to look to the health, education and moral welfare of the rising generation'.[4] The establishment of youth groups was one way of dealing with the perceived problem.

The best known of these youth groups was the Boy Scout movement founded by Robert Baden-Powell in 1908. Baden-Powell, a British army officer, started this movement in response to the interest that boys had shown in his 1899 army training manual, *Aids to Scouting*. He was also inspired by the model of the Boys' Brigade, which was launched by William Alexander Smith in 1883 in Glasgow. Smith used military drill and discipline as a way of providing guidance to the boys who attended his Scottish Free Church Sunday School. Baden-Powell, in contrast, put less *overt* emphasis on militarism. Instead he focused on outdoor activities and personal development in order to counter what he saw as the moral and physical decline of the upcoming generation. He also wanted to train boys

1 I would like to thank the Irish Research Council for the Humanities and Social Sciences for its financial support, which enabled me to undertake research for this chapter. 2 For more in-depth discussion of the Fianna, see J. Anthony Gaughan, *Scouting in Ireland* (Dublin: Kingdom Books, 2006), pp 33–77, and Marnie Hay, 'The foundation and development of Na Fianna Éireann, 1909-16', *Irish Historical Studies*, 36:141 (2008), 53–71. 3 David Fitzpatrick, 'Militarism in Ireland, 1900–1922', in Thomas Bartlett and Keith Jeffrey (eds), *A Military History of Ireland* (Cambridge: CUP, 1996), pp 382–3. 4 Colin Heywood, *A History of Childhood* (Cambridge: Polity, 2005), pp 29–30.

to be better citizens.[5] Whether his main concern prior to 1920 was training citizens or future soldiers has sparked much scholarly debate.[6]

Irish nationalists viewed such British imports as the Boys' Brigades and the Boy Scouts as a threat that could be turned into an opportunity. In 1903 Arthur Griffith (1871–1922) condemned the Catholic Boys' Brigades as a recruiting ground for the British Army, but recognized that if 'properly conducted', boys' brigades could be turned into 'a great national force', contributing to 'the intellectual and physical good of the young'.[7] Griffith saw such potential in what was actually the first incarnation of Na Fianna Éireann.

This was a boys' hurling club founded by Hobson in Belfast in 1902. The excitement surrounding the club's inaugural meeting convinced Hobson that the fledgling organization was something that could be moulded 'into a strong force to help in the liberation of Ireland'.[8] But due to lack of money and the pressures of his various cultural and political commitments, the Belfast organization lapsed before it could live up to this dream.

By 1909 circumstances had changed and Hobson jumped at the opportunity to re-establish Na Fianna Éireann with Markievicz in Dublin. Their aim was to counteract the influence of Baden-Powell's pro-British body. The new militarized Fianna was a nationalist, non-sectarian youth organization designed to appeal to boys between eight and eighteen,[9] although a girls' *sluagh*, or troop, was later started in Belfast.[10] The Fianna went on to play an important role in helping to prepare boys (and some girls) for their future role in the fight for Irish freedom. It not only provided them with an Irish nationalist education and military training, but also promoted role models for them to emulate.

This chapter will examine advanced nationalist propaganda produced by Na Fianna Éireann in the period 1909–26. For the purposes of this study, the term 'propaganda' refers to written material intended to influence the attitude and opinion of readers. As members of the Fianna tended to come from families with

5 Richard A. Smith, 'Robert Baden-Powell', in John Cannon (ed.), *The Oxford Companion to British History* (Oxford: OUP, 1997), p. 72; Robert A. Smith, 'Boy Scouts' and 'Boys' Brigade', in Cannon (ed.), *Oxford Companion*, p. 119; Henry Collis, Fred Hurll and Rex Hazlewood, *B.-P.'s Scouts: an official history of the Boy Scouts Association* (London: Collins, 1961), pp 48, 55.   6 See Michael Rosenthal, 'Knights and retainers: the earliest version of Baden-Powell's Boy Scout scheme', *Journal of Contemporary History*, 15 (1980), 603–17; Allen Warren, 'Sir Robert Baden-Powell, the Scout movement and citizen training in Great Britain, 1900–1920', *English Historical Review*, 101 (1986), 376–98; John Springhall, 'Baden-Powell and the Scout movement before 1920: citizen training or soldiers of the future?', *English Historical Review*, 102 (1987), 934–42; Anne Summers, 'Scouts, Guides and VADs: a note in reply to Allen Warren', *English Historical Review*, 102 (1987), 943–7; Allen Warren, 'Baden-Powell: a final comment', *English Historical Review*, 102 (1987), 948–50.   7 *United Irishman* (24 Jan. 1903), 1.   8 Hobson, *Ireland Yesterday and Tomorrow* (Tralee: Anvil Books, 1968), p. 15.   9 Eamon Martin, Bureau of Military History (BMH) witness statement, n.d. (National Archives of Ireland [NAI], BMH, WS 591).   10 James Connolly's daughters Nora and Ina were leading members of this girls' troop in Belfast.

advanced nationalist and/or republican views, Fianna propaganda was more likely to reinforce an existing nationalist sentiment rather than convert readers to advanced nationalism. In addition, much of the material under consideration was designed to provide an Irish nationalist alternative to popular British youth publications, such as Baden-Powell's *Scouting for Boys* (1908) and periodicals like the *Boy's Own Paper*,[11] by subverting the conventions of such literature.

From its inception in 1909 up until the 1916 Easter Rising, the official Fianna organization, as well as individual members, published propaganda aimed mainly at boys in their pre-teen and teen years in advanced nationalist newspapers, such as *Bean na hÉireann* (1908–11), *Irish Freedom* (1910–14) and the *Irish Volunteer* (1914–16), in the boys' paper *Fianna* (1915–16), and in the *Fianna Handbook* (1914). During this time the Fianna served as a training ground for future members of the Irish Volunteers, a nationalist paramilitary organization founded in 1913 which later became known as the Irish Republican Army (IRA).

As a result of the Rising's 'propaganda of deed' and Irish abhorrence of the British reaction to the insurrection, the Fianna attracted an all-time high of over 30,000 members by June 1917.[12] However, there was a lull in Fianna publications during the period between the Rising and the achievement of independence in the 26 counties because the organization was preoccupied with re-grouping and then making an active contribution to the War of Independence (1919–21).

From about 1922 onwards, propagandist publications, such as a revived version of the *Fianna* paper, commemoration souvenirs and a new edition of the handbook, began to appear again. Particularly after the Irish Civil War (1922–3), the Fianna, which had opposed the 1921 Anglo-Irish Treaty, was keen to emphasize its educational, rather than military, value in a newly independent Irish Free State, where the Baden-Powell Boy Scouts continued to attract higher membership figures, and in Northern Ireland where Fianna troops, despite having been outlawed in 1923, remained in existence.[13] The June 1926 issue of *Fianna* emphasized the continuing need for republican youth propaganda when it complained about the presence in Ireland of 50,000 Freemasons and 36,000 Boy Scouts, who represented 'the Vanguard of British imperialism in this country'.[14]

---

11 For more on nationalist propaganda aimed at youth, see Marnie Hay, 'This treasured island: Irish nationalist propaganda aimed at children and youth, 1910–16' and Michael Flanagan, '"There is an isle in the western ocean": the Christian Brothers, *Our Boys* and Catholic/nationalist ideology', in Mary Shine Thompson and Celia Keenan (eds), *Treasure Islands: studies in children's literature* (Dublin: Four Courts, 2006), pp 33–52. 12 Pádraig Mac Fhloinn, 'The history and tradition of Fianna Éireann', *Fianna Éireann Handbook* (Dublin: Fianna Éireann, 1988), p. 14. 13 Ibid., p. 18. 14 'Editorial', *Fianna* (June 1926), 1. Four years earlier Fianna membership stood at 26,000, though this was probably an inflated figure ('Report of the Fianna convention', *Fianna* [June 1922], 5).

Although the newspapers *Bean na hÉireann*, *Irish Freedom* and the *Irish Volunteer* were primarily aimed at an adult audience, they provided a forum for Na Fianna Éireann to report its news and views.[15] Markievicz and Hobson were contributors to *Bean na hÉireann*, which was published by the nationalist women's organization Inghinidhe na hÉireann (Daughters of Erin). Various Fianna members and supporters produced articles for *Irish Freedom*, which was the mouthpiece of the Irish Republican Brotherhood (IRB), a secret society whose goal was the achievement of an Irish republic through the use of physical force if necessary. Fianna officers Liam Mellows and Pádraig Ó Riain wrote regular columns for the *Irish Volunteer*, the official organ of the Irish Volunteers. These papers kept members up to date on the activities of troops around the country and changes to official Fianna policy, with the *Irish Volunteer* publishing articles providing instruction on topics such as field sketching and map reading.[16] Such coverage of Fianna activities may have attracted new members to the organization.

Irish Freedom also ran a monthly column for youth under twenty, entitled 'Grianán na nÓg' (or the 'Sunroom of Youth'). Written by a young woman identified as 'Neasa', it featured monthly competitions and suggested ways in which young people could further the struggle for Irish independence, such as was proposed on one occasion, by joining the Fianna or setting up a similar organization for girls.[17] As it happened, it was not until the early 1930s that a girls' group, Cumann na gCailíní, was started by the nationalist women's organization Cumann na mBan.

It is impossible to say for certain how many members of the Fianna read these papers, which were probably purchased by older family members. Hobson's estimate that there were over 1,500 members of the IRB in 1912 suggests that *Irish Freedom* had a potential adult audience of at least that number.[18] Contemporary police reports surmised that the *Irish Volunteer* had at the very least a total circulation of 3,937 in November 1915 and 4,615 in February 1916.[19]

In 1914 the Fianna started to produce its own publications to disseminate propaganda aimed at youth, particularly boys. Its first venture was the launch of the *Fianna Handbook*, which was issued by the Fianna's Central Council and compiled by Honorary General Secretary Pádraig Ó Riain.[20] Priced at one

15 For an example of these Fianna news reports, see Ruaidhri, 'Na Fianna Éireann', *Bean na hÉireann* (Jan. 1911), 12–13, which discusses the drawing of the Goose Club prizes at the Fianna Hall on Camden Street in Dublin and the recent growth and activities of three Belfast troops. 16 For instance, a series of articles on map reading appeared in early 1916. See Ó Riain, 'Na Fianna Éireann', *Irish Volunteer* (22 Jan. 1916, 29 Jan. 1916, 5 Feb. 1916, 12 Feb. 1916), 8. 17 Neasa, 'Grianán na nÓg', *Irish Freedom* (June & July 1912), 3.   18 Hobson, *Ireland*, p. 36. 19 Breandán Mac Giolla Choille (ed.), *Intelligence Notes, 1913–16* (Dublin: Republic of Ireland State Papers Office, 1966), p. 163.   20 Bulmer Hobson, BMH witness statement (15 Oct. 1947) (NAI, BMH, WS 31).

shilling, it provided detailed information about the Fianna organization, such as its aims, structure, rules and tests of skill, and practical instruction on topics related to military training and camping, including drill, first aid and even swimming.[21] While Markievicz's introduction was directed towards 'young people' in general,[22] the remainder of the text referred to boys only, highlighting the controversy over female membership in the organization.[23] Prominent nationalists such as Patrick Pearse (1879–1916), Douglas Hyde (1860–1949) and Roger Casement (1864–1916) also contributed chapters. The handbook's editor proudly reported that Catherine M. Mahon, the former president of the Irish National School Teachers' Organization Society (the Irish National Teachers' Organization), had not only written a favourable review of the book, but urged 'all national school teachers to read [it] and to set about starting branches of the Fianna in connection with local Volunteer corps'.[24]

The *Fianna Handbook* was billed as 'the first, the largest and the only illustrated military publication issued for the use of Irish nationalists', implying that its content would be of use to adults (such as the Irish Volunteers) as well as youth.[25] It was designed to replace Baden-Powell's 1908 book *Scouting for Boys* and British War Office manuals, which were the few written sources for instruction previously available to the Fianna. Both the *Fianna Handbook* and *Scouting for Boys* covered topics such as camping, first aid, patriotism and chivalry, but the interpretation differed, particularly of the latter two topics. Baden-Powell promoted patriotism in the context of the British Empire and medieval knights as models of chivalry. In contrast, the *Fianna Handbook* encouraged Irish youth to direct their patriotic impulses toward the foundation of an independent Irish state and hailed the chivalry of Fionn Mac Cumhaill's Fianna warriors. Unlike *Scouting for Boys*, the *Fianna Handbook* included an illustrated section on rifle exercises, revealing the overtly militant nature of the Irish organization.[26]

When the *Fianna Handbook* was re-issued in 1924, most of the content remained largely the same. A key difference, however, can be seen in the declaration to be made by new Fianna members, which reflected the changed political circumstances in Ireland and post-Treaty divisions within Irish nationalism. In 1914 members promised 'to work for the independence of Ireland, never to join England's armed forces, and to obey [their] superior officers'.[27] Ten years later they pledged their 'allegiance to the Irish Republic and promise[d] to do all in

21 See Pádraig Ó Riain (ed.), *Fianna Handbook* (Dublin: Central Council of Na Fianna Éireann, 1914). 22 Countess Markievicz, 'Introduction', in Ó Riain (ed.), *Fianna Handbook*, pp 6–8. 23 For a discussion of this controversy, see Hay, 'The foundation and development of Na Fianna Éireann, 1909–16', 60–2, and Margaret Ward, *Unmanageable Revolutionaries: women and Irish nationalism* (London: Pluto, 1995), pp 104–6. 24 'Boy Scouts', *Irish Volunteer* (24 Oct. 1914), 16. 25 'Boy Scouts', *Irish Volunteer* (12 Sept. 1914), 3. 26 See Ó Riain (ed.), *Fianna Handbook*, pp 53–74. 27 Ibid., p. 13.

[their] power to protect her from all enemies, whether foreign or domestic, and not to relax [their] efforts until the Irish Republic is universally recognized'. The promise to obey their superior officers remained the same.[28] More significant changes in content were made to later editions published in 1964 and 1988.[29]

In addition to the appearance of the first handbook, the year 1914 witnessed the publication of a Fianna Christmas annual, entitled *Nodlaig na bhFiann*. Edited by Fianna members Percy Reynolds and Patsy O'Connor, the annual was not issued by Fianna Headquarters but did have official sanction.[30] The annual proved a financial success, but drew criticism from Ó Riain who deemed it 'the most unboyish boys' paper I have ever seen'. He slated 'two rather heavy articles' by James Connolly (1868–1916) and Hobson ('The chief merit of both is that they are brief') and complained that the annual's title was the only line of Irish that appeared in the publication. On a more positive note Ó Riain praised Markievicz's article on the formation of the Fianna and enjoyed reading 'an amusing escapade of four members of the Dublin Fianna' who decided to annoy 'the aristocracy of Rathmines and neighbourhood' through their carol singing.[31]

Reynolds and O'Connor continued to take heed of Hobson's recommendation that 'every boy in the Fianna should be a propagandist for the Irish nation',[32] going on to launch *Fianna*, a monthly paper for boys, in February 1915.[33] The paper published fiction, poetry and jokes, articles on Irish history and folklore, and Fianna news and views, though it was not an official organ of Na Fianna Éireann. Ó Riain's criticism regarding the absence of Irish in the Christmas annual was addressed by including a monthly column on folklore written in Irish. Among the serials that the paper ran was 'The Wandering Hawk', a school story by Pearse about a popular teacher in a Catholic boys' boarding school who was a Fenian on the run, and 'The Boys of Wexford', a series of tales about 'a brave band of boys' who fought during the 1798 Rebellion.[34] *Fianna*'s editors,

28 *Fianna Handbook*, 2nd ed. (Dublin: Central Council of Fianna Éireann, 1924), p. 7.   **29** See *The Young Guard of Erin: the Fianna Handbook* (Dublin: Na Fianna Éireann, 1964) and *Fianna Éireann Handbook* (Dublin: Fianna Éireann, 1988).   **30** Liam Mellows, 'Boy Scouts Organising Notes', *Irish Volunteer* (21 Nov. 1914), 15.   **31** Willie Nelson (Pádraig Ó Riain), 'Na Fianna Éireann', *Irish Volunteer* (19 Dec. 1914), 8.   **32** Fergus Mac Leda (Bulmer Hobson), 'Letters to members of Na Fianna Éireann', *Irish Freedom* (Mar. 1913), 6.   **33** Contemporary newspaper articles identified Reynolds and O'Connor as the initial editors of the paper, with O'Connor resigning from the editorship sometime prior to his death in June 1915 (Willie Nelson, 'Na Fianna Éireann', *Irish Volunteer* [9 Jan. 1915, 26 June 1915], 8; 'In memoriam', *Fianna* [July 1915], 3). Reynolds may have secured another editorial partner. Although Virginia E. Glandon and Ben Novick have cited Hobson as the editor of *Fianna*, Hobson does not verify this in his memoirs, perhaps wishing to maintain the impression that the paper was produced by Fianna members (Virginia E. Glandon, *Arthur Griffith and the Advanced Nationalist Press: Ireland, 1900–1922* [New York: Peter Lang, 1985], p. 269; Ben Novick, *Conceiving Revolution: Irish nationalist propaganda during the First World War* [Dublin: Four Courts, 2001], p. 30; Bulmer Hobson, BMH witness statement [15 Oct. 1947] [NAI, BMH, WS 31]).   **34** Pearse's serial started in the Feb. 1915 issue of *Fianna* while 'The Boys of Wexford' by Croghan Kinsella began in April of that

however, found it difficult to compete against popular British boys' periodicals, such as the *Boys' Friend*, which they declared were 'killing Irish Nationalism'. Despite attempts to boost circulation by offering incentives such as free copies of the *Fianna Handbook* to readers who attracted four new subscribers,[35] they were forced to widen their target audience to include adult men as well from July 1915 onwards.[36] By November 1915 the British authorities estimated that the paper had a circulation of at least 859, which grew to 1,094 by February 1916.[37]

Fianna was later revived as an official organ of the youth group in June 1922. Its editor outlined some of the challenges facing the organization in light of the changed circumstances in a (partially) independent Ireland:

> Conditions in recent years rendered it necessary that the Fianna should act more like a military organization than they would be expected to do in normal times. The educational side of our programming has been completely neglected. For instance, how many of our officers or boys have qualified to wear the Fáinne? To develop on educational lines a paper is more needed than ever. While still keeping in view military training we must devote more of our time to the training of the mind and body. Physical training has had to be cut out; Gaelic games have been neglected, both necessary if we are to raise up strong and virile Irishmen fit to take a soldier's part in the national struggle of tomorrow.[38]

The revived paper included the usual Fianna news and views, as well as poetry, competitions, and articles about republican heroes, old and new, such as Theobald Wolfe Tone (1763–98) and Liam Mellows (1892–1922).[39]

A competition in the June 1922 edition betrayed the organization's continuing sexist attitude towards the role of females in the nationalist movement, despite Markievicz's position as Chief of the Fianna and the notable contributions made by women to the Irish Revolution in the preceding years. The premise of the competition was that Kathleen, 'a good Irish cailín', needed help in choosing a husband on the basis of the answers provided by her suitors Kevin, Lorcan and Brendan to the question 'Why did you become a soldier of the IRA?' Entrants were to write an essay on which soldier gave the best answer to the question and by extension which man Kathleen should marry.[40]

Inherent in the foundation of the Fianna by Markievicz and Hobson had been the recognition that youth were the future of the Irish nationalist movement. Thus, education and training were meant to be an important part of the organization, in terms of both its written propaganda and its regular activities such as

year. **35** 'Killing Irish nationalism', *Fianna* (Mar. 1915), 4. **36** 'From the editors', *Fianna* (June 1915), 3. **37** Mac Giolla Choille (ed.), *Intelligence Notes*, p. 163. **38** 'Editorial', *Fianna* (June 1922), 3. **39** 'Tone: episodes in his life', 'The objects of Tone', *Fianna* (June 1922), 8–9; 'Liam Ó Maoil Íosa', *Fianna* (June 1926), 1. **40** 'Fianna-tion', *Fianna* (June 1922), 10.

weekly meetings, route marches and camping trips. To move up within the ranks of the Fianna (at least during 'peace time'), members had to pass tests on Irish language and history, as well as on military drill, first aid and other skills necessary for scouting and camping.[41] Therefore, Fianna propaganda sought to educate young people about Irish history and folklore in order to teach them about their own unique heritage, to familiarize them with Ireland's long struggle against British occupation, and to introduce them to Irish heroes worthy of emulation. Practical instruction on topics such as signalling, map reading and handling weapons was provided both at weekly meetings and in the *Fianna Handbook* and articles included in the *Irish Volunteer*. Members learned how to govern themselves by being responsible for the running of the organization, preparing them for citizenship, possibly even leadership, in an independent Ireland. To this end, the *Fianna Handbook* outlined the policy, organizational structure and constitution of the youth group.[42] In taking the initiative to produce *Nodlaig na bhFiann* and *Fianna*, Reynolds and O'Connor demonstrated that Fianna membership could help youths to develop the ability and self-confidence to communicate the message of Irish nationalism and separatism to their own age cohort. However, none of these publications provided any Irish language instruction, though they did include some Irish language content and urged Fianna members to learn Irish.

In addition to providing an Irish nationalist education and military training, Fianna propaganda endorsed suitable role models for Irish boys. In general, it promoted an idealized image of Irish nationalist youth that emphasized the importance of patriotism and morality. A Fianna member was to learn 'all about his country, its history and language, its resources and industries, and his one aim in life [was] to serve it to the best of his ability'. He should also keep his body and mind 'clean and pure'.[43] Such propaganda urged members never to 'do anything that would bring discredit upon Ireland or upon the Fianna'.[44] According to the Fianna Code of Honour, which was developed in 1921, members of the Fianna were to embody the following twelve traits: patriotism, reliability, diligence, kindness, obedience, cheerfulness, thrift, bravery, cleanliness, humility, temperance and punctuality.[45] Such qualities were similar to those promoted by Baden-Powell's Boy Scouts, which included self-discipline, obedience, loyalty, sobriety and cleanliness.[46] Despite these obvious parallels, however, advanced nationalist propaganda from this period highlighted a moral dichotomy between Ireland and Britain, criticizing the alleged 'degenerate and debased nature of British and pro-British people'.[47]

41 See Ó Riain (ed.), *Fianna Handbook*, pp 17–21.   **42** Ibid., p. 14.   **43** Fianna Code of Honour (1929) (National Library of Ireland [NLI], MS 10,910).   **44** Ó Riain (ed.), *Fianna Handbook*, p. 14.   **45** Fianna Code of Honour (1929) (NLI, MS 10,910).   **46** Lieut.-General R.S.S. Baden Powell, *Scouting for Boys: a handbook for instruction in good citizenship*, fifth impression (London: C. Arthur Pearson, 1908), p. 266.   **47** Novick, *Conceiving Revolution*, p.

As part of this idealized image of nationalist youth, Fianna members were to be prepared to make the ultimate sacrifice to attain Irish independence. In her introduction to the first *Fianna Handbook*, Markievicz predicted that members of the Fianna would not 'flinch' if the 'path to freedom' led to their death, as it had for Wolfe Tone and Robert Emmet (1778–1803).[48] Those current or former members of the organization who died as a result of their involvement in the Easter Rising, the War of Independence or the Irish Civil War were not only praised in post-1916 Fianna propaganda, but promoted as worthy role models for future generations.[49] For instance, a 1922 Easter Week commemoration souvenir programme declared that Fianna officers Sean Heuston and Con Colbert, who were executed for their roles in the 1916 Rising, 'met their deaths, happy that it was for Ireland, sure of the heaven that awaited them. In boyish simplicity and purity, and with manly courage, they faced the firing squad.'[50] Markievicz's foreword to the second edition of the *Fianna Handbook* encouraged members to follow 'the example and teachings of our heroic dead'. She reported that Liam Mellows, who was executed in 1922 during the Civil War by the Irish Free State as a reprisal for the murder of a Dáil deputy, 'always urged on the Fianna the importance of educating and training their minds, in the principles and ideals that governed Gaelic Ireland'.[51] Future Fianna propaganda continued to glorify martyrs to the cause, with a Fianna Roll of Honour listing the names of 54 members 'who gave their lives for Ireland's freedom' between 1915 and 1981.[52] The first name on the list is former *Fianna* editor Patsy O'Connor, whose death in 1915 was believed to have resulted from a head injury that he received when he was batoned by the police while administering first aid to a worker during the 1913 Lock-out in Dublin.[53]

It is difficult to provide an empirical assessment of the effectiveness of any type of propaganda. There are, however, indications that the Fianna's propaganda was effective to some degree. That the editors of *Bean na hÉireann*, *Irish Freedom*, the *Irish Volunteer* and *Fianna* chose to publish, and continued to publish, propaganda aimed at Fianna members in particular and youth in general, suggests that they believed there was a potentially receptive audience for their message. Although *Fianna*, unlike the Christian Brothers' *Our Boys*, clearly failed in its attempt to provide a successful Irish nationalist alternative to popular

169. **48** Markievicz, 'Introduction', in Ó Riain (ed.), *Fianna Handbook*, p. 8. **49** See *Easter Week 1916–1922 Commemoration Aeridheacht Souvenir Programme*, 23 April 1922 (Dublin: Fianna Éireann Dublin Brigade, 1922), and Cathal O'Shannon (ed.), *Souvenir of the Golden Jubilee of Fianna Éireann, 16 Aug. 1909–16 Aug. 1959* (Dublin: Na Fianna Éireann, 1959). **50** *Easter Week 1916–1922 Commemoration Aeridheacht Souvenir Programme*, p. 7. **51** Countess Markievicz, 'Foreword', *Fianna Handbook*, 2nd ed., pp 4–5. **52** 'Fianna Roll of Honour', in Robert Holland, 'A short history of Fianna Éireann', n.d. [*c.*1981], pp 25–6 (NLI, MS 35,455/3/12A). Na Fianna Éireann produced this photocopied booklet, which features a memoir written in 1949. **53** Willie Nelson, 'Na Fianna Éireann', *Irish Volunteer* (26 June 1915), 8; Mac Fhloinn, 'History and tradition', p. 10.

British boys' papers, it made gains in circulation after it widened its focus to become a paper geared towards boys and men. After the outbreak of the First World War the authorities in Dublin Castle were so worried about the effect of 'seditious' newspapers that they suppressed *Irish Freedom*, issued a warning to the printer of the *Irish Volunteer*, and began tracking the rising circulation of *Fianna*.[54] That members of the Fianna served as leaders, combatants, scouts and messengers during the Easter Rising and later in the War of Independence also attests to the effectiveness of Fianna propaganda: nine Fianna members died during the Rising and twenty-one during the War of Independence.[55] Such propaganda may have contributed to the role of youth and the pre-dominance of young men within the IRA, which has been noted in recent studies of the Irish Revolution.[56] Although the Fianna laid down its arms in May 1923, it did not surrender its commitment to a 32-county Irish republic. Instead, it revived its educational programme through activities such as the publication of republican youth propaganda.

The propaganda produced by the Fianna in the period 1909–26 served a similar purpose to advanced nationalist propaganda aimed at children and youth in general. It provided Fianna members with an Irish nationalist education and military training; promoted specific role models as well as an idealized image of Irish nationalist youth that members could emulate; and, just like the Fianna organization itself, offered an Irish nationalist alternative to British youth culture. As much of this propaganda was generated by the youthful members themselves, participation in its production also empowered them to seize control of their own destinies, both individual and national.

54 Mac Giolla Choille (ed.), *Intelligence Notes*, pp 116, 163.   **55** 'Fianna Roll of Honour', in Holland, 'A short history of Fianna Éireann' (NLI, MS 35,455/3/12A).   **56** See Peter Hart, *The IRA and its Enemies* (Oxford: Clarendon, 1998); Joost Augusteijn, *From Public Defiance to Guerrilla Warfare: the experience of ordinary volunteers in the Irish war of independence, 1916–1921* (Dublin: Irish Academic, 1996); Marie Coleman, *County Longford and the Irish Revolution* (Dublin: Irish Academic, 2003); and David Fitzpatrick, *Politics and Irish Life, 1913–1921* (Cork: Cork UP, 1998).

'Tales told in the turflight': the Christian Brothers, *Our Boys* and the representation of Gaelic authenticity in the popular culture of the Irish Free State

MICHAEL FLANAGAN

The Kitty the Hare stories by Victor O'Donovan Power, the prolific contributor to popular Irish periodicals, which first appeared in *Our Boys* in November 1924, encapsulate the spirit of pastoral idealism which permeated the early years of the Free State.[1] These tales were to become a central feature of the magazine for the next sixty years (though Power died in 1929). Power's fictional creation, Kitty the Hare, was a travelling woman who roamed the countryside of Munster. Each issue found her recounting a tale, either from the comfort of her own fireside or the hearth of a household she was visiting. This was a woman who was received warmly by those who lived in isolated farmsteads. In a pre-technology era such travellers were appreciated: being bearers of news and gossip, they brightened up the routine of everyday life. In that age, news had a certain currency, and was treated as such by those who made a living moving from place to place. Power's chosen title for his series, 'Tales Told in the Turflight', conveys much of its atmosphere. This was an essentially rural world, a timeless place in which the established mores of folklore governed the lives of the country people. Many of the elements of the social, economic and cultural tenets through which the newly independent Ireland defined her distinct identity are to be found in these tales of magic and mystery, fairies and mischievous spirits such as púcas. The heroes and heroines of these tales live among the hills of west Cork and Kerry. Their lives are governed by the harsh reality of existence at a time of widespread poverty, high mortality (which explains, to a degree, the number of ghost stories among the material) and mass emigration. This is a popular literary version of an official ideal that Roy Foster has described:

---

1 *Our Boys* was a magazine for boys first published in 1914 by the Christian Brothers with the stated aim of competing for the hearts and mind of Irish youth against the perceived imperialist orientation of the British *Boys' Own* genre. Victor O'D. Power contributed fiction to *Irish Lamp*, *Irish Emerald, Irish Fireside, Shamrock, Weekly Freeman, Catholic Times, Donohoe's Magazine, Ireland's Own* and *Our Boys*. The Kitty the Hare series was popular even in the early 1980s. He was also a popular playwright and published two novels.

De Valera's vision, repeated in numerous formulations, was of small agricultural units, each self-sufficiently supporting a frugal family; indus- trious, Gaelicist and anti-materialist. His ideal, like the popular literary versions, was built on the basis of a fundamentally dignified and ancient peasant way of life.[2]

A central belief in the nationalist creed was that the 'real' Ireland, the 'authentic' Ireland was not to be found in the streets of Dublin, Cork or Galway: the defin- itive form of true Irish community was located on an idealized western seaboard, far from the decay and corruption of what was perceived as the alien influence of modern metropolitan culture.

There were literally dozens of stories in this series extending across the broad range of Irish folklore. The series featured ghost stories such as 'Pat Kearney's Promise', 'By Little Nan's Grave' and 'The Ghost of Ownahincha'; mystery stories like 'The Mystery of Eily Forde', 'The Midnight Thief' and 'The Mystery of Denis Maguire'; and stories of supernatural influence such as 'Seamus Buckley and the Good People', 'The Stolen Child and Theigue Maguire' and 'The Banshee'. For all the variation of material, these tales have some broad similarities in terms of structure. The iconography of landscape is a central feature of the series. There is a pronounced signification of the Irish cottage, and the supernatural is invoked frequently, the forces of the other world interfering occasionally in human affairs, often with complex and terrifying results. Finally, there is frequent use of what Raymond Williams terms 'magical resolution' - the surprising appearance of a missing character, for example, or an unexpected legacy as a narrative device.[3]

In evoking the Western landscape Power's stories may be seen in the context of the formation of a national sense of identity and of self-image in the early days of the State.[4] The Christian Brothers' placing of the 'Turflight Tales' in the setting of a youth magazine indicates a further sense of commitment on their part to the promulgation of the dominant ideology (rural, Gaelic and Catholic)

---

2 Roy Foster, *Modern Ireland, 1600–1972* (London: Penguin, 1988), p. 538. 3 Raymond Williams, *The Long Revolution* (London: Hogarth, 1992), pp 65–7. Williams describes the role of the Empire as a narrative device in British popular fiction from the 1840s onwards: a universally available escape route, for example, or the source of an unexpected legacy. I would argue that emigration to America played a similar role in Irish popular fiction, many examples of which are to be found in 'Tales Told in the Turflight'. 4 This desire for some form of 'national authen- ticity' was not an exclusively Irish concept. It may be seen as an aspect of what Kenneth McConkey identifies, in the context of Britain, as 'the late-Victorian bourgeois impulse to return to rusticity'. See his 'Haunts of ancient peace', in David Corbett, Ysanne Holt and Fiona Russell (eds), *The Geographies of Englishness: landscape and the national past, 1880–1940* (London: Yale UP, 2002), pp 65–91. See also James Vernon, 'Border crossings: Cornwall and the English Imagination', in Geoffrey Cubit (ed.), *Imagining Nations* (Manchester: Manchester UP, 1998), pp 153–72.

that had been central to their ethos almost from the inception of the order and certainly from the 1870s onwards. This was the vision of Ireland that *Our Boys* marketed in the 1920s. In doing so, the magazine may be seen as part of a collective policy of illusion, whereby much of what the dominant ideology rejected was ignored in terms of the development of nationalist iconography – *Our Boys* continued to avoid the lifestyles of urban children, for example. In this it was not alone. Irish art, if it may be said to have had a cohesive ideology at this period, was also dominated by matters pastoral and by themes which reflected the concerns of those recently arrived in the corridors of power. Mainly rural, Gaelic and Catholic, the newly dominant class of bureaucrats and business men wished to see their ideals reflected in the work of Irish artists. Although they did not constitute an organized nationalist school of painting, the works of artists like Sean Keating (1889–1977), Paul Henry (1876–1958), Maurice MacGonigal (1900–79), Charles Lamb (1893–1964) and Patrick Touhy (1894–1930) helped to create in visual terms a 'corporate identity' for independent Ireland.[5]

What was now sought from all kinds of artistic representation was the concept of a range of symbolism which would define the aesthetic parameters of the new state, as Yeats had sought to achieve in his poetry, for example. In this new order there was little room for compromise on the part of such writers as Liam O'Flaherty (1896–1984), who vehemently opposed George Russell's management of the periodical, the *Irish Statesman*, on the grounds that his editorial policy of giving equal space to both Gaelic and Anglo-Irish traditions was 'not representative in any respect of the cultural forces, in all spheres, that are trying to find room for birth in this country at present'.[6]

A good example of the style of art which might have found O'Flaherty's approval is Paul Henry's 'A Sunny Day in Connemara', painted in 1940. In this painting he captures the whole sentiment of the landscape: in the humble dwellings depicted with their gathered stacks of turf for fuel and their general suggestion of a basic but satisfying way of life, unsullied by technological advancement and other trappings of 'civilization', is a view which fits perfectly with the temper of the time.[7] 'Tales Told in the Turflight' may also be viewed in the light of independent Ireland's pursuit of an image by which the state could define itself. While there are no political references in these stories, or at least little of overt nationalism, there is a highly defined sense of place, particularly local place, as Kitty travels across a deeply symbolic landscape. This is a sacred landscape – it is the point of contact with another world, so many of the local place-names redolent with the meaning of a set of beliefs that can only be rural, only Gaelic, and therefore carry the weight of identification with so much of the

5 See Brian P. Kennedy, 'The Irish Free State 1922–49: a visual perspective', in *Ireland: art into history* (Dublin: Town House, 1994), pp 132–52. 6 *Irish Statesman* , 20 June 1925, cit. Brian Kennedy, 'Irish landscape painting in a political setting', in Myrtle Hill and Sarah Barber (eds), *Aspects of Irish Studies* (Belfast: Institute of Irish Studies, QUB, 1990), pp 47–8. 7 Ibid., p. 48.

ethnic/revivalist iconography that contributed to the development of national consciousness at this crucial period, the early decades of the twentieth century.

There is no modernization in this setting; there are no motor cars, no cities. Kitty the Hare walks the little roads of West Cork and Kerry, mediating between the external world and the other world. On the road between such 'real' places as Dunmanway and Drimoleague lie such points of contact as Lis na Shee, Lis an Urra, Lis Beg, Liscloone, Lis na Corriga and Glauna Shee, whose etymologies associate them with fairies and fairy dwellings. They symbolize a hidden Ireland, a deeper, older and therefore different, more valuable world to that of the modern, the metropolitan, the Anglified. The folklore revival element of the national movement encouraged the Catholic middle class to look to its past, to travel to the isolated West in pursuit of the authentic and the meaningful.[8] The peasantry held the key to a fuller understanding of funda-mental 'Irishness'; their stories carried the secrets of an ancient code, through which the new Ireland would throw off the shackles of alien values.[9] In publishing the stories of Victor O'Donovan Power, the Christian Brothers brought these values to the readers of *Our Boys* and in this process contributed to the 'nationalizing' of the Irish landscape.

Kitty the Hare comes out of the landscape and is part of the fabric of the countryside. It is by the fireside, however, that the most important acts of the mediation process that define Power's stories take place. In a pre-electric period, a place that was only opening up to the standardization of the outside world at the start of the twentieth century, the traveller, whether peddler, tinsmith or in Kitty's case, of indefinable livelihood apart from her social role as storyteller, had a significant function in the economy of news exchange and social intercourse. In the ideology of the Free State there is an understanding that the Irish farmhouse *is* home, the only authentic expression of the domestic ideal. Kitty comes in and out of this fixed point, frequently informing us at the beginning of her nightly story that we are, on this occasion, in her own home, 'in ould Ballyroe, near the lapping waters o' Corran Lake'.

8 The attractions of the peasant community of the west for the new middle class of independent Ireland are outlined in Diarmuid Ó Giolláin's *Locating Irish Folklore: tradition, modernity, identity* (Cork: CUP, 2000), pp 142–64. See also Yvonne Scott, introductory essay, *The West as Metaphor* (Dublin: Royal Hibernian Academy, 2005), pp 7–52.   9 The extent to which the peasantry subscribed to this code in their daily lives is outlined by Richard P. Jenkins, 'Witches and fairies: supernatural aggression and deviance among the Irish peasantry', *Ulster Folklife*, 23 (1977), 33–56. Many of the stories were examples of supernatural aggression. Deviance from the accepted norm, as in the case of a fairy path being disturbed, could result in mystical retribution. These forms of aggression took two main forms, attacks by either witches or fairies. Witches were generally believed to operate in the communal, inter-familial sphere of relationships. Fairies normally attacked within the family. Other kinds of deviance, for example an incursion onto a *rath* or fairy fort, or misbehaviour could lead to being 'taken'. Directly flouting fairies normally led to correspondingly direct retribution. See also Jacqueline Simpson, 'Rationalized motifs in urban legends', *Folklore*, 92:2 (1981), 203–7.

It may be argued that these stories contribute to the creation of a sense of home, and by extension, homeland, at this particular juncture in Irish social and cultural history, from the early 1920s. This is an idea that has had profound and long-lasting consequences in the national psyche. In the cultural propaganda of the Free State the harsh reality of rural life was ignored. Rather, the rapturous images in the work of artists such as Keating, Lamb and Henry (and even, it may be argued, including John Hinde's unique style of nostalgic representation) treated the white-washed cottage in such reverent terms as to make it a shrine to the aspirations of de Valera's Ireland:

> The thatched, whitewashed cottage that looked so well on calendars became a shrine. Pamela Hinkson listed its qualities: 'the whitewashed walls within have always a warm tinge in them from the turf fire, out of sight which is the life of the house ... the open door, the shining dresser, the movement about the floor of animals and fowl, are all symbols of welcome ... That tumbledown cottage with its door open was more truly the castle of the Irishman and woman than any English cottage ever was.'[10]

Successive generations of *Our Boys* readers, particularly those who had no experience of the reality of country life, would have absorbed a highly romanticized image of the Irish cottage:

> An' my ould friends the (the O'Driscolls) lived in an elegant, thatched farmhouse, in a sheltered corner o' Farnagilla, with big beech trees all around the *boan*, among the branches o' which the winter storms roared an' moaned an' *ullagoned*, many an' many a night, when *myself* sat in the cosy chimney corner with poor Donal O'Driscoll an' his wife, Miereadh, an' his handsome sons an' daughters an' we all *chanachiachthing* in the light o' the blazing turf an' bogwood long, long ago.[11]

Here is another example of Power's romantic treatment of the cottage, this time a typical introduction to a story set in Kitty's cottage, by her own fireside:

> An' after that, *imbeersa*, I made my way to the spot I always loved, the ould house o' Ballyroe, close to the lapping waters o' Corran Lake. An' you might say I got a warm welcome from all the *sgoriachters* gathered in that night an' me in my *own* corner, ('Kitty the Hare's' corner as they used to say, why!) alongside o' the big turf fire. An' that night, begannies, I fell in with an ould man o' ninety seven; an' he told me one o' the quarest stories I ever listened to since I was born.[12]

---

10 Peter Somerville-Large, *Irish Voices: 50 years of Irish life, 1916–1966* (London: Chatto and Windus, 1999), p. 133.   11 *Our Boys*, July, 1929, vol. 15, 827.   12 *Our Boys*, Sept. 1928, vol. 15,

The tradition of folk tales in Ireland existed in a different social and cultural setting from that found in the metropolitan region of Britain.[13] The Irish genre was of an oral nature, surviving to a great extent in its original, natural milieu. As Angela Bourke has pointed out, one feature 'which makes fairy-legends so tenacious in a changing cultural environment is the concision and vivid memorability of their central themes. Another is their connection to real, named, people, and to real places in a known landscape. Yet another reason why they survive is that their narratives interact so intimately with the practicalities and emotional realities of daily life.'[14]

'Viewed as a system of interlocking units of narrative, practice, and belief', she continues,

> fairy-legend can be compared to a database: a pre-modern culture's way of storing and retrieving information of every kind, from hygiene and childcare to history and geography. Highly charged and memorable images like that of a woman on a white horse emerging from a fairy dwelling are the retrieval codes for a whole complex of stored information about land and landscape, community relations gender roles, medicine, and work in all its aspects: tools, materials and techniques. Stories gain verisimilitude, and storytellers keep their listeners' attention by the density of circumstance they depict, including social relations and the technical details of work. Most stories, however, are constructed around the unexpected, and therefore the memorable, happenings in people's lives. Encounters with or interference by the fairies in stories remind listeners (and readers) of everything in life that is outside human control.[15]

The oral tradition that supported such a complex narrative structure was sensitive to change. Through a process of natural attrition and the shifting sense of social and cultural values that were natural by-products of the modernization of Irish society, the fire-side arena gradually became a thing of the past. *Our Boys*, by publishing these tales, and perhaps equally importantly by recycling them to generation after generation, maintained a point of contact between fairy lore and the many generations of Irish youth who would otherwise have known little or nothing of this crucial aspect of their collective past. This concept – the 'collective past', was dear to the official policy makers of the newly formed Free State. In 1922, for example, the new government declared that its education

---

26. 13 The transition from folk to fairy tale in Britain is described by Robert Leeson as part of a 'refining' process whereby the newly evolving urban middle class of the Victorian era sought to distance themselves from their rural roots. See Robert Leeson, *Reading and Righting: the past, present and future of fiction for the young* (London: Collins, 1985), pp 84–7. 14 Angela Bourke, *The Burning of Bridget Cleary* (London: Pimlico, 1999), p. 29. 15 Ibid.

policy was to give the 'language, history, music and tradition of Ireland their natural place in the life of Irish schools'.[16]

Parallel with such visible state-inspired initiatives to develop a national consciousness as the design of Irish stamps and coins, in which Gaelic cultural ideology played a central role,[17] there was another, less visible, but, it was hoped, equally crucial pioneering innovation in the field of education. State policy from the earliest days of self-government proposed a systematic attempt to Gaelicize the education of Irish children.[18] The early years of the Free State witnessed an increasing awareness of the importance of Irish folklore in any attempt to define the nature of a nationalist ideology. The rationale behind such a project was outlined by the Department of Education:

> The collection of the oral traditions of the Irish people is a work of national importance. It is but fitting that in our Primary schools the senior pupils should be invited to participate in the task of rescuing from oblivion the traditions which, in spite of the vicissitudes of the historic Irish nation have, century in, century out, been preserved with loving care by their ancestors. The task is an urgent one, for in our time most of this important national oral heritage will have passed away for ever.[19]

Such an interest in the area of folklore was a reaction to the process of modernization, and had significant elements of nationalism. In the case of the collection and dissemination of Irish folklore from the point of independence onwards, an understanding of an official sense of identification with the rural and the traditional, as the formally validated and perceived cultural identity of 'Ireland' is important in an effort to place 'Tales Told by the Turflight' in the broader context of national iconography spanning the foundation, and subsequently, the early decades of the Free State.

Declan Kiberd contends that James Joyce turned his back on Gaelic Ireland in order to address, on his own terms, the many aspects of that land with which he could not agree. Kiberd comments that: 'For Joyce, writing was a measure of his own exile from Ireland, but also of that Ireland from its past, of Hiberno-English from standard languages, and of writing itself as a fall from oral culture – emigration simply emblematizing these denials.'[20] The condition of exile was

16 John Coolahan, *Irish Education: its history and structure* (Dublin: IPA, 1981), p. 41.   17 See, for example, Liam Miller and William Kane (eds), *Postage Stamps of Ireland, 1922–1982* (Dublin, Ireland: Philatelic Section, Dept of Posts and Telegraphs); William Butler Yeats, *Coinage of Saorstát Éireann; report of the committee appointed to advise the government on coinage designs* (Dublin: Stationery Office, 1928).   18 See Coolahan, *Irish Education*, pp 223–6.   19 Seán Ó Súilleabháin, *Irish Folklore and Tradition* (Dublin: Department of Education, 1937), p. 3.   20 Declan Kiberd, *Inventing Ireland: the literature of modern Ireland* (London: Vintage, 1997), p. 333. See also G.J. Watson, *Irish Identity and the Literary Revival* (London: Croom Helm, 1979),

a common one in the early years of the Free State. Massively high emigration figures showed just what the youth of Ireland thought of their lot of frugal self-sufficiency, which was the ideal of the Fianna Fáil and its leader, Eamon de Valera.[21] Between 1911 and 1926 405,000 people had left Ireland. This momentum was to slow in the following decade to 167,000, nevertheless resulting in a combined aggregate figure of 572,000 emigrants in the two decades around the foundation of the Free State.[22] Many of those young men and women, for whom their country had little to offer in the initial years of its independence (and for many decades after), chose to go to England. As they travelled through the English night, on the railway line to Newcastle or London, they may perhaps have gazed out the window of their carriage and allowed their thoughts to turn to home. As the train halted at the platform of Chester or Crewe the young Irish emigrant may have been surprised to see that among the various advertising posters, for 'Ovaltine' or 'Hovis', say, that decorated the station wall, there was a familiar image, that of a typical scene in the west of Ireland; a winding road, purple mountains in the distance, their rugged edges softened by a western sky, the brown of the bog, the whitewashed walls of the cottages with turf stacked at the gable end.[23] The poster was one of those scenes from the quintessentially Irish iconography of Paul Henry.

It was during this period, the early 1920s, that these images were achieving popularity both at home and abroad. This particular one, entitled 'Connemara' (1924–5), had been adopted by the London Midland and Scottish Railway Company and was reproduced on a widely distributed tourism poster. The *Irish Times* of August 1925 declared:

> If thousands of people in Great Britain and in North America have been led this summer to think over the claims of Ireland as holiday ground it is largely through the lure of Mr Paul Henry's glowing landscape of a Connemara scene.[24]

pp 151–245.   21 Fianna Fáil's 1932 manifesto announced that 'all sections of the community' had to be content with 'frugal living'. See Mary E. Daly, *Industrial Development and Irish National Identity, 1922–1939* (New York: Syracuse UP), p. 60.   22 F.S.L. Lyons, *Ireland since the Famine* (Glasgow: Fontana/Collins, 1976), p. 405.   23 Jackson Lears describes the advertising of such products as Hovis and Ovaltine to the urban consumer during this period as 'sentimental agrarianism.' See his *Fables of Abundance: a cultural history of advertising in America* (New York: Harper Collins, 2000), especially pp 102–33.   24 Cited in S.B. Kennedy, *Paul Henry* (London: Yale UP, 2000), p. 95. Kennedy would maintain that the mass reproduction of Henry's 'Connemara' used in this campaign, the first of many reproductions of the artist's work, marked the beginning of his wider recognition of his stature as a painter. However, by over-popularizing his treatment of the western landscape to the extent that he became a prisoner of his own success, it was 'Connemara' that, in the long run, marked the onset of a decline in the quality of his work. See also Luke Gibbons, 'Synge, country and western: the myth of the west in Irish and American culture', in Chris Curtin et al. (eds), *Culture and Ideology in Ireland* (Galway: Galway UP, 1984);

The landscapes of Henry satisfied the need of metropolitan culture to view the west as a remote, unspoilt and timeless Ireland both at home and abroad. The landscapes that these pictures constructed resemble the settings of J.M. Synge's plays, which were poetic expressions of the very difficult lives led by the population of the west of Ireland.

Many of the plays performed in the flagship institution of Irish theatre, the Abbey, also drew on this location for their inspiration.[25] Depicting peasant life theatrically, as Synge had done, was very much to the taste of the new middle class of Dublin.

What was the rationale behind the desire to see lives of the peasantry played out on the national stage? The employment opportunities provided by the structures of the new state system would certainly appeal to a different type of recruit than was the case under the British government. D.P. Moran had long claimed that there was a Protestant-inspired system of discrimination against Catholics in all walks of life.[26] This was no longer the case. Now the various arms of the Free State regime threw open the doors of secure and pensionable employment to their own. The newly formed police force, the army, the civil service, and perhaps most obviously, the vanguard of the state's ultimate aspiration of Gaelicization, the teaching profession, all attracted employees who met the nationally revised criteria.

Thus many of the members of the Abbey audience were themselves from the countryside, not from Dublin where they lived. Many in fact were from those parts that had been in the past excluded from this high table. Now that times had changed, to be from the west implied a certain cachet, a fluency in Irish for example having a much greater market value in the corridors of power of the new government than had previously been the case – Irish was adopted as the official language alongside English in 1922. So they came from the country to the city. And in doing so, as they took on a different lifestyle, assuming the aspirations and values of an embryonic ruling middle class, they were, in fact, in exile.

As Joyce looked to Ireland from the focal point of Paris, as tired and lonely emigrants gazed with bemusement at the surprising image of Connemara on the station wall at Crewe, so too did the new middle class of ever-expanding Dublin

Gibbons, *Transformations in Irish Culture* (Cork: Cork UP, 1996); Brian P. Kennedy, 'The Irish Free State 1922 – 1949: a visual perspective', in Brian P. Kennedy, and Raymond Gillespie (eds), *Ireland – Art into History* (Dublin: Town House, 1994), pp 132–54; David Scott, 'Posting images', *Irish Arts Review Yearbook, 1990–1991*, 188–95; Terence Brown, *Ireland: a social and cultural history, 1922–2001* (London: Preennial, 2004); Brian Kennedy, 'The traditional Irish thatched house: image and reality', in A. Dalsimer (ed.), *Visualizing Ireland: national identity and the pictorial tradition* (Boston: Faber, 1993), p. 176; Mike Crang, *Cultural Geography* (London: Routledge, 1998); Joseph Lee, *The Modernization of Irish Society* (Dublin, 1983). **25** Anthony Roche, 'The two worlds of Synge's "The well of the saints"', in *The Genres of the Irish Literary Revival* (Dublin: Wolfhound, 1980), p. 27. **26** See D. P. Moran, *The Philosophy of Irish Ireland*, 1st pub. 1905 (Dublin, 1905; UCD Press, 2006), introduction by Patrick Maume.

suburbia look to the Ireland they idealized, the Ireland they had left behind with its white-washed cottage walls and unspoilt landscape. The artistic, literary, theatrical and educational forms of iconography that were either official or semi-official products of this process of adjustment, this period of national reorientation, all speak of the inner desire to define Ireland, of a national longing for home.

'In the Turflight' became an institution in *Our Boys*. Part of the reason for its continued success was that the series addressed a compelling need – a rurally rooted class in exile could enjoy their monthly, timeless images of winding Munster roads, fairy changelings and pookas, Kitty the Hare forever rambling down the boreen, the patter of rain on the cottage window, the howl of the wind as the storm increased in ferocity and that eternal source of comfort, of security, of physical and emotional warmth, the blazing turf fire, in whose light the story was told, its ever-changing shadows dancing on the kitchen walls.

Recovering a heroic past: the *Táin* retold

CIARA NÍ BHROIN

The *Táin Bó Cuailgne* (Cattle Raid of Cooley) is the centre-piece of Irish heroic literature and one of the oldest vernacular epics in Western literature. The public debate generated by a stage production of the saga during the 2005 Dublin theatre festival[1] attests to its contemporary relevance as do the numerous retellings which have been published in recent years.[2] Its hero, Cuchulain, has remained a potent figure for Irish writers in both languages, including Eileen O'Faoláin, Thomas Kinsella, Seán Ó Tuama and Nuala Ní Dhomhnaill.[3] All treatments of Cuchulain, as Declan Kiberd has pointed out, are explorations of contemporary issues by means of a narrative set in the remote past.[4] This paper aims, in light of this statement, to explore the two earliest versions of the saga addressed at a young readership, Standish James O'Grady's (1846–1928) Cuchulain trilogy – comprising *The Coming of Cuculain*[5] (1894), *In the Gates of the North* (1901) and *The Triumph and Passing of Cuculain* (1920) – and Lady Augusta Gregory's (1852–1932) *Cuchulain of Muirthemne* (1902), published during the Irish Literary Revival and struggle for national independence.

The *Táin* belongs to what in modern times has been classified as the Ulster Cycle of tales, which recount the heroic deeds of the Ulster tribal warriors who dominated the northern part of Ireland in pre-historic times until their defeat

---

1 In an *Irish Times* review of 7 Oct. 2005, Fintan O'Toole described Michael Keegan-Dolan's stage adaptation as 'a scintillating new satire on Celtic Tiger Ireland, a profound reflection on the continuing resonance of Irish mythology, a raw, fast-paced Irish crime thriller, a vastly impressive exercise in avant garde physical theatre.' 2 Among them are: Liam MacUistin, *The Táin* (Dublin: O'Brien, 1990); Aogan Ó Muircheartaigh, *Táin Bó Cuailgne* (Dublin: Coiscéim, 1992); Michael Scott, *Irish Myths and Legends* (London: Warner, 1992); Frank Murphy, *The Big Fight, the Story of the Táin* (Dublin: O'Brien, 1999); Eoin Neeson, *An Táin, Cuchulain's Saga, the Imperishable Celtic Epic* (Dublin: Prestige, 2004); Carlo Gébler, *The Bull Raid* (London: Egmont, 2004); Colmán Ó Raghallaigh, *An Táin* (Mayo: Cló Mhaigh Eo, 2006); Ciaran Carson, *The Táin* (London: Penguin, 2007). 3 Eileen O'Faoláin, *Irish Sagas and Folk Tales* (London: OUP, 1954); Thomas Kinsella, *The Táin* (Oxford: OUP, 1969); Seán Ó Tuama's poems in praise of Christy Ring in *An Bás I dTír na nÓg* (1988) compare the legendary Cork hurler to the Ulster hero drawing particularly on imagery relating to Cuchulain's battle rage or warp spasm; Nuala Ní Dhomhnaill deconstructs the hero myth in five poems sometimes subtitled the Atáin to offer a modern, feminist perspective. Cuchulain is a 'small, dark, rigid man', in one poem and a bored stone-throwing delinquent in another. See *Rogha Dánta/Selected Poems*. (Dublin: Raven Arts Press, 1988), pp 110–25. 4 Declan Kiberd, *Irish Classics* (London: Granta, 2000), p. 401. Kiberd cites Patricia Kelly, 'The Táin as literature', in J.P. Mallory (ed.), *Aspects of the Táin* (Belfast, 1992). 5 O'Grady omits the 'h', in his spelling of the hero's name. Except when

some time in the fifth century. It tells of the invasion of Ulster by Queen Maeve of Connacht in pursuit of the Brown Bull of Cooley and the single-handed defence of the province by its foremost champion, Cuchulain, while Ulster's Red Branch warriors are under a spell of weakness. [6] The saga is thought to have been first written down in the eighth century by Christian scribes and survives in three main manuscript recensions from the twelfth and fourteenth centuries in the Book of the Dun Cow, the Book of Leinster and the Yellow Book of Lecan.[7] The stories of the Ulster Cycle were particularly popular among the elite of Gaelic society and Cuchulain was undoubtedly the national hero of Ireland until the eleventh century, after which Fionn MacCumhail of the Fenian cycle became increasingly popular, particularly among the ordinary people.[8] With the suppression of the bardic schools and the exile of the learned classes in the seventeenth century, Irish mythology became largely a folkloric tradition and the Cuchulain tales became less well known.[9] The scholars of the Royal Irish Academy in the late eighteenth century, supplemented by those of the Ordnance Survey, most notably Eugene O'Curry (1796–1862), in the nineteenth century, unearthed these ancient tales with the aim of preserving them through translation. Tales from the living peasant oral tradition were collected and recorded by folklorists including Crofton Croker (1798–1854), Lady Gregory and Douglas Hyde (1860–1947). The writer credited with resurrecting the heroic figure of Cuchulain is Standish James O'Grady, author of the apocalyptic and highly influential two-volume *History of Ireland; the heroic period* (1878) and *Cuculain and His Contemporaries* (1880). O'Grady's Cuchulain trilogy for younger readers marked the beginning of a process that was to gain momentum during the Literary Revival and continues to the present day – the retelling of Ireland's ancient myths and legends for children.

directly quoting from his text, I use the more conventional spelling which is that used by Lady Gregory.   6 For concise information about the *Táin* see Pronsias MacCana, 'Early and Middle Irish literature', in Seamus Deane (ed.), *The Field Day Anthology of Irish Writing*, vol. 1 (Derry: Field Day, 1991), pp 1–7; Robert Welch (ed.), *The Oxford Companion to Irish Literature* (New York: OUP, 1996), pp 551–3; Miranda J. Green, *A Dictionary of Celtic Myth and Legend* (London: Thames and Hudson, 1992), pp 70–1.   7 The Book of the Dun Cow and the Book of Leinster are twelfth-century manuscripts and the Yellow Book of Lecan is from the fourteenth century. For more detailed information about the three recensions see the introduction to Cecile O'Rahilly's *Táin Bó Cúalnge from the Book of Leinster* (Dublin: Dublin Institute for Advanced Studies, 1967), pp ix–iv.   8 Peter Berresford Ellis, *A Dictionary of Irish Mythology* (London: Constable, 1987), p. 11.   9 Cuchulain is not mentioned at all in the brief summary of the *Táin* in Mary Frances Cusack's *An Illustrated History of Ireland from AD 400–1800* (1868, London: Bracken, 1995), pp 92–4. Stories of Cuchulain are also less popular in nineteenth century Anglo-Irish literature than the romantic stories of Fionn and the Fianna. However, Cuchulain is mentioned in Joseph Cooper Walker's *Historical Memoirs of the Irish Bards* (1786), in Charlotte Brooke's *Reliques of Irish Poetry* (1789), in Lady Mary Ferguson's *The Story of the Irish before the Conquest* (1868) and in Aubrey de Vere's *The Foray of Queen Maeve* (1882).

Cormac Mac Raois has outlined some of the challenges facing writers in retelling Irish myths for children.[10] Foremost of these is that the original stories were intended for adults and their style and subject matter reflect the adult interests and values of a very different era. The *Táin* depicts a pre-Christian culture in which brutal warfare is central to survival, military prowess is celebrated and human life is expendable. It is a story of great carnage and graphic violence. Furthermore, it reflects the sexual mores of an era in which virility was admired and celebrated. There are frequent references to copulation and seduction and there is a suggestion of incest in how Cuchulain was begotten.[11] Cuchulain, while betrothed to Emer, has an affair with Uathach and begets a son by his enemy, Aoife.[12] Maeve's seduction of Fergus is regarded by her husband, Ailill, as expedient in ensuring the warrior's loyalty.[13] Deirdre's desire for Naoise is so strong that she forces him to take her away with him.[14] The explicit violence and sexuality central to the *Táin* pose challenges for writers attempting to retell the saga for a young readership. For writers of the Victorian era like O'Grady and Lady Gregory such challenges were particularly acute.

Further difficulties relate to questions of style and language. The *Táin*'s origin in an oral culture is reflected in its episodic construction and in inconsistencies and repetitions in the narrative. In its translation from an oral to written literature[15] and from Old Irish to modern English, the saga has undergone a number of striking metamorphoses. Cecile O'Rahilly has pointed out that the saga is uneven because some parts have been expanded and stylistically embellished.[16] In the introduction to his own critically acclaimed translation, Thomas Kinsella argues that, because of its relative completeness and despite its florid and adjectival style, the Book of Leinster has received disproportionate attention from translators, including Lady Gregory.[17] Anglicization of the ancient Gaelic names has complicated the situation by producing numerous spellings or versions of the same name. More importantly, 'each period of translation like each period of literary activity has implicit or explicit norms that determine what is acceptable literary or translation practice'.[18] In his study of translation in Ireland, Michael Cronin refers to the different translation strategies of fidelity, expansion, contraction, naturalization and paraphrase,[19] all of which have been applied to the *Táin* with varying degrees of success. Whatever strategy is

10 'Old tales for New People: Irish mythology retold for children', in *The Lion and the Unicorn*, 21 (1997), 330–40. 11 See Thomas Kinsella, *The Táin*, p. 23. 12 Ibid., pp 30–3. 13 Ibid., p.103. 14 Ibid., pp 11–13. 15 Pronsias MacCana points out that the relationship between oral and written literature was complex from the outset. With writing came, not only a new technique, but also new (Christian) values and a different concept of literary aesthetics. See 'Early and Middle Irish literature', in *The Field Day Anthology of Irish Writing*, vol. 1, p. 5. 16 See the introduction to O'Rahilly's *Táin Bó Cúalnge from the Book of Leinster* (Dublin: DIAS, 1967), p. xxv. 17 Thomas Kinsella, *The Táin* (Oxford: OUP, 1969). 18 Michael Cronin, *Translating Ireland: translation, languages, cultures* (Cork: CUP, 1996), p. 19. 19 Ibid., p. 21.

employed, however, translation is always implicitly political. According to Cronin, translators 'can be viewed as revolutionaries or conservatives, dangerous subversives or reliable guardians of public morality'.[20]

Ironically, O'Grady's portrayal of Cuchulain proved revolutionary by default. A staunch Unionist, anti-democratic and keenly interested in the preservation of the privileged Anglo-Irish Ascendancy class to which he belonged, O'Grady was decidedly conservative in his political motivations.[21] The late nineteenth century was a period of accelerated change in Ireland. The failure of British governmental policy and the ineptitude of the landlord class during the Great Famine of 1845–9 had caused increasingly fraught relations between Ireland and England and between the Anglo-Irish and native Irish populations. The disestablishment of the Church of Ireland in 1869, the Land War of the 1880s and the campaign for Home Rule had threatened the security of a minority Ascendancy class ever more wary of an increasingly self-assured and powerful Catholic majority. O'Grady, like Charlotte Brooke (1740–93) and Samuel Ferguson (1810–86) before him, saw in ancient Irish culture a means of uniting Anglo-Irish and native Irish and of enhancing esteem and partnership between Ireland and England within the context of Empire. The theories of Matthew Arnold on the complementary natures of Celt and Saxon[22] lent weight to a vision of Union that accommodated and indeed encouraged Celtic difference; the romantic and artistic Celtic spirit ennobled the philistine Saxon, whose rationalism and practicality in turn made him suitable to govern. Moreover, a shared Celtic identity rooted in the distant past transcended Anglo-Irish/native Irish divisions. Writers like O'Grady, such as W.B. Yeats (1865–1939), Æ (aka George Russell, 1867–1935) and Lady Gregory 'sought to popularize a view of Irish identity that might soften the stark outlines of politics, class and sectarianism in the benign glow of culture',[23] and therefore turned to an ancient, heroic Ireland in which 'unity of culture was manifest in a pagan, mythic, rural paradise'.[24]

The romanticism that infuses O'Grady's trilogy is anticipated in the preface to *The Coming of Cuculain*, in which 'Cuculain and his friends' are described as 'historical characters, seen as it were through mists of love and wonder'.[25] The association of Henry Grattan, 'thundering in the Senate', with 'these antique heroes', imbues O'Grady's retelling with contemporary significance. His young readers are clearly encouraged to recognize in the Anglo-Irish aristocracy the rightful descendants of Ireland's ancient aristocratic heroes. The book opens with a description of these heroes that emphasizes their nobility, their physical

20 Ibid., p. 111.   21 R.F. Foster, *The Irish Story: telling tales and making it up in Ireland* (Oxford: OUP, 2002), pp 13–16.   22 Matthew Arnold, *On the Study of Celtic Literature and Other Essays* (London: Dent, 1919; 1st pub. 1867).   23 Terence Brown, 'Cultural nationalism', in *The Field Day Anthology*, vol. II, p. 517.   24 Ibid., p. 517.   25 *The Coming of Cuculain* (London: Methuen, 1894), p. 9.

beauty, the glory of their 'banqueting attire', but above all their unity and inviolability:

> They rejoiced in their glory and their might, and in the inviolable amity in which they were knit together, a host of comrades, a knot of heroic valour and affection which no strength or cunning, and no power, seen or unseen, could ever relax or untie. (13)

A powerful wish-fulfilment clearly underlies this portrayal of the Red Branch Knights, whose inviolability contrasts with the insecurity of the declining Anglo-Irish Ascendancy. It emerges, however, that the Red Branch Knights are themselves in a state of crisis. Fergus addresses the assembly and (like O'Grady) bemoans the lack of heroism among his contemporaries. The morning hunts and 'unearned feastings at night', of which Fergus has become weary, reflect the dissipated lifestyle of the debilitated nineteenth-century Anglo-Irish landlord class. Just as Fergus urges the Red Branch Knights to live up to the heroism of their noble ancestors, O'Grady tries to inspire his class to heroic leadership of the masses.

In presenting the Iron Age heroes of the Ulster saga as shining exemplars for the nineteenth-century Ascendancy, O'Grady endows them with Victorian virtues and removes the flaws which are central to the motives for conflict in the *Táin*. All elements of treachery, vengeance, jealousy and desire, around which much of the action revolves, are erased from the tale, thus reducing its powerful dramatic import. The trickery of Ness in obtaining the kingship for her son is omitted. Instead Fergus willingly abdicates the throne in recognition of Concobar's inherently superior skills at governance. Concobar is consistently portrayed as a wise and just ruler, whose authority should not be questioned. His sinister role in the tragic fate of Deirdre is underplayed. He is motivated, not by his own desire to possess Deirdre, but by his duty to protect her chastity and to uphold the law, for 'without chastity valour faileth in a nation, and lawlessness in this respect begetteth sure and rapid decay'. (95) Maeve's seduction of Fergus is omitted as is any marital discord between Maeve and Ailill, including the rivalry that instigated the cattle raid in the first place. Rather ludicrously, Fergus at one stage calls for a robe with which to cover Maeve when she runs out 'thinly clad'. O'Grady's sanitization of the saga reflects the restrictive middle-class sexual mores of his time, as does his association of licentiousness with the lower orders of society, 'of whom no man maketh any account'. (95) The imposition of a prudish Victorian sensibility on the heroes of the Ulster cycle diminishes their heroic stature, reinventing them as thinly disguised Victorian gentlemen.

Indeed, what most distinguishes O'Grady's Cuchulain from other portrayals of the hero is his extreme refinement, sensitivity, modesty and obedience to his elders – hardly characteristics of an epic warrior. The classical writers Diodorus

Siculus and Strabo both describe the warlike qualities of the Celts including their boastfulness, their extreme courage and their custom of sometimes going into battle naked.[26] Totem and head hunting were common practices. O'Grady's Cuchulain, however, is Christ-like. He is 'gentle exceedingly' with 'more of love in his heart than war'. (103) The young Setanta weeps when the boys of Emain Macha do not make him welcome. His yellow curls and pure white skin, combined with his innocence and gravity, endow him with Romantic angelic qualities directly antithetical to those with which the young Setanta is more typically associated. He is portrayed as a peace-maker who averts conflict between Concobar and Culain after the slaying of Culain's hound. No account of the actual killing of the hound is given. Setanta enters Culain's dun blood-stained and injured. Although in severe pain, he 'made a reverence as he had been taught, to the man of the house and to his people and went backwards to the upper end of the chamber.' (60) Such lessons in courtesy and good breeding are encoded in the narrative throughout and provide a reductive didactic subtext at odds with the grand spirit of epic literature.

Proinsias Mac Cana describes the main protagonist of early Irish hero tales as 'essentially a lone wolf, who, even though … associated with a warlike fraternity within the tribe and … frequently represented as the tribal kingdom's protector, operates primarily on his own initiative'.[27] O'Grady's Cuchulain is singularly lacking in initiative and is no lone wolf. He is a family man, a faithful husband and dutiful father. The tragic, unwitting killing of his only son, which was the subject of Yeats' play *On Baile's Strand* (1904), does not occur in O'Grady's version. Indeed, Connla is presented as the legitimate son of Cuchulain and Emer and is provided with a younger sister to create an idealized Victorian family unit. Father-son relationships are harmonious throughout the trilogy and marital accord is everywhere evident. O'Grady's promulgation of Victorian patriarchal family values as central to social order is nowhere more apparent than in his portrayal of the women in the saga. Kinsella has suggested that the greatest achievement of the *Táin* and the Ulster cycle is the series of women on whose strong personalities the action continually turns. 'It may be as goddess-figures ultimately that these women have their power; it is certainly they, under all the violence, who remain most real in the memory.'[28] O'Grady's domesti-cation of the female characters and his eradication of their sexual agency disempower and reduce them. Cuchulain's mother and wife both run orderly households, an important Victorian female virtue lacking in Maeve, for which Fergus chides her: 'Fitter for thee, O Queen, to have remained in thy own dun and seen to the government of thy household.'[29] Maeve's warriors follow her

26 Cited in the introduction to Cecile O'Rahilly, *Táin Bó Cúalnge*, p. x.   27 'Early and Middle Irish literature', in *The Field Day Anthology*, vol. 1, p. 5.   28 Thomas Kinsella, *The Táin* (Oxford: OUP, 2002), p. xv.   29 O'Grady, *In the Gates of the North* (Dublin: Talbot Press, 1938), p. 34.

lead only because they are bewitched by her beauty and 'will not let a tress of her golden hair be harmed'. (34) The fierce Irish goddess of sovereignty and war[30] has been transformed by O'Grady into an English medieval lady in need of protection by chivalrous knights.

Indeed, the medieval feudal system is idealized by O'Grady, who strongly opposed Gladstonian democracy and wished to revive feudal values in nineteenth-century Ireland, including fealty to an English king.[31] In December 1881 he organized a convention of landlords to resist the implementation of the Gladstone Land Acts which would transfer minimal rights to tenants. O'Grady's solution to the difficulties of the tenantry was to awaken a sense of responsibility in the landlord class, on whose largesse tenants should rely. In Concobar Mac Nessa's court at Emain Macha, 'it was the custom that the weak should accept the protection of the strong and submit themselves to their command. So slaves received masters, so runaways and fugitives got themselves lords and sheltered themselves under their protection and paid dues.'[32] The privileged position of the Ascendancy is implicitly legitimized here and landlord-tenant relationships naturalized within an imperial system portrayed as beneficial to the lower social orders in particular. However, the contempt for the lower classes that in reality underpinned that system is all too apparent in O'Grady's description of 'the vast and slavish multitude in whose souls no god has kindled the divine fire by which ... the glory and prosperity of nations are sustained'.[33] The torpor and confusion from which the Ulster warriors eventually awaken is a metaphor for the debilitation of the Ascendancy, in whom 'the divine fire of leadership' needs rekindling.

In 1882 O'Grady warned that Irish nationalist politics would lead to 'anarchy and civil war ... [and] a shabby sordid Irish republic, ruled by corrupt politicians and the ignoble rich'.[34] His disillusionment with the socio-political situation in early twentieth-century Ireland[35] is evident in the last book of the trilogy, *The Triumph and Passing of Cuculain*, published in 1920 during the War of Independence (1919–21). In a surreal scene Cuchulain and his charioteer visit the city of Dublin and are shocked at the squalor and poverty of the masses, who in turn are in awe of the heroes: 'Would that we had they or such as they to rule over us whom we can see with our eyes to be so much greater and nobler than ourselves.'[36]

30 Pronsias Mac Cana argues that the meaning of Maeve's name – 'The Intoxicating One' – as well as many features of her legend identify her as the goddess of sovereignty and war. See 'Early and Middle Irish literature', p. 5. O'Grady's deliberate disempowerment of the saga's female characters coincides with the rise of the suffragette movement and the growing prominence of strong Irish women such as Maud Gonne and Countess Markievicz. 31 R.F. Foster, *The Irish Story*, p. 13. 32 *The Coming of Cuculain*, p. 42. 33 Ibid., p. 50. 34 Foster, *The Irish Story*, p. 13. 35 O'Grady spent the last decade of his life (1918–28) in exile on the Isle of Wight. Æ, a disciple of O'Grady's, later became disillusioned with the new Ireland and moved to England in 1932. 36 *The Triumph and Passing of Cuculain* (Dublin: Talbot Press, 1938), p. 97.

That such an interpretation of the Cuchulain saga should inspire a separatist nationalist movement and ultimately the republican ideals of the 1916 revolutionary, Patrick Pearse,[37] proves Michael Cronin's contention that the consequences of translation are rarely predictable.[38] O'Grady's efforts to rehabilitate the Ascendancy were ultimately instrumental in the rise of modern Irish nationalism which led to their demise. His achievement was as a literary catalyst who awoke his contemporaries to the existence of an epic Irish literature. He was the vital link between the antiquarianism of the eighteenth and nineteenth centuries and the Literary Revival in which heroic myth was central. However, his intended audience was the Anglo-Irish gentry and not the despised masses. Indeed, he urged Yeats and the playwrights of the Abbey Theatre to 'leave the heroic cycles alone and not bring them down to the crowd'.[39] In direct contrast to O'Grady was Lady Augusta Gregory, a passionate nationalist, whose *Cuchulain of Muirthemne* (1902) was aimed at popularizing epic literature among the general public. Drawing on both the living oral folkloric tradition and the scholarly written tradition, Lady Gregory succeeded in reaching a wide readership and, like O'Grady, influenced many writers of the Literary Revival, most notably W.B. Yeats and J.M. Synge (1871–1909).

While O'Grady's portrayal of Cuchulain was aimed at conserving the social order, Lady Gregory's intent was more subversive. *Cuchulain of Muirthemne* was written primarily to refute disparaging statements about the Irish language and Irish literature made by Doctors John Mahaffy and Robert Atkinson of Trinity College to the Vice-Regal Inquiry into Irish and Intermediate Education in 1899. In response to the demands of Douglas Hyde and the Gaelic League that Irish language and literature should be taught in secondary schools, they dismissed the language as a *patois* and Irish literature as silly, obscene and lacking in idealism and imagination. That Atkinson was a philologist was significant, as P.J. Mathews has pointed out; language and race are inextricably linked in philology which emerged as a discipline at the end of the eighteenth century to support the European imperial agenda and was used in this instance by Atkinson to implicitly support English interests in Ireland.[40] Interestingly, Atkinson suggested that if Irish language texts were really required, an Irish translation of Daniel Defoe's *Robinson Crusoe* 'or some book of that kind' would be preferable to folklore, all of which 'is at the bottom abominable'.[41] Determined to prove the

37 See Ruth Dudley Edwards, *Patrick Pearse, the Triumph of Failure*, 1st pub. 1977 (London: Faber, 1979), pp 123, 133, 175, 296. 38 *Translating Ireland*, p. 2. Cronin points out that O'Grady had only a scant knowledge of Irish and was heavily dependent on the translations of O'Curry, O'Halloran and others. His achievement was as a mediator for the translation scholarship of earlier generations. See p. 138. 39 O'Grady, *All Ireland Review*, 3:6 (12 April 1902), 84. Cited in Declan Kiberd, *Irish Classics* (London: Granta, 2002), p. 402. 40 P.J. Mathews, *Revival: the Abbey Theatre, Sinn Féin, the Gaelic League and the Co-operative Movement* (Cork: CUP, 2003), p. 38. Mathews refers here to Edward Said's *Orientalism: Western concepts of the Orient* (1978). 41 Cited in Mathews, *Revival*, p. 39. For a detailed account of the Vice-Regal

inherent worth of Irish literature, the Gaelic League asked Yeats to undertake a retelling of tales from some of the principal sagas but he was busy with his own work and declined. Lady Gregory, who was more proficient in the Irish language than Yeats or, indeed, O'Grady, undertook the task of translating transcripts of the Cuchulain tales recorded by Eugene O'Curry and collating them with other nineteenth-century translations of manuscripts, primarily those of Henri d'Arbois de Jubainville (1827–1910), Whitley Stokes (1830–1909) and Kuno Meyer (1858–1919).

The association of myth with the sacred, and epic with the heroic, made Lady Gregory's choice of form alone an effective answer to any allegation of lowness of tone in Irish literature.[42] Yeats' preface to the book abounds with classical and biblical allusions that endow the saga with literary significance and the spiritual charge of the sacred. He echoes O'Grady in elevating the imagined past of mythology over the actual events of history. Implicit in the preface is Yeats' belief that the recovery of a nation's imagined past is an essential step towards imagining and thereby shaping its future. The importance of myth to postcolonial national rehabilitation has been well documented.[43] In delving into a mythic pre-colonial past, the writer uncovers 'beyond the misery [of the present] ... some very beautiful and splendid era' whose existence rehabilitates the nation and 'serves as a justification for the hope of a future national culture'.[44] That *Cuchulain of Muirthemne* was written for children is doubly significant; moulding the consciousness of the young is a powerful way of shaping the future of a nation.

Lady Gregory's desire to make epic literature available to the masses was a direct contradiction, not only of those like O'Grady, who saw it as the rightful heritage of the upper classes, but equally of those who held it as the preserve of scholars and antiquarians. Scholars from imperial institutions such as the Royal Irish Academy[45] and the Ordnance Survey[46] undoubtedly played a central role in

Inquiry and an analysis of the language controversy and its consequences see pp 33–45. **42** I discuss this at greater length and from a postcolonial perspective in 'Championing Irish literature, a postcolonial critique of Lady Augusta Gregory's *Cuchulain of Muirthemne*', in *Bookbird: A Journal of International Children's Literature* 43:2 (2005), 13–21. **43** See Frantz Fanon, *The Wretched of the Earth*, 6th ed. (London: Penguin, 2001; 1st pub. 1962). **44** Ibid., p. 169. **45** The Royal Irish Academy was founded in 1785 for the promotion and investigation of the sciences, polite literature and antiquities. It encouraged scholarly work in the collection and study of Irish manuscripts. Distinguished members included Sir William Wilde, George Petrie, Whitley Stokes and Kuno Meyer. For more information see F.S.L. Lyons, *Ireland since the Famine* (Glasgow: Fontana, 1971), pp 224–5; R.F. Foster, *Modern Ireland, 1600–1972* (London: Penguin, 1989), p. 184. See also www.ria.ie/about/background html. **46** The Ordnance Survey was established in Ireland in 1824 to survey and map the entire country for land valuation and taxation purposes. Scholars John O'Donovan and Eugene O'Curry were employees who, in addition to their surveying duties, collected a vast amount of folklore and oral literature from around the country. See Ulick O' Connor, *Celtic Dawn. A portrait of the Irish Literary renaissance* (London: Black Swan, 1985), p. 99.

the preservation of manuscripts and folklore but their primary concern was to make archaic Irish literature accessible to other scholars and not to the reading public. It is arguably in the interests of the colonial power to preserve and thus control native tradition, maintaining it in a state of antiquity and preventing its development into more vital and possibly subversive channels.[47] Indeed, the explicit identification of many eighteenth- and nineteenth-century Ascendancy intellectuals with native Irish culture is described by David Cairns and Shaun Richards as a deliberate strategy amounting to 'little less than an act of cultural appropriation', an attempt to shape and control the emerging discourse in the interests of their own class.[48] O'Grady publicly urged his fellow landlords to reclaim what he saw as their rightful heritage, warning that they continue to ignore native culture at their peril.[49] The underlying motives, therefore, of writers such as O'Grady and, before him, Brooke and Ferguson – the preservation of their own class and of the Union and the naturalization of landlord/tenant relationships – were no different from those of Ascendancy writers who rejected native culture such as Maria Edgeworth (1767–1849). Lady Gregory, in contrast, wished to validate native Irish culture through use of epic mythology which could be enjoyed by the masses through a living and distinctively Irish literature.

In dedicating the Irish edition to the people of Kiltartan, Lady Gregory very deliberately addresses a native audience, a small local community, in an act which is the antithesis of the provincialism of Mahaffy and Atkinson, who looked to the imperial capital. She distances herself from the male Trinity College establishment, which represented imperial hegemony, and closely identifies herself with the local peasant community in a manner similar to that of the oral storyteller. Indeed, she later wrote to Yeats that she had 'done all from the peasant point of view',[50] a claim, however questionable, that nevertheless serves to highlight the contrast with O'Grady. However, Lady Gregory's rather unconvincing description of herself in the dedication as 'a woman of the house that has to be minding the place, and listening to complaints, and dividing her share of food', illustrates the difficulty of the Ascendancy intellectual wishing to connect with the native peasantry.[51] Any attempt to identify with the peasant perspective, particularly use of dialect, held the risk of unconsciously appearing patronizing.

47 See David Cairns and Shaun Richards, *Writing Ireland: colonialism, nationalism and culture* (Manchester: Manchester University Press, 1988), pp 29–41. See also Fanon, *Wretched of the Earth*, pp 195–96. 48 Cairns and Richards, *Writing Ireland*, p 30. 49 See Kiberd, *Irish Classics*, p. 402; O' Connor, *Celtic Dawn*, pp 130–1. 50 Cited in Daniel Murphy's forward to *Cuchulain of Muirthemne* (Gerrards Cross: Colin Smythe, 1970), p. 8. 51 Fanon has described the precarious position of the native intellectual wishing to reconnect with the peasantry but alienated by an assimilative colonial education. See *Wretched of the Earth*, pp 175–81. The position of the Anglo-Irish intellectual, who was both settler and native was doubly precarious. Cairns and Richards refer to difficulties facing members of the colonial elite wishing to dissociate themselves from the class of their birth. Citing Albert Memmi's concept of 'the colonizer who refuses', they

What is most subversive about Lady Gregory's translation, however, is precisely the Kiltartenese dialect in which it is rendered.[52] In the preface Yeats writes of the difficulties he experienced in writing stories of medieval Irish life with no language available to him but 'raw, modern English'. The search for a fitting language to express ancient Irish experience was a challenge facing writers like O'Grady and Lady Gregory. O'Grady writes in an overblown style of English and his epigraphs are drawn largely from Romantic English poetry. His is a story of glowing palaces, forest glades, noble steeds, modest maidens and chivalrous knights – in short a Victorianized medieval romance. The topographical element of the *Táin*, characteristic of early and middle Irish liter-ature, is greatly underplayed by O'Grady. Indeed, the use of derived literary modes and forms renders O'Grady's evocation of the ancient Gaelic past a rather bland mirror image of the British imperial present. In contrast, Irish place names and their meanings and origins occupy a central position in *Cuchulain of Muirthemne*, as emphasized by Yeats in the book's preface.[53] Lady Gregory's use of native literary modes[54] and idiom reshapes the imperial language, allowing 'the target language, the language of the colonizer, to be colonized in its turn by the language of the colonized'.[55]

Lady Gregory was highly influenced in her choice of idiom by the prose translations in Hyde's *Love Songs of Connacht* (1893) and developed a style deriving partly from the speech of the local community of Kiltartan and partly from her knowledge of the Irish language and her experience of translation. Her distinctively Irish rendering of the English language seemed truer to the original transcripts and to the native oral tradition than previous translations and similar to the living dialect of the peasantry. Unusually, Lady Gregory's aristocratic heroes and heroines speak in a peasant idiom, yet with ancient nobility. The idiom was enthusiastically received by many writers of the Revival and singled out for particular praise by Yeats in the book's preface:

point out that unconscious attitudes and assumptions frequently surface to reveal 'the refuser' to share the fundamental assumptions of the class which has been nominally rejected. See *Writing Ireland*, p. 25. **52** *Cuchulain of Muirthemne* was initially rejected for publication because of its idiom. Lady Gregory courageously resisted pressure from Murray publishers to popularize the book for the English market. That she chose to address a native audience in a native idiom was significant in that it posed a deliberate challenge to imperial hegemony. **53** The primacy of the geographical in the imagination of anti-imperialism is emphasized by Said in 'Yeats and decolonisation'. See Denis Walder (ed.), *Literature in the Modern World* (Oxford: OUP, 1990), pp 34–41. Said argues that colonialism results in 'the loss to an outsider of the local place, whose concrete geographical identity must thereafter be searched for and somehow restored'. The topography of the *Táin*, in this context, takes on added significance. For cultural nationalists of the Revival, Irish mythology was the key, not only to imaginative repossession of the past, but to emotional reconnection with local places and by implication imaginary repossession of the land. **54** In addition to *dinnseanchas* (topography), Lady Gregory includes the *caoineadh*, an Irish poetical form of lament. **55** Cronin, *Translating Ireland*, p. 141.

> Lady Gregory has discovered a speech as beautiful as that of Morris,[56] and
> a living speech into the bargain … It is some hundreds of years old, and age
> gives a language authority. We find in it the vocabulary of translators of the
> Bible, joined to an idiom which makes it tender, compassionate and
> complaisant, like the Irish language itself.[57]

Cronin argues that 'translation relationships between minority and majority
languages are rarely divorced from issues of power and identity'.[58] In the case of
native and imperial languages such issues are further accentuated. In radically
altering the English language to give a new voice to awakening nationalist
consciousness, translations such as those of Hyde and Lady Gregory 'mark a
transition from translation as an act of exegesis to translation as an agent of
political renewal. Translations no longer simply bore witness to the past; they
were to actively shape a future'.[59]

The ultimate symbol of national renewal and regeneration was Cuchulain.
Lady Gregory's Cuchulain is semi-divine, characterized most notably by youth
and energy, but also by beauty, valour and loyalty. He has access to the supernatural aid of the sidhe in times of trouble and is outrageously glorious in battle
and successful in love. Such qualities made him the ideal icon to regenerate a
nation disillusioned with parliamentary politics following the deposition of
Charles Stewart Parnell (1846–1891) as leader of the Home Rule Party in 1890
and the defeat of Gladstone's second Home Rule bill in 1893. Indeed, it is highly
likely that Parnell's charismatic leadership and tragic demise inspired Lady
Gregory's portrayal of Cuchulain as tragic hero. While O'Grady's portrayal of
Cuchulain is marred by sentimentality, Lady Gregory magnifies the tragic
import of his short but intensely lived life and heroic death. Cathbad, the druid,
prophesizes great fame and early death for Cuchulain on the very day he takes
up arms. Cuchulain's heart-rending battle with his foster brother Ferdiad (which
is underplayed in O'Grady's version) and the unwitting killing of his only son
(omitted by O'Grady, as mentioned previously) are all the more tragic to the
modern reader in light of the Irish civil war (1922–3) and the conflict that
continued in Northern Ireland until recent years. Cuchulain's death – tying
himself to a pillar in order to die in an upright position – is the ultimate Irish
image of heroic self-sacrifice and is immortalized in the famous bronze statue by
Oliver Sheppard in Dublin's General Post Office.[60] *Cuchulain of Muirthemne*
contains none of the disillusionment evident near the end of O'Grady's trilogy
and concludes with a joyful image of the hero's immortality:

56 Yeats refers here to the English writer William Morris (1834–96), a socialist associated with
the Pre-Raphaelite Brotherhood and the English Arts and Crafts Movement.   57 *Cuchulain of
Muirthemne* (Gerrards Cross: Colin Smythe, 1970), p. 12.   58 Cronin, *Translating Ireland*, p. 4.
59 Ibid., pp 135–6.   60 This statue is the subject of satirical allusion in Samuel Beckett's novel
Murphy (1938).

> But the three times fifty queens that loved Cuchulain saw him appear in his
> druid chariot, going through Emain Macha; and they could hear him
> singing the music of the Sidhe.[61]

While *Cuchulain of Muirthemne* was a seminal book of the Literary Revival and
remained the best-known version of the saga until Thomas Kinsella's (1929–)
translation in 1969, it contains numerous pre-tales at the expense of the *Táin*
itself, which seems inadequately represented. However, it is undoubtedly a more
inspirational retelling of the saga than O'Grady's didactic and prudish version.
That Lady Gregory herself subscribed to Victorian sensibilities in sanitizing
much of the sexual material of the saga is undeniable.[62] Indeed, her bowdlerization of the text drew censure from critics at the time, most notably Kuno
Meyer.[63] The myth of multiple fathers is omitted by both Lady Gregory and
O'Grady, as is any hint of incest in the conception of Cuchulain. While
Cuchulain's sexual vigour is at least implied by Lady Gregory, who emphasizes
his attractiveness to women and hints at his numerous love affairs,[64] it is nevertheless greatly underplayed. References to female sexuality are even more heavily
censored. When Scathach's daughter, Uathach, first beholds Cuchulain, she
blushes at the sight of his beauty and, instead of inviting him to share her bed,
expresses a wish that he return safely to his family. Such attention to matters of
sexual morality was a feature of translation activity of the period and not unique
to Ireland. However, the colonial critique of native literature as obscene placed
additional pressure on Irish writers and translators to prove the inherent purity
and morality of Irish writing. Furthermore, Lady Gregory was no doubt
conscious in addressing a native audience that the majority of the Irish
population had voted only a few years previously to depose Parnell due to his
affair with a married woman. Indeed, in her dedication to the people of Kiltartan
Lady Gregory openly, and rather patronizingly, admits that she omitted material
that she believed they may have found offensive. That *Cuchulain of Muirthemne*
was intended for use in schools may also have been a consideration in her sanitization of the text.

It is ironic, nevertheless, that in challenging the colonial critique of Mahaffy
and Atkinson, Lady Gregory reveals the extent to which she herself had inter-
nalized it. P.J. Mathews argues that the Mahaffy/Atkinson dismissal of Irish
literature as inherently immoral and the reaction of those who sought to project

---

61 *Lady Gregory's Complete Irish Mythology* (London: Bounty, 2004), p. 541. **62** Although
Cronin's assessment in *Translating Ireland* (p. 152) seems to me to be unduly harsh. See Kiberd's
more sympathetic analysis of *Cuchulain of Muirthemne* in *Irish Classics*, pp 300–419. **63** See
Cronin, p. 139. See also Kiberd, p. 412. Meyer was particularly critical of Lady Gregory's
omission of the description of the heroine's naked body in the wooing of Etain. See *Lady
Gregory's Complete Irish Mythology*, pp 385–6. **64** See *Lady Gregory's Complete Irish
Mythology*, pp 360, 497–507, 509.

an idealized Irishness set the terms within which the cultural debate of the following decade took place.

> In this classic post-colonial situation, emerging nationalists felt obliged to refute the imperial conception of Irish culture by idealizing it and exaggerating its inherent morality, but in the process often replicated in nationalist guise the very colonial thinking which they sought to dislodge.[65]

The romanticism of the noble Celt portrayed by writers such as O'Grady and Lady Gregory fed into imperial Arnoldian notions of Irish exceptionalism, defining Irishness in discursive terms set by the colonial context.[66] Furthermore, the reactionary nature of Irish nationalism was to continue throughout the early decades of independence.

In twenty-first-century Ireland, where Irishness is rapidly metamorphosing in response to the challenges of modernization and multiculturalism, there appears to be a renewed interest in retelling our ancient tales, especially the *Táin*, for our young people. Cormac Mac Raois has expressed reservations about retelling for children myths originally intended for adults. Referring to the *Táin* in particular, already censored by Christian scribes, he fears that in the 'further toning down required for children's versions there is a risk of presenting a narrative of unappealing blandness'.[67] However, with the influence of the Christian churches waning in twenty-first-century Ireland, the prevalence of more liberal sexual mores and the exposure of children to television programmes, videos and playstation games featuring violence, the need to censor sexual, violent and occult[68] elements of the *Táin* would appear to be considerably less than that deemed necessary in Victorian times. This is certainly apparent in the two most recently published versions for young readers at the time of writing, Carlo Gébler's *The Bull Raid* (2004) and Colmán Ó Raghallaigh's *An Táin* (2006), both of which are characterized by the earthiness and frankness of older versions.[69] Interestingly, Ó Raghallaigh, uses the modern genre of graphic novel to retell the ancient saga for today's young people in the Irish language. While the revival of the saga through translation into English was an important consideration for writers like O'Grady and Lady Gregory a century ago, the revival of the Irish language through retelling the now well-known saga is a priority for Colmán Ó Raghallaigh in twenty-first-century Ireland.

65 *Revival*, p. 45.   **66** For writers of the Revival Cuchulain embodied an ancient, spiritual Irishness directly antithetical to modern British philistinism. I discuss this further in 'Championing Irish Literature', in *Bookbird*, 43:2 (2005), 19–20.   **67** Mac Raois, 'Old tales for new people; Irish mythology retold for children', in *The Lion and the Unicorn*, 21 (1997), 332. **68** Cuchulain's occult distortions or warp spasms are not described by either O'Grady or Lady Gregory, with the latter explaining instead that his appearance changed to that of a god.   **69** Ó Raghallaigh's *An Táin* is more sexually sanitized than Gebler's very sexually forthright version.

Kate Thompson, James Stephens and the Irish literary landscape

ANNE MARIE HERRON

English-born writer Kate Thompson (1956–) has declared herself 'lucky to have been accepted by the Irish as an Irish writer'.[1] But perhaps this acceptance can be attributed more to her wholehearted espousal of Irish music, culture, history and landscape, than to any presence of luck. Thompson has written prolifically for children and teenagers and, as winner of the prestigious Whitbread Children's Book Award (2005), Guardian Award (2005) and Bisto Book of the Year Award (2005/6), has attained both Irish and international acclaim. In much of her writing, and particularly in her novel *The New Policeman* (2005), she examines Irish traditions, shows appreciation of the topography of the Irish countryside and links modern and mythological aspects of Irish heritage.

This focus on Ireland and on things Irish prompts an investigation into the degree to which she can be said to share in Irish literary traditions. In particular, it explores the literary influences that the writer James Stephens (1880–1950) exerts on Thompson.

IRISHNESS AND THE ANGLO-IRISH TRADITION

Dermot McCartney's interpretation of Irishness as 'a changing and fluid state or attitude of mind induced by the shared experiences, political, social, cultural, religious and economic' of the Irish people[2] is an inclusive one. Equally broad is Richard Fallis' assertion that Irish literature is 'any literature written by a person of Irish birth, or a person born elsewhere who chooses to live in Ireland, identify himself or herself with Ireland, and write in a way which seems particularly meaningful in an Irish context'.[3] But when a writer is from an English background, it is tempting, given the historical and geographical proximity of the two countries, to deploy the term 'Anglo-Irish literature'.[4] While James Joyce

---

1 Anne Marie Herron, interview with Kate Thompson. MA Thesis, St Patrick's College, 2007. Appendix p. iii. 2 D. McCartney, 'The quest for Irish political identity: the image and the illusion', *Irish University Review*, 9:1 (1979), 13–22, at p. 13. 3 Richard Fallis, *The Irish Renaissance: an introduction to Anglo-Irish literature* (Dublin, 1978), p. x. 4 The term 'Anglo-Irish' relates to persons of English descent born or resident in Ireland or descendants of mixed English and Irish parentage. 'Anglo-Irish literature' describes Irish writing in English to

judged the notion as 'a botheration',[5] the term is now so accepted that, as W.J. McCormack states, 'it is too late to purge it from our critical vocabulary'.[6] According to A. Norman Jeffares, Anglo-Irish literature is 'a body of literature in English ... generally speaking bound up with Ireland'. And while he also sees it primarily as 'writing in English by Irish authors', he recognizes it also as the 'inheritance of two traditions'.[7] Such broad definitions allow us to include Kate Thompson as an Irish literary voice and to place her with some confidence on the continuum of the shared Anglo-Irish tradition.

The late nineteenth and twentieth centuries saw a literary renaissance in Ireland, as writers, among them W.B. Yeats (1865–1939), J.M. Synge (1871–1909) and Lady Augusta Gregory (1852–1932), attempted to create a national literature 'drawn upon the resources of the indigenous tradition'.[8] These writers were conscious of two powerful and contentious cultures, namely, the 1,500-year old Gaelic literary tradition, along with Irish literature in the English language, which developed from the seventeenth century onwards. At a time when Ireland was asserting its nationhood and had finally achieved independence from Great Britain with the Anglo-Irish Treaty of 1921, the literary revivalists sought to create a 'distinctive national literature' and to uncover 'a national imagination which was distinctively Irish'.[9] Irish folklore became the central impulse behind the movement, with Yeats lauding the folktale as 'at once the Bible, the Thirty-Nine Articles, and the Book of Common Prayer'.[10] Poet Seamus Heaney recognizes that Yeats, during what was known as this 'Celtic Twilight' phase, 'sought a badge of identity for his own culture', found it in 'the magical world-view of the country people', and resolved to 'restore a body of old legends and folk beliefs that would bind the people of the Irish place to the body of their world'.[11] Yeats believed that because this literature was regional and reflected the speech of the native population, the Irish sense of identity was restored. In Heaney's view, this formed 'the beginning of a discovery of confidence in our own ground, in our place, in our speech, English and Irish'.[12] The Anglo-Irish cultural revival performed a vital function in developing a new literature and in breeding successive generations of celebrated Irish writers during the twentieth century.

Thompson concedes her debt to the Anglo-Irish writers who perpetuated this tradition and, while familiar with Yeats' work from an early age, she sees Lady Gregory 'as a bigger and more immediate influence', finding her translations or

distinguish this tradition from English literature and literature in Gaelic.   5 W.J. McCormack, 'Yeats and a new tradition', *The Crane Bag Book of Irish Studies*, 3:1 (1978), 30–40, at p. 36.   6 Ibid.   7 A. Norman Jeffares, *Anglo-Irish Literature, Macmillan History of Literature* (Dublin: Macmillan, 1982), pp 1, 2.   8 Tomás Ó Cathasaigh, 'Between god and man: the hero of Irish tradition', *The Crane Bag Book of Irish Studies*, 211–12 (1978), 72–9, at p. 72.   9 Fallis, *Irish Renaissance* p. 5.   10 W.B. Yeats, *The Message of the Folk-Lorist* (1893), p. 284; in Mary Helen Thuente, *W.B. Yeats and Irish Folklore* (Dublin, Jersey: Gill and Macmillan, 1980), p. 2.   11 Seamus Heaney, *Precoccupations: selected prose, 1968–1978* (London: Faber, 1984), pp 101, 135. 12 Ibid.

versions of early Irish material 'enormously exciting' and 'wonderfully lyrical'.[13] Thompson, as a former outsider who believes that modern cynicism has dismissed much of this folkloric tradition, perhaps more than most appreciates what may be lost in the long term if she and other writers were to fail to interpret and revive such heritage.

JAMES STEPHENS' INFLUENCE ON KATE THOMPSON

Although influenced by the general ideas of Yeats and Gregory, a more obvious precedent for Thompson's writing, as seen in *The New Policeman*, is found in the work of Dublin-born author and poet James Stephens. Regarded within literary circles as a wit and raconteur, Stephens was also admired greatly for his delightful expositions of Irish fairytales and mythology with their mixture of lyricism and humour. But he is perhaps best remembered for his novels *The Charwoman's Daughter* and in particular, *The Crock of Gold*, both published in 1912, which have had enduring popularity.

Augustine Martin points out that many viewed Stephens merely as 'a fey emanation of the Celtic Twilight as it flickered to a close in the new light of the twentieth century',[14] but he also states that others recognized that Stephens 'brought into Irish literature ... a naturalism that was fresh as it was engaging'.[15] Stephens' temperament and experience as a storyteller and conversationalist made him 'a natural fantasizer'.[16] However, with hindsight, he was more highly regarded as 'the important bridge between the first Irish writers of the Celtic Twilight period and the new more sophisticated writers'[17] like James Joyce, Liam O'Flaherty and Flann O'Brien, whose legacy lives on in post-modern times. *The Crock of Gold*, in particular, was seen as highly sophisticated, complex and ground-breaking for its time and proved inspirational to new generations of writers. The work has been lauded by critics, among them poet Walter de la Mare, who praised its ingenuity as 'crammed full of life and beauty' and 'a delicious, fantastical, amorphous, inspired medley of topsy turvydom'.[18] But this is not to undermine its depth. Fallis notes that despite it being 'naively wonderful', we should not be blinded to the fact that the book 'is a profound and joyful account of our inner lives'.[19] Jeffares too remarks on its 'idiosyncratic mixture of the apparently ephemeral and the profoundly serious'.[20]

13 Anne Marie Herron, interview with Kate Thompson, 2007, p. ii. 14 Augustine Martin, *James Stephens: a critical study* (Dublin: Gill and Macmillan, 1977), p. x. 15 Padraic Colum, 'Preface', in L. Frankenberg (selector), *James Stephens: a selection* (London, 1962), p. ix. 16 Fallis, *Irish Renaissance*, p. 153. 17 Hilary Pyle, *James Stephens: his work and an account of his life* (London: Routledge, 1965), p. x. 18 Walter de la Mare, foreword to *The Crock of Gold* (London, 1953), pp 7, 8. 19 Fallis, *Irish Renaissance*, p. 154. 20 Jeffares, *Anglo-Irish Literature*, p. 178.

Stephens gained a familiarity with Irish myth and legend from his contempo-
raries, and 'plunged into the seas of mythology along with Yeats and the rest'.[21]
But the genesis of his ideas goes back to poet William Blake (1757–1827) whom
Stephens hailed as a genius. Stephens' work is evidence of his 'deep adherence
to Blake's tenets' [22] and the recognition that he was 'under the powerful sway of
Blake's philosophy'.[23] And just as he saw in Blake a writer he could admire and
emulate, Kate Thompson pays tribute to her Irish predecessor, stating that
'Stephens was the very best of them … He had everything – imagination, vision,
humour'.[24]

In comparing the writings of Thompson and Stephens, one can identify
shared ideology and genre, as well as elements of style, language, music, wit,
characterization and an all-pervading fairytale atmosphere. In *The New
Policeman*, Thompson articulates her admiration by drawing on the ideas and
tone of Stephens' work and by echoing the approach and style of *The Crock of
Gold*.

GENRE

Thompson distances herself from the term 'fantasy', preferring to align herself
with the fairytale or indeed with its near equivalent, the German wonder tale,[25]
but it can be argued that her work answers to many of the criteria of the fantasy
genre. Her stories incorporate the personal quest, the inner development of the
young person on his or her journey towards self-discovery, all hallmarks of
fantasy. Her protagonists follow the Jungian pattern of initial isolation, they
embark on journeys, confront the shadow, or negative aspect of the personality,
descend into darkness and finally achieve ultimate transformation. Furthermore,
in Thompson's writing the real is interpreted and understood through the
mythological and the supernatural.

This interweaving of fact and fancy is a well-recognized characteristic of
fantasy. As Peter Hunt states, 'the one thing that can rarely be said of fantasy is
that it has nothing to do with reality'.[26] He also believes that 'alternative worlds
must *necessarily* [his italics] be related to, and comment on, the real world'. In this
way, fantasy can be seen as a 'heightening of reality',[27] a means of coping with
our existence and of arriving at the truth. Kathryn Hume goes further, saying

---

21 Herbert A. Kenny, *Literary Dublin: a history* (Dublin: Gill and Macmillan, 1991; 2nd ed.), p.
164. 22 Pyle, *James Stephens*, p. x. 23 John Cronin, *Irish Fiction, 1900–1940* (Belfast:
Appletree, 1992), p. 51. 24 Herron, Interview, 2007, iii. 25 Ibid. 26 Peter Hunt and
Millicent Lenz, *Alternative Worlds in Fantasy Fiction, Contemporary Classics of Children's
Literature* (London, New York: Continuum, 2001), p. 7. 27 U.K. Le Guin, *The Language of the
Night: essays on fantasy and science fiction* (New York: Harper Collins, 1992), p. 79.

that the interaction between realism and fantasy is such that creating divisions between them is 'as impracticable as separating the dancer from the dance'.[28]

Stephens, in his time, understood this relationship and created narratives that allowed for 'the intermingling of the fantastic or mythic and the realistic' in a manner that was 'sober and understated'.[29] Martin notes that in his work, 'magic, mystery and miracle are fused with the quotidian and the domestic', and that his fantasy world retains 'its own laws or its own indigenous anarchies'. *The Crock of Gold*'s characters portray the many facets of human beings, their sensual and emotional core, their intellectual and spiritual being, their conventions and logic and their innocence. Stephens used his work to comment on society and to parody some of its figures. The musings and diatribes of his Philosopher allow him to expound wittily on a wide range of topics, including sleep, hunger, nakedness, daughters, policemen, the intelligence of dogs and finally, the nature of philosophy itself.[30] His repeated use of aphorisms comments ironically on societal values. Echoing Blake, Stephens 'mourned the advance of what modernity calls civilization', that which 'enslaves mankind and perverts Nature'.[31] This apparent anti-modernity might suggest escapism on the writer's part, but Lloyd Frankenburg emphasizes his firm grip on the real world, describing him as 'one of the masters of looking-glass reality'.[32] Behind the veil of the mythical story, Stephens mischievously and playfully criticizes pomposity and materialism and questions the values of his generation.

Similarly, Thompson balances the fantastic with the real. In *The New Policeman,* she too is interested in the problems of her society and the demands of the modern, fast-paced world where people are 'tyrannized by time', where there is no time for 'mooching along country lanes', nor even 'time to talk about time'.[33] More than that, she bemoans the loss of traditional mores, the loss of enjoyment in simple pleasures and the pressures of life in the twenty-first century. Although her character JJ stumbles into *Tír na nÓg*, the Land of Eternal Youth, his quest in search of time is credible and unsentimental. The fantasy world, as she creates it, maintains a rationality suited to modern readers and she provides explanations for its workings. However ethereal, it is as easily imagined as the real, allowing us to visualize it. Her fantastic inventions of 'sky doors' and 'time skin'[34] are predicated upon a logic that make them acceptable to the reader. The clever invention of mutual amnesia,[35] which allows the characters to forget their experiences in their opposing worlds, means that they can retain their identities and their secrets. It also helps the reader to believe that these worlds can exist independently alongside each other.

28 Kathryn Hume, *Fantasy and Mimesis: responses to reality in Western literature* (London: Methuen, 1984; 2nd ed.), p. 21.   29 Martin, *James Stephens*, pp 43, 38.   30 James Stephens, *The Crock of Gold* (London: Macmillan, 1926; 1st published 1912), pp 26, 67, 75, 48, 150, 158, 76.   31 Cronin, *Irish Fiction*, p. 52.   32 Lloyd Frankenberg, *James Stephens*, p. xxix.   33 Kate Thompson, *The New Policeman* (London, 2005), pp 141, 34, 35.   34 Ibid., p. 337.   35 Ibid., p. 171.

Stephens has been deemed 'a fabulist'[36] and seen as belonging to the realms of 'imaginative realism'. However, no such definitive tag has been accorded to Thompson. While it is tempting to apply the term 'realistic fantasy' to her work, this is somewhat tautological, given the complementary and fused nature of the real and the fantastic as already described. Perhaps Thompson with her analytical style belongs within the realms of a form of psychological realism infused with the fantasy genre.

INTRODUCING MYTHOLOGY TO NEW GENERATIONS

Both Stephens and Thompson are conscious of their contemporary audiences. Stephens, like the other Anglo-Irish revivalists writing at a time of great political change, looked to the past to illuminate his present, sought to 'free the true sprit of Ireland'[37] and to 'discover the native ideology' of his country.[38] Believing that the writer 'who creates a new world must create a new art to express it,'[39] Stephens found this art by breathing new life into the world of the gods and fairies. With tongue in cheek, he announced that he wanted to give to modern Ireland 'a new mythology to take the place of the threadbare mythology of Greek and Rome',[40] and so he 'resurrected characters portrayed 800 years before and made them real for his own time',[41] setting them in a 'psychic landscape'[42] of his own creation.

Following the maxim that 'to understand the present we must possess the past',[43] Thompson too, writing at a time of social change in Ireland and seeking to treat contemporary themes, resorts to the mythological world. She introduces Irish mythology to a new audience that has grown away from the culture of fairy forts, changelings, ancient stories of the *Fianna* and the notion of a land of eternal youth. Now at the beginning of the third millennium, she unearths the cultural treasury of folk memory once again. In re-introducing mythology to young people, Kate Thompson aspires to a future firmly linked to our past. She sees many of the stories that children encounter today as 'the mental equivalent of junk food' lacking 'the crucial nutritional elements' of fairy stories, myths and legends, that is, the psychological maps which feed children's understanding of what it is to be human and helps them to cope with 'moral choice'.[44] In her work she shows appreciation for this precious tradition, first revived by Gregory and her contemporaries, and places it in a credible setting for young people today.

In *The New Policeman*, she allows young JJ, who is 'torn between normal

36 Martin in Cronin, *Irish Fiction*, p. 50.   37 Pyle, *James Stephens*, p. 27.   38 Ó Cathasaigh, in *Crane Bag*, p. 220.   39 Pyle, *James Stephens*, p. 111.   40 Frankenburg, *James Stephens*, p. xxiv. 41 Pyle, *James Stephens*, p. 101.   42 Cronin, *Irish Fiction*, p. 51.   43 Robert Scholes & Robert Kellogg, *The Nature of Narrative* (Oxford, New York: OUP, 1968), p. 57.   44 Herron, Interview, p. i.

teenage pastimes and the call of his heritage',[45] to question his family history, and through him, explains to a new generation the traditions of 'older more primitive beliefs'.[46] While JJ is a normal teenager faced with the attractions of the modern world, he enters into the fairy world of *Tír na nÓg* and converses with the characters who are 'convincingly robust as well as endearingly whimsical'.[47] Mimicking Alice's tumble through the rabbit hole and into Wonderland, JJ passes through the souterrain to discover another world. But unlike Alice, JJ can fully accept this world as an extension of his own, a part of his heritage waiting to be discovered. In fact, this other world manages to make sense of what is happening in the reality of his life where time is inexplicably escaping at an alarming rate.

TOPOGRAPHICAL EVIDENCE OF LITERATURE AND LORE

The inspiration of the landscape is particularly evident in the Irish traditional genre of *dinnseanchas*, that is, 'poems and tales which relate the original meanings of place names and constitute a mythological etymology'.[48] In the landscape itself, a topographical record of literature and lore are inscribed which, in Heaney's view, is a marriage of 'the legendary and the local'. He speaks of the sacred nature of place, 'a sacramental sensing', which allows for 'the foundation of a marvellous or a magical view of the world'.

Just as Yeats did in poetry, Stephens, in *The Crock of Gold*, forges strong links between history, mythology and place. His setting is one peopled with gods whose homes he conceals. His Angus Óg is found wandering lonely on the hills, leaving the sense of his presence in 'the holes of the rocks and the dark caves of the sea'.[49] Thompson's landscapes are also those in which 'the present is suffused with the past'.[50] We have the sense of treading on hallowed ground, a ground echoing the many traditions of Ireland – the pagan, the legendary and the Christian. With the 'inspirational range of limestone of the Burren' as a backdrop to the story, we soon learn that we are close to 'older more primitive beliefs',[51] and that this is a place where anything is possible. This gives credence to Heaney's notion that the rich oral and literary tradition that we share makes us all 'inhabitants not just of a geographical country but of a country of the mind'. This 'nourishment which springs from knowing and belonging to a certain place'[52] is one which is central to Thompson's beliefs. She uses

45 Jan Mark, 'Where the sun stands still', [The Guardian Digital Edition, 2005], p. 2. Accessed 23 Mar. 2006. http:// books.guardian.co.uk/reviews/childrensandteens/0.612II519186.oohtml. 46 Thompson, *New Policeman*, p. 79. 47 Julia Eccleshare, 'The Music of Time', *Inis*, 14 (Winter 2005), 38. 48 Heaney, *Preoccupations*, pp 131, 133. 49 Stephens, *Crock of Gold*, p. 113. 50 Thompson, *New Policeman*, p. 141. 51 Ibid., pp 33, 79. 52 Heaney, *Preoccupations*, pp 132, 136.

geographical maps to provide the psychological maps she deems necessary for her fantasy worlds. She articulates this in an earlier novel, *Wild Blood* (1999) when she speaks of the 'immortal ones', 'older even than the ancient mountain ... who lived and would continue to live beneath the green fields of Ireland'. For her, the historical map which lies under the modern is 'a fairy map, made up of leylines and *sidhes* and the strongly radiating focal points of magical powers'.[53] Her writing asserts the pervasiveness of the supernatural. She speaks of 'a magic energy in the Burren' and, in its souterrains, burial mounds and fairy forts, she sees visible signs of the otherworld, 'remains of old civilizations'.[54] In addition, she perceives the landscape as Heaney does, as one which retains the memory of everything that has happened in it. For Thompson, place is not just a touchstone but an underlying influence, a character in itself, breathing life into her writing and providing what William Wordsworth called 'a prospect of the mind'.[55] Moreover, the Burren, with 'its delicate environmental balance' acting as backdrop to this story, serves as a metaphor for the delicate cultural balance between old and new. And while 'environmental protection legislation'[56] exists to maintain the physical environment, we must depend on writers to provide protection for the mythological and the cultural, by refocusing our attention on it.

In *The New Policeman* readers become conscious that the rural landscape is home not only to the traditions of story and song but also contains physical evidence of 'the other side'. They are never far from reminders of that world. JJ can imagine 'Fionn and the Fianna walking around in these grey hills with their broadswords and their beards'[57] just as Yeats reminded his fellow Irish that they were all around them 'in the places where we go riding and go marketing'.[58] Heaney supports John Montague's view that 'the whole of the Irish landscape is a topographical record, a manuscript which we have lost the skill to read'.[59] Thompson, by paying attention to the visible signs of mythology in the landscape and summoning up the spirit of the land, is equipping her readers with the vision and vocabulary to read this geographical document of place and time. Like Stephens, she makes use of the dual time of the fairy world and the human world, allowing us to vacillate between the physical present and the mystical past, while also giving continuity into the future. Her story, like *The Crock of Gold*, ends with a fairy-tale happiness and we rest content in the knowledge that *Tír na nÓg* would stay 'basking for ever in this warm golden evening'.[60]

53 Thompson, *Wild Blood* (London: Bodley Head, 1999), pp 532, 535.   54 Herron, Interview, p. ii.   55 Heaney, *Preoccupations*, p. 20.   56 Thompson, *New Policeman*, p. 57.   57 Ibid., pp 134, 241.   58 Yeats, Preface p. xvii., to Gregory, *Cuchulain of Muirthemne* (London, 1902). 59 Heaney, *Preoccupations*, p. 132.   60 Thompson, *New Policeman*, p. 366.

MUSIC

Stephens had 'an ardent desire for gaiety and *joie de vivre*' [61] and music permeates *The Crock of Gold* like the fairies themselves. The leprecauns [*sic*] dance for joy, and the pipes of Pan are heard 'calling and sobbing and making high merriment on the air'. Throughout, there is dancing and the climax of the book is an apocalyptic dance when, in the tone of Yeats' 'Stolen Child' (1886), we are urged to 'Come away! Come away!', to join with the people and the gods in this harmonious scene. As the music gathers momentum, it brings with it not only increased understanding and knowledge of where truth lies, but also freedom and love. In this final scene we witness the healing power of the music as well as its ability to enchant and beguile. The culmination of the story is one of Blakean joy, where gaiety and uninhibited happiness prevail as the characters dance 'telling their sunny tale'. Nature partakes fully in this merry scene 'as the sun laughs down into the valley and the sea leaps upon the shingle, panting for joy'.[62]

Thompson's writing echoes this belief in the power of music. She states that music is 'the touchstone for communication between the fairy and the human domains'.[63] In *The New Policeman*, it naturally traverses the boundaries between the traditional and the new, the real and the imagined, the young and old. The author perpetuates the notion that 'our music – our jigs and reels and hornpipes and our slow airs – was given to us by the fairies'. The whole book is structured around traditional tunes that draw her readers in and allow them to enter in as performers. Music enchants as musicians are 'taken over by the spirit of that wild anarchic music' with its 'tunes demanding to be played'. The performance of music and dance releases a power, a magic which takes hold, 'electrifying, energetic, graceful'.[64] It draws the people, young and old, into a celebration reminiscent of Stephens' merry dances 'of uncontrollable gaiety'[65] and brings this book to a similar musical climax, with the assembled characters dancing 'both separately and together', forming 'a perfectly circular whole'.[66]

CHARACTERS

Thompson's choice of setting, her use of music, her belief in the mythological and in the fairy world, all pay homage to the work of Stephens, as do the characters she chooses and the book's title. The policeman, as Stephens' *bête noire* and 'the butt of his imagination and wit',[67] was the vehicle that allowed him

61 Cronin, *Irish Fiction*, p. 53. **62** Stephens, *Crock of Gold*, pp 78, 228. **63** Anne Marie Herron, Notes taken on discussion between Kate Thompson and Robert Dunbar, Hugh Lane Gallery, 17 June 2006. **64** Thompson, *New Policeman*, pp 80, 21, 162. **65** Stephens, *Crock of Gold*, p. 222. **66** Thompson, *New Policeman*, p. 162. **67** Pyle, *James Stephens*, pp 59, 62.

to question human law. In one of the Philosopher's diatribes, he questions whether policemen are necessary to civilization at all. Thompson continues this commentary with her policeman questioning his role and place in society. Stephens was also disparaging about the clergy, stating that 'the difference between a priest and a policeman is too slight to talk about'.[68] Thompson too casts the priest in the role of villain who sets out to destroy traditional culture and 'the devil's music' because they are 'dangerous and subversive'.[69]

Readers encounter some of the same Irish mythological figures in both *The New Policeman* and *The Crock of Gold*, in the personages of Angus Óg (or Aengus) and Dagda, the Tuatha dé Danann and the Shee, although Stephens gave further depth to his story by introducing the Greek God Pan. While both books refer to animal figures, in particular to the goat or *púka*,[70] Stephens takes a more fantastical approach with a more eclectic mix of gods, humans and talking animals. Most significantly however is the fact that characters in both stories are on quests of various sorts, not for the tangible, but for meaning. Stephens' Philosopher is seeking happiness, love and joy; the New Policeman is looking for 'that [unnamed] elusive thing',[71] and JJ, the modern young hero, is in search of time. These two writers are posing bigger questions about the meaning of life and what it means to be human at particular times in our history. By re-discovering the past under the mantle of myth and tradition they help readers to understand their present and their possible future.

STYLE OF EXPRESSION

Not only are parallels discernible between both authors in their belief in the mythological and choice of characters and themes, but also in their style of writing. Stephens' inventive use of language has been widely acknowledged and Frankenberg praises his 'absolutely right and delightful writing', stating that 'he originates prose. He creates speech, words that rise from the page like a steam of breath'.[72] His work has been described as 'refreshing' and injecting into the poetic idiom 'a stream of vigorous down to earth language'.[73] Stephens has also been noted as 'a man who has entertained words and can let them crowd the doorways and sills of the mind'.[74] And yet his lyricism was never at the expense of plot which he could deliver 'in a fashion that would be beguiling enough to hold us'.

As a poet of some note, Stephens had the lyrical ability to raise the ordinary to the extraordinary so that his descriptive passages become indelibly patterned

68 Ibid., p. 59.   69 Thompson, *New Policeman*, p. 162.   70 Púca, pooka, puck: variously described as a hobgoblin or ghost, often taking the form of a goat.   71 Thompson, *New Policeman*, p. 72.   72 Frankenburg, *James Stephens*, p. xxxi.   73 Pyle, *James Stephens*, pp 31, 175.   74 Frankenburg, *James Stephens*, pp xix, xviii.

on the mind of the reader. His description of 'the first white peep of the dawn', the 'sickle moon, a tender sword' or the trees with 'their earnest whisper'[75] are memorable.

Thompson has expressed her admiration for Stephens' 'beautiful rich language'. She goes on to state that 'every word is poetry. His work speaks directly to the soul, bypassing the mental filters'.[76] While not as breathtaking in its originality as that of Stephens, nonetheless Thompson's work contains many lyrical passages, particularly in relation to nature. Descriptions such as those of the water as 'pewter-grey with muddy bronze glints', 'its surface ragged' and of the clouds as 'mottled shapes ... moving like a school of fish gliding through the black depths of the sea'[77] are evocative. Jan Mark has praised the 'matter-of-fact voice of the author, her robust sense of fun, and the sheer energy of her writing'.[78] But it is the very spare quality and apparent simplicity of her writing that primarily gives it power, as in the 'the beehive buzz of a dozen conversations' or the family secrets succinctly described as 'hidden territories, so cleverly concealed'.[79]

WIT AND HUMOUR

Along with his lyrical expression, Stephens, in *The Crock of Gold*, displays his 'capricious wit' or what has been described as an 'impish sense of fun or ... a witty contrariness',[80] which carries the reader along at a fast pace. His sense of the ridiculous is highly developed and he appears to enjoy his zestful romp through the novel with his host of eclectic characters. His tone is simultaneously ironic, mocking, playful and humorous and the pomposity of his Philosopher allows him to exhibit all of this.

Although lacking the anarchic nonsense of Stephens, Thompson also displays her own a sense of the absurd with coloured socks as landmarks, a goat that becomes a bodhrán, furniture which continues to grow and Tony Stradivarius as a great fellow to make a fiddle from 'chiming maple'. Her description of teaching Aengus the rules for worrying forms a wry commentary on the obsessions of modern life, as do her references to the vagaries and regulations of the European Union and the economic phenomenon of Ireland's 'Celtic Tiger'.[81]

It has been noted that Stephens 'lacked the solemnity of his elders'[82] and did not treat the Celtic gods and heroes as reverently as did Gregory and Yeats. Similarly, Thompson pokes fun at Aengus, showing him as petulant and naive. While Thompson's humour is not of the hearty variety, there is an underlying

75 Stephens, *Crock of Gold*, pp 39, 210. 76 Herron, Interview, p. iii. 77 Thompson, *New Policeman*, pp 9, 16. 78 Jan Mark, 'Where the sun stands still', p. 3. 79 Thompson, *New Policeman*, pp 9, 109. 80 Pyle, *James Stephens*, p. 177. 81 Thompson, *New Policeman*, pp 238, 170, 212, 374, 185, 108. 82 Martin, *James Stephens*, p. 40.

wit that surfaces unexpectedly, bringing a lightness of touch to the serious issues she addresses.

ATMOSPHERE

Thompson's work resonates with the influence of James Stephens in terms of themes, characters and mythology, and she also manages to evoke a similar mood. In creating the 'pastoral idyll' or 'the Irish Arcadia'[83] of *The Crock of Gold*, Stephens makes extensive use of sunlight and its power to create atmosphere. This otherworld is 'wrapped in sunshine and peace',[84] a place of 'sunlit wisdom and instinctive happiness',[85] contrasted only with the sinister walk of the Philosopher into darkness. The final chapter is replete with references to the light of the early morning sun and the 'bright and happy beings'[86] bathed in the glow of sunlight.

Thompson's *Tír na nÓg* is similarly suffused with a golden glow. At times the sun is 'blindingly bright' and it impacts on the landscape with its 'lush green farmlands' or 'sun drenched mountains'.[87] This light brings to the book a certain hallucinatory quality giving 'the sensation … of watching a dream slip away after waking'.[88] The consciousness that it could be ended by time seeping in makes us value it all the more, knowing that the disappearance of the sun will bring pain and suffering to a perfect world.

CONCLUSION

Thompson's heritage as a writer draws from two cultures. With her background in both Ireland and England and her insight into the two traditions, she exemplifies the shared linguistic heritage of Ireland and Great Britain.

Modern Ireland, as depicted by Thompson for her young audience, is characterized by change. This change is certainly of a different nature to that which faced the Irish nation a century earlier but, nonetheless, one where new realities of consumerism and time poverty must be accommodated. The challenge of forging national identity is ongoing and evolving and takes account of changing political, social and economic status.

James Stephens understood the necessity of looking to earlier literary heroes for guidance. In commenting on his own indebtedness to William Blake, he stated wittily: 'I make no monstrous claims for Blake as a poet … but he is still

83 Ibid., p. 41.   84 Stephens, *Crock of Gold*, p. 227.   85 Seamus Deane, *A Short History of Irish Literature* (London, 1986), p. 201.   86 Stephens, *Crock of Gold*, p. 224.   87 Thompson, *New Policeman*, pp 145, 233, 139.   88 Jan Mark, 'Where the sun stands still', p. 3.

... very good to steal from; and let it be conceded that theft is the first duty of man'.[89] Thompson, with similar admiration for Stephens' work, admits to being 'a huge fan' and jokingly declared herself willing to become 'the head of any James Stephens revival movement'.[90]

As witness to this admiration, her writing pays homage to him in many ways and she acknowledges Stephens' guidance in her evocation of fairies and legend. In doing so she emerges as a flame-carrier for such mythological interpretation, rejuvenating the spirit of his writing for a new generation of readers and in the process, justified her own place within the Irish literary landscape.

89 Cronin, *Irish Fiction*, p. 51.   90 Interview with Kate Thompson, *Rattlebag*, 15 June 2006. RTÉ.

Irish and European echoes in Oscar Wilde's fairy tales

ANNE MARKEY

Since the 1980s, one of the major paradigms guiding Oscar Wilde studies has been the contribution made by Wilde's Irishness to the style and content of his work.[1] In particular, a link has been posited between Irish folklore and what are commonly known as his two collections of fairy tales, *The Happy Prince and Other Tales* (1888) and *A House of Pomegranates* (1891).[2] While Wilde's Irish background is an important context for the consideration of his work, it is equally important to remember that he was a cosmopolitan figure who described himself as 'a most recalcitrant patriot'.[3] Born in Dublin in 1854, he lived most of his adult life in England, preached his gospel of aesthetics on both sides of the Atlantic, and died in Paris in 1900. Since his death, his life and work have increasingly become the focus of international criticism. Wilde, in effect, is a cultural hybrid whose continuing appeal transcends the division between popular icon and academic object of enquiry. An examination of his fairy tales will show that they too are cultural hybrids whose combination of Irish folkloric and international literary echoes adds to their aesthetic complexity and enriches their exploration of selflessness and self-absorption.

The roots of Wilde's cultural hybridity lie in his Irish background. Born into the caste known as the Anglo-Irish, he became, as Jerusha McCormack points out, 'adept at living on both sides of the hyphen'.[4] Young Oscar had access to his father's large library, which included selections of European literature and volumes on numerous subjects of Irish interest.[5] His parents' shared interest in Irish history and popular traditions alerted their son to the wealth of Ireland's cultural heritage. Oscar also spent long periods on family property in the west of Ireland where he came in contact with local servants who enriched his knowledge of Irish popular culture and folklore.[6] His formal education in Portora Royal

1 See, for example, Davis Coakley, *Oscar Wilde: the importance of being Irish* (Dublin: Town House, 1994); Richard Pine, *The Thief of Reason: Oscar Wilde and modern Ireland* (Dublin: Gill and Macmillan, 1995); Jerusha McCormack (ed.), *Wilde, the Irishman* (New Haven and London: Yale UP, 1998); and Eiléan Ní Chuilleanáin (ed.), *The Wilde Legacy* (Dublin: Four Courts Press, 2003). 2 For examples of this suggested link, see Sally Brown, *Oscar Wilde, 1854–1900* (London: British Library, 2000), pp 22–3 and John Sloan, *Authors in Context: Oscar Wilde* (Oxford: OUP, 2003), pp 79–80. 3 Merlin Holland and Rupert Hart Davis (eds), *The Complete Letters of Oscar Wilde* (London: Fourth Estate, 2000), p. 371. 4 Jerusha McCormack, 'Introduction: the Irish Wilde', in Jerusha McCormack (ed.), *Wilde the Irishman* (New Haven: Yale UP, 1998), pp 1–5, p. 1. 5 See *Catalogue of the Library of the Late Rev. Tho. Hamblyn Porter and of the Late Sir William Wilde, 1879* held in TCD Library. 6 Coakley, *Oscar Wilde*, pp 94–9.

School, Enniskillen, at Trinity College Dublin and Magdalen College Oxford gave him access to English, continental and classical literature. From childhood, then, Oscar had access to a variety of cultural influences that resurface in his later work.

In what follows, I will distinguish between elements that are found in the international folklore tradition and European literary sources, including the literary fairy tale, and those that seem to point to a source special to Irish folklore. Wilde's first published work of prose fiction was *The Happy Prince and Other Tales*, published in 1888, and containing 'The Happy Prince', 'The Nightingale and the Rose', 'The Selfish Giant', 'The Devoted Friend' and 'The Remarkable Rocket'. All five stories contain structural features of the folktale as they generally follow a sequence that begins with a lack and leads towards the liquidation of that lack. [7] In addition, they contain some motifs, such as the triadic repetition of the statue's requests to the swallow in the title story, which are associated with the folktale in general. However, Wilde's recourse to Irish folklore in particular is most evident in the stories' ongoing focus on selflessness and childlike innocence. Seán Ó Súilleabháin points out that Irish religious folktales feature miraculous occurrences, focus on the power of innocence, and show that charity and generosity are abundantly rewarded while neglect of those virtues is punished.[8] 'The Happy Prince' and 'The Selfish Giant' feature miraculous occurrences, highlight the value of childlike innocence, and show that charity and generosity are divinely rewarded.

Two specific details suggest that 'The Selfish Giant' draws on the Irish folk narrative tradition. Wilde's story contains the phrase, 'Years went over', which is unusual and unwieldy in English.[9] That may well be because it is a literal translation of the Irish phrase 'Chuaigh blianta thart', suggesting that Wilde was drawing on memories of stories originally told in Irish but later translated into English. Pádraig Ó Héalaí points out that apocryphal stories based on characters and events described in the New Testament abound in the oral Irish tradition. One of the apocryphal occurrences to which Ó Héalaí refers, recorded in songs and stories collected in counties Galway and Mayo where the Wilde family spent considerable amounts of time, tells of the tree that bent down low in response to a request from the unborn infant Jesus.[10] 'The Selfish Giant', which features a tree that bends to accommodate a little child who later bears the prints of nails on his hands and feet, alludes directly to this apocryphal folk tradition. It also recalls a religious folktale, called 'The Priest's Soul', anthologized by Lady Wilde, Oscar's mother, in 1887. This story concerns a learned priest whose pride

---

7 See Vladimir Propp, *Morphology of the Folktale* (Austin: University of Texas Press, 1971), p. 53. 8 Seán Ó Súilleabháin, *Storytelling in Irish Tradition* (Cork: Mercier, 1973), pp 18, 43, 44. 9 Ian Small (ed.), *Oscar Wilde: complete short fiction* (London: Penguin, 2003), p. 22. 10 Pádraig Ó Héalaí, 'An Crann a Chrom: Scéal Apacrafúil', in Pádraig Ó Fiannachta (ed.), *Léachtaí Cholm Cille XIV: Ár Scéalaíocht* (Maynooth: An Sagart, 1983), pp 151–72, pp 151, 154.

leads him to deny the existence of purgatory, heaven, hell, God and the human soul. On the eve of his death, an angel tells him that he may only escape eternal damnation if he can find one person who believes in the existence of the soul. Eventually, he meets a child from a far country who reasons that 'if we have life, though we cannot see it, we may also have a soul, though it is invisible'.[11] The priest rejoices, knowing his soul is safe. Lady Wilde's story foregrounds the necessity for repentance and the redemptive potential of a little child, themes which recur in her son's story of 'The Selfish Giant'.

While 'The Selfish Giant' draws directly on the Irish folk narrative tradition, and 'The Happy Prince' alludes to it in its divine vindication of generosity, the influence of Irish folklore on the other stories in *The Happy Prince and Other Tales* is negligible. As they contain stylized, elaborate descriptions that are not essential to the plot, digressions, and ambiguous endings, they are more readily aligned with the genre of the literary fairy tale than with the folk narrative tradition. Their structural complexity results in multi-layered stories that can be read at more than one level. The focus of all five stories on selflessness and self-absorption facilitates a cumulative exploration of issues including the use and abuse of power, the value of philanthropy, the purpose of education, and the function of art. Despite their vague settings in relation to time and place, the stories thus critically engage with ideological issues relevant to the Victorian reader who was invited to question the values that govern society. They raise questions that are equally relevant to later readers, because they relate to the fundamental values on which all societies are based. Wilde provides no easy answers as the stories not only contain internal oppositions, but also challenge each other. The vindication of selflessness conveyed in 'The Happy Prince' and 'The Selfish Giant' is undermined by unpunished selfishness and pointless sacrifice in other stories, as instanced by the student's treatment of the rose in 'The Nightingale and the Rose', by the death of little Hans in 'The Devoted Friend' and by the Remarkable Rocket's refusal to see himself as others see him. The inclusion of a variety of international literary echoes enhances the interpretative ambiguity inherent in the stories.

Wilde's contemporary reviewers compared *The Happy Prince and Other Tales* to the work of Hans Christian Andersen but noted that Wilde's tales were more satirical than the Dane's.[12] Wilde deliberately evokes Andersen but the expected match between their stories never materializes. 'The Happy Prince' features a little match girl, who unlike the child in Anderson's story, does not die, but runs home laughing. 'The Nightingale and the Rose' alludes to a number of Andersen stories, including 'A Rose from Homer's Grave', 'The World's Most Beautiful

11 Lady Wilde, *Ancient Legends, Mystic Charms & Superstitions of Ireland with Sketches of the Irish Past*, 2 vols (London: Ward and Downey, 1887), i, p. 65.   12 Karl Beckson (ed.), *Oscar Wilde: the critical heritage* (London and New York: Routledge and Kegan Paul, 1970), pp 60–1.

Rose', 'The Nightingale', and 'The Swineherd', only to complicate Andersen's vision of the relationship between love and death, nature and artifice. 'The Devoted Friend' invokes Andersen's 'Big Claus and Little Claus' but departs completely from Andersen's literary rendition of an international folktale by its reversal of the poor peasant's triumph over his rich neighbour, and by its inclusion of a narrative frame that focuses on the power and limitations of story-telling. The investigation of vanity in 'The Remarkable Rocket' recalls Andersen's similar project in 'The Darning Needle' but while Andersen's reader is coerced into abandoning the needle as she lies on the cobblestones at the end of the story, Wilde's final sentence highlights the consolatory power of narcissism: '"I knew I should create a great sensation", gasped the Rocket, and he went out'.[13] Wilde and Andersen deal with similar themes, including the relationship between nature and artifice, the effects of narcissism, and the connection between love and sacrifice. Wilde's approach to these issues within his fairy tales does not echo Andersen but rather reflects his own developing, and sometimes contradictory, philosophy. The deliberate evocation of Andersen is refracted by Wilde to produce distinctive stories whose tone and emphasis vary considerably from the Dane's. Wilde's satiric tone, which depends largely on a pervasive use of irony, creates stories which expose political, social and moral hypocrisies. The deliberate allusions to Andersen can be seen as part of this ironic strategy as they create narrative expectations that Wilde's fairy tales consistently undermine. References to other narrative and literary traditions dilute the obvious allusions to Andersen and complicate Wilde's investigation of the relationship between art and life. These references are most apparent in 'The Happy Prince' and 'The Nightingale and the Rose'.

The Charity Children in 'The Happy Prince' are not unlike those described in Blake's 'Holy Thursday' in *Songs of Innocence*. This Blakean tradition of childhood faith and radiance had been updated for the Victorian reader by George MacDonald's description of a Christ-like child who flies over London in *At the Back of the North Wind* (1871). The swallow's description of death as the brother of sleep in 'The Happy Prince' is taken from the opening lines of Percy Shelley's *Queen Mab*. This intertextual allusion to a poem that criticizes corrupt, tyrannical political systems enhances Wilde's criticism of the self-aggrandizing venality of the Town Councillors. The oriental imagery of 'The Happy Prince' may partly reflect Wilde's admiration of the fourteenth-century Persian poet, Hafiz.[14] It also reflects the pervasive influence of *The Arabian Nights* on the European literary imagination and the particular Victorian interest in the Orient fanned by Edward Fitzgerald's 1859 translation of *The Rubaiyat of Omar Khayyam*. Here, Wilde uses exotic imagery to highlight the harsh reality of life in a northern city and thereby emphasize the unselfish nature of the swallow's

13 Small, *Short Fiction*, p. 46.   14 Holland and Hart Davis, *Complete Letters*, p. 621.

decision to stay there. The swallow's evocation of the orient recalls Théophile Gautier's 'Ce que disent les hirondelles'. In this poem, a group of swallows describe the wonders of Egypt while the speaker compares himself to a captive bird who cannot escape to warmer climes. This intertextual echo aligns the figure of Wilde's swallow with the artist whose vocation can be seen as a liability.

The setting of 'The Nightingale and the Rose' in a university town and its description of the misadventures of a lovelorn student recall E.T.A. Hoffman's 'The Golden Top'. We know from Wilde's letters that he greatly admired the German Romantic writer.[15] Hoffman's story, like Wilde's, pits the deflationary recalcitrance of ordinary life against the ecstatic, but often disquieting, life of the imagination, and contrasts a rare, idealized form of love with the more shallow emotion that forms the basis of most human relationships. By placing a nightingale at the centre of the action, Wilde alludes to the Greek myth of Philomela, who, in Ovid's version in Book 6 of *Metamorphoses*, is transformed into a suffering nightingale. This classical myth considers inter alia the source of artistic inspiration and its effect on human lives. In Wilde's story, the nightingale can be seen as the figure of the ideal artist who goes against nature to produce a beautiful artefact that has no practical use and whose value goes unnoticed in the real world. The story also evokes John Keats' 'Ode to a Nightingale', in which pain and suffering are ineluctable elements of human existence from which the poet longs to escape with the immortal nightingale. In Wilde's story, the Nightingale is not immortal, but willing to suffer and die for the sake of an ideal love so Wilde subtly reverses the terms by which Keats explores suffering and perfection, life and art, death and immortality. The varied intertextual allusions unobtrusively woven into the fabric of both 'The Happy Prince' and 'The Nightingale and the Rose' greatly add to their aesthetic complexity.

Wilde described his second collection of fairy tales, *A House of Pomegranates*, containing 'The Young King', 'The Birthday of the Infanta', 'The Fisherman and his Soul' and 'The Star-Child', as rather like his first, 'only more elaborate'.[16] The increased range of literary allusions contained in these stories contributes in part to the greater sense of elaboration and enriches their ongoing exploration of the effects of selfishness and the need for, but also the tragedy of, selflessness. All four stories deliberately eschew clear identification with late Victorian society. Nevertheless, the issues they raise and the questions they provoke were relevant to Wilde's contemporary readers, and continue to be relevant to all readers interested in the interaction between individual freedom and social constraint.

With the exception of 'The Birthday of the Infanta', they all contain biblical allusions: the outraged nobles scorn the Young King as 'a dreamer of dreams', recalling the false prophet of Deuteronomy 13:1–10, the Fisherman's

---

15 Ibid., p. 393.   **16** Ibid., p. 493.

description of love as being more precious than riches is prefigured in Corinthians 13:1–2, while the falling star that leads the woodcutters to the child's resting place recalls the similar star that led the wise men to Bethlehem. This biblical frame of reference is reinforced by Wilde's use of parallel phrases and archaic pronouns, which echo the sonorous cadences of the King James Bible: 'And the people fell upon their knees in awe, and the nobles sheathed their swords and did homage, and the Bishop's face grew pale, and his hands trembled. "A greater than I hath crowned thee", he cried, and he knelt before him'.[17] This cadenced syntax heightens the sense suggested by the direct and indirect biblical allusions contained in the stories that their appreciation requires an acknowledgement of their spiritual dimension. Nevertheless, the aesthetic focus of all four stories on beauty in various forms heightens the sense that they are not intended as simplistic or didactic Christian allegories. In particular, the deliberate evocation of the timeless, magical world of the folktale in stories which feature foundlings, magical helpers, talking animals, magicians, witches and triadic repetition of various types, suggests that they cannot be read as conventional Christian morality tales. The range of diverse literary allusions contained in the stories reinforces the sense that they are carefully crafted works of art that counterpoint the fascination of aestheticism with the radiance of spirituality.

'The Young King' evokes the Catholic medieval world of chivalric romance. Through naming the palace 'Joyeuse', which recalls the Castle of Joyous Gard in *Morte d'Arthur*, Wilde alludes to Thomas Malory's accounts of knights, including Perceval and Gareth, who are recognized after being brought up far from court. As 'the dead staff blossomed' at the end of the story, it also refers to the Tannhauser legend.[18] According to this legend, which inspired Richard Wagner's 1848 opera, a German knight confesses his love for Venus to the Pope, who says a dry staff will sprout before God forgives the sinner. Tannhäuser leaves, the staff sprouts, and the Pope is condemned to eternal punishment.[19] The reference to the blossoming staff also alludes to the English mystery tradition in which Joseph is recognized as Mary's spouse, a belief that itself provides a New Testament analogue of the Old Testament representation of David as the flower of Jesse's stem. These allusions suggest that the story's investigation of honour, responsibility and repentance are rooted in European literary and religious tradition. The Young King's initial solipsistic worship of art and later attempt to purge his guilt echo Alfred Tennyson's 'The Palace of Art'. This change of heart is brought about by a sequence of three dreams, two of which draw on the rhetoric and imagery of a poem by Lady Wilde, Oscar's mother, called 'The Famine Year'. This poem, which emotively describes the

17 Small, *Short Fiction*, p. 96.   18 Ibid., p. 95.   19 Carl Lindale, John McManus and John Lindow (eds), *Medieval Folklore: an encyclopaedia of myths, legends, beliefs and customs*, 2 vols (Santa Barbara, CA: ABC–CLIO, 2000), i, pp 968–70.

heartbreak of the Irish Great Famine, opens with the following line: 'Weary men, what reap ye? – Golden corn for the stranger', and goes on to say that while others enjoy the fruits of the workers' labour, 'our children swoon before us'.[20] The weaver in the King's first dream complains: 'We sow the corn, and our own board is empty', with the result that 'our children fade away before their time'.[21] The poem's unlamented famine victim who dies 'without a tear, a prayer, a shroud, a coffin or a grave' is like the pearl diver whose body is unceremoniously thrown overboard in the story. The description of the diver's death, as 'blood gushed from his ears' also recalls John Keats' 'Isabella; or, the Pot of Basil', based on the fifth story of the fourth day in Bocaccio's *Decameron*. In Keats' poem, Isabella's two brothers are rich, acquisitive, murderous merchants for whom 'the Ceylon diver held his breath' until 'his ears gushed blood'.[22] The various inter-textual echoes within the story enrich its juxtaposition of pleasure and responsibility and enhance its critique of exploitation and imperialism.

'The Birthday of the Infanta' engages with the classic fairy tale of 'Beauty and the Beast', which became popular after it was published by Jean Marie Le Prince de Beaumont, a French woman working as a governess in England, in *Magazine des Enfants* in 1757. Wilde inverts this source's vindication of love's capacity to see beneath an ugly surface. As Christopher Nassaar notes, Wilde gives us 'a beauty who is a heartless egocentric and a beast who remains a beast and dies of a broken heart'.[23] By eschewing the conventional happy ending, Wilde suggests that destiny is bleaker than fairy tales generally acknowledge. This ugly duckling never becomes a swan, as, like Frankenstein's creature, his physical deformity ensures rejection. By contrasting the dwarf's ugly appearance with his inner beauty, Wilde finds 'le beau dans l'horrible', a concept associated with Charles Baudelaire, whom he greatly admired. He cited two lines from 'Un Voyage à Cythere' in his Oxford notebook: 'O Seigneur! Donnez-moi la force et le courage De contempler mon corps et mon coeur sans degout'.[24] In 'The Birthday of the Infanta', he explores this theme, showing how the dwarf's inability to contem-plate his body without disgust results in his broken heart. In presenting the dwarf as a clown, Wilde is perhaps alluding to the tradition of the Shakespearean fool as social critic. However, in presenting the dwarf as a clown who is never taken seriously and who is ultimately disillusioned and destroyed, he is mining a rich seam of nineteenth-century French literature. In works such as Charles Baudelaire's 'Une Mort Héroïque' and Victor Hugo's *Le Roi S'Amuse* (1832) and *L'Homme qui Rit* (1869), the clown is a performer, sometimes gifted, sometimes

20 Jane Francesca Wilde, *Poems by Speranza*, new and revd ed. (Dublin: M.H. Gill, no date), p. 10. 21 Small, *Short Fiction*, p. 87. 22 Miriam Allott (ed.), *The Poems of John Keats* (Harlow: Longman, 1972), p. 333. 23 Christopher Nassaar, 'Andersen's "The Ugly Duckling" and Wilde's "The Birthday of the Infanta"', *The Explicator*, 55:2 (1997), 83–5, p. 83. 24 Philip E. Smith II and Michael S. Helfand (eds), *Oscar Wilde's Oxford Notebooks: a portrait of the mind in the making* (Oxford, 1989), p. 135.

not, who is destroyed by a mixture of his own ingenuousness and the cruelty of others. Wilde's dwarf can be seen as the figure of the misunderstood artist destroyed by his own *naïveté* and the indifference of those on whose patronage he depends.

'The Fisherman and His Soul' alludes to not only Hans Christian Andersen's 'The Little Mermaid', but also to Friedrich de la Motte Fouqué's literary version of the traditional Undine legend, first translated into English in 1818. Wilde's story reworks the theme of the divided self, previously explored in Adelbert von Chamisso's variation of the Faust legend, *Peter Schlemihl*, and in Andersen's 'The Shadow'. Wilde's preoccupation with the fisherman's relationship with his soul is foreshadowed in the work of his mother. In a footnote to a poem entitled 'Undine' included in her collection, *Poems*, Lady Wilde notes: 'Love gives soul to a woman but takes it from a man'.[25] The Undine legend is closely to folktales concerning the marriage of a man to a supernatural woman, versions of which abound in Irish folklore, particularly in those western regions where the Wilde family spent long periods on their properties.[26] Lady Wilde included one version, 'The Dead Soldier', which tells of a young fisherman whose peace of mind is shattered by an encounter with a seductive mermaid, in *Ancient Legends*. As we have seen, in 'The Priest's Soul', contained in the same collection, Lady Wilde's protagonist queries the nature and existence of the soul. Her son develops this interrogation in 'The Fisherman and his Soul', a story which complicates its investigation of the power of love and the relationship between the soul and the body through its allusions to the Irish folk narrative tradition as mediated by his mother, to traditional legends mediated by German Romantic writers, and to the work of Hans Christian Andersen. In his descriptions of the soul's travels, Wilde exploits the exotic imagery of the east familiar from *The Arabian Nights*. However, the soul's descriptions of precious stones and commodities echo the elaborate descriptions found in the seventeenth-century fairy tales of the French courtier, Madame d'Aulnoy, and reflect the influence of Wilde's more recent decadent French literary masters, Théophile Gautier and J.-K. Huysmans. Through its combination of national and international, narrative and literary traditions, 'The Fisherman and His Soul' stands at the confluence of various cultural flows, which it re-channels in provocative ways.

'The Star-Child' opens in the type of forest landscape associated with German folktales, such as 'Hansel and Gretel'. The story repeatedly employs the type of triadic repetition associated with the folktale; the Star-Child is rebuked three times for his lack of charity; he asks three animals if they have seen his

25 Jane Wilde, *Poems by Speranza*, p. 139. **26** See Bo Almqvist, 'The Mélusine Legend in Irish Folk Tradition', *Béaloideas*, 67 (1999), 13–70, pp 21, 66; Bo Almqvist, 'Of mermaids and marriages', *Béaloideas*, 58 (1990), 1–74, at p. 5.

mother; he is given three tasks, in which he is aided by an animal helper, and by a magician who seems to have been imported from *The Arabian Nights*. While evoking the generic, timeless world of the international folktale, 'The Star-Child' also invokes the national Irish folk tradition through its inversion of Irish changeling lore as reported by Wilde's mother. Her version of a story called 'The Fairy Changeling' tells how a man overhears two women discussing how they have swapped an ugly, dead fairy child for the local lord's son. The man rescues the stolen infant and brings it home to his mother: 'Now the mother was angry at first, but when he told her the story, she believed him and put the baby to sleep'.[27] The child is returned amid great rejoicing and goes on to rule justly and well, as his descendants do after him. 'The Star-Child' retains the details of the rescued child of noble lineage being brought home to an initially reluctant, female caregiver. Like the lord's son, the Star-Child is restored and, acclaimed by his people, becomes a just ruler. Wilde, however, eschews the happy ending: 'Yet ruled he not long [...] And he who came after him ruled evilly'.[28] Wilde also dispenses with the most basic trope found in changeling lore – that of the exchange of a sickly fairy infant for a healthy human child. Although the woodcutter's wife calls the infant a changeling and is afraid that it will bring her family bad fortune, the Star-Child is not, as Richard Pine claims, actually a changeling.[29] A changeling, as described by Lady Wilde, 'is an ugly, wizened little creature', who 'is generally hated by all the neighbours for its impish ways'.[30] The Star-Child, by contrast, is revered by his companions, 'for he was fair and fleet of foot'.[31] As he could 'dance, and pipe, and make music', he does, however, possess attributes which Lady Wilde describes as characteristic of a child who is half-human, half-fairy: 'But the children of the Sidhe and a mortal mother are always clever and beautiful, and specially excel in music and dancing. They are, however, passionate and wilful'.[32] While the description of the Star-Child's wilfulness reflects the Irish folk tradition, it also has analogues in modern European literature. Wilde's description of a wilful child who enjoys inflicting pain on animals but who goes on to repent his cruelty and to achieve redemption through kindness to a leper echoes the story of St Julian recounted in Gustave Flaubert's 'La Légende de St. Julien l'Hospitalier'. The various national and international intertextual echoes in 'The Star-Child' greatly enrich its complex and ambiguous exploration of human cruelty, repentance and compassion.

It could be argued that the inclusion of these echoes results in stories that cannot be appreciated by a child reader, and the issue of Wilde's intended readership was a factor in the initial reception of both collections. Alexander Galt Ross, reviewing *The Happy Prince and Other Tales* shortly after its publication,

27 Lady Wilde, *Ancient Legends*, i, pp 10–11.   **28** Small, *Short Fiction*, p. 164.   **29** Pine, *The Thief of Reason*, p. 177.   **30** Lady Wilde, *Ancient Legends*, i, p. 173.   **31** Small, *Short Fiction*, p. 153.   **32** Ibid.; Lady Wilde, *Ancient Legends*, i, p. 173.

claimed that 'no child will sympathize at all with Mr Wilde's *Happy Prince*', because 'children do not care for satire, and the dominant spirit of these stories is satire'.[33] By contrast, an anonymous contemporary reviewer announced in the *Athenaeum* that 'a child would delight in the tales without being worried or troubled by their application, while children of larger growth will enjoy them and profit by them'.[34] Objecting to 'the rather "fleshly" style of Mr Wilde's writing', another reviewer asked: 'Is *A House of Pomegranates* intended for a child's book?'[35] The issue remains disputed, with Michelle Ruggaber, for example, claiming that '*A House of Pomegranates* is more appropriate for an adult audience than for the young audience suggested by the title *The Happy Prince and Other Tales*', while Jarlath Killeen describes both as 'collections of children's literature'.[36] Regardless of Wilde's intended audience, the inclusion of intertextual allusions not only enhances the satiric effect of the fairy tales, but also ensures that they can be read from different perspectives and at different levels. The reader does not have to recognize the allusions to Gautier's 'Ce que disent les hirondelles' to enjoy 'The Happy Prince', but appreciation of the swallow's plight is undoubtedly heightened by recognition, as Wilde draws on the imagery of that poem in a fairy tale that, inter alia, questions the function and nature of art.

In 1885, Wilde proposed a provocatively plagiaristic theory of artistic creativity, claiming: 'It is only the unimaginative who ever invent. The true artist is known by the use of what he annexes, and he annexes everything'.[37] In his two collections, *The Happy Prince and Other Tales* and *A House of Pomegranates*, Wilde annexes elements of national and international, oral and literary traditions to produce complex, hybrid literary fictions that expand the boundaries of the fairy tale. Since these stories were published over a century ago, as Ian Small points out, 'literary critics have had little to say about them: either they are dismissed as juvenilia, or they are simply overlooked'.[38] Like the portrait of Dorian Gray, Wilde's fairy tales have been consigned to the nursery but they have the power to challenge, charm, and disturb older readers. Like that portrait, they are lovingly produced, finely crafted works of art that contain hidden depths and surprising powers of revelation. Wilde wrote of his tales: 'I did not start with an idea and clothe it in form, but began with a form and strove to make it beautiful enough to have many secrets, and many answers'.[39] The form he chose was that of the fairy tale, and one of the ways he strove to make it beautiful, mysterious, and revelatory was through the inclusion of national and international intertextual echoes.

33 Beckson, *Critical Heritage*, p. 61.   **34** Ibid., p. 60.   **35** Ibid., p. 113.   **36** Michelle Ruggaber, 'Wilde's *The Happy Prince* and *A House of Pomegranates*: bedtime stories for grown-ups', *English Language in Transition*, 46:2 (2003), 141–54, p. 143; Jarlath Killeen, *The Fairy Tales of Oscar Wilde* (London: Ashgate, 2007), p. 1.   **37** Anya Clayworth (ed.), *Oscar Wilde: selected journalism* (Oxford: OUP, 2004), p. 54.   **38** Small, *Short Fiction*, p. xxx.   **39** Holland and Hart Davis, *Complete Letters*, p. 354.

Narnia: the last battle of the imaginative man

JANE O'HANLON

> The imaginative man in me is older, more continuously operative, and in that sense more basic than either the religious writer or the critic [...] And it was of course, he who has brought me, in these last few years, to write the series of Narnia stories for children.[1] (C.S. Lewis, 1954)

With the release of the film version of C.S. Lewis' children's book, *The Lion, the Witch and the Wardrobe*[2] in December 2005, Harper Collins issued 170 Lewis-related publications in 60 countries.[3] In a survey coinciding with the film release, the book entitled *The Lion, the Witch and the Wardrobe* topped the poll as people's favourite read.[4] A simultaneous poll of favourite books commissioned by the National Literacy Trust in the United Kingdom placed The Chronicles of Narnia's series of seven books second only to Enid Blyton's Famous Five series.[5] This bears out the statement that the *Narnia* series, first published between 1950 and 1956, still possesses 'that magical degree of readability'[6] longed for by every writer, and achieved by very few, Blyton, Lewis and J.K. Rowling among them. This essay grapples with the ongoing fascination with the Chronicles of Narnia, addressing some of the more troubling aspects of the books through a deeper understanding of Lewis himself and his relation to other writers of the period.

Lewis was born in 1898 in Belfast, 'a Northern Ireland protestant',[7] who was Professor of Medieval and Renaissance Literature at Cambridge University from 1954 until his premature death in 1963. In person he was a bright, though bullish, intellectual, not much given to introspection.[8] He was also a complex, compartmentalized individual. With friends and students he was warm and generous and he enjoyed simultaneous careers as a highly successful and formidable medieval scholar, a renowned literary critic, a popular Christian apologist and later, following his conversion back to Christianity in 1930, a popular broad-

---

1 Humphrey Carpenter, *The Secret Garden* (London: George Allen & Unwin, 1987). 2 Andrew Adamson (director), *The Chronicles of Narnia: The Lion, the Witch and the Wardrobe* (Walt Disney Pictures, 2005). 3 Paul Harris, 'Holy War Looms over Disney's Narnia', *Observer*, 16 Oct. 2005. Accessed 20 Nov. 2005. All citations of *The Guardian* and *The Observer* from http://www.guardian.co.uk. 4 David Ward, 'The Magnificent Seven', *The Guardian*, 25 Aug. 2005. Accessed 20 Nov. 2005. 5 John Ezard, 'Famous Five tops pole', *The Guardian*, 21 Dec. 2005. Accessed 3 Jan. 2006. 6 A.N. Wilson, 'Right thinking', *The Guardian*, 31 Dec. 2005. Accessed 7 Feb. 2006. 7 Carpenter, *Secret Garden*, p. 50. 8 See Humphrey Carpenter, *The Inklings: C.S. Lewis, J.R.R. Tolkien, Charles Williams and their friends* (London: George Allen & Unwin, 1978); and A.N. Wilson, *C.S. Lewis: a biography* (London: Norton, 1990).

caster. His better known writings include the allegorical fiction, *The Pilgrim's Regress* (1933), and the satirical *The Screwtape Letters* (1942), which became a popular text in many Christian schools in the 1960s. A veteran of the First World War, its effect on his writing was considerable: it caused him to elide the horrors of the War, and to glorify conflict and violence both in his writings and in the views he expressed:

> What I cannot understand is this sort of half-hearted pacifism you get nowadays which gives people the idea that though you have got to fight, you ought to do it with a long face as if you were ashamed of it. It is that feeling which robs lots of magnificent young Christians in the Services of something they have a right to, whole-heartedness.[9]

SHORTCOMINGS

In the Narnia series, Lewis chose to rework the central myth at the heart of Christianity through the medium of a children's story.[10] His retellings are located within an 'unrepentantly conservative' world, and his view has been characterized as 'a 1930s vision of a hierarchical society where everyone [... has] their rightful place'.[11] Much criticism has been heaped upon the form of muscular Christianity and the explicit iconography much in evidence in the books. Philip Pullman has commented that, with their 'dying god' and valorization of martyrdom and unhealthy preoccupation with sadistic violence linked to a Christian message, they are 'one of the most ugly, poisonous things I have ever read – a peevish blend of racist, misogynistic and reactionary prejudice' lacking 'Christian charity'.[12] Pullman echoes an earlier critical commentator, David Holbrook, who remarked that:

> there is a particular emphasis on a *continual* aggressive stance: indeed, in a sense, nothing happens in the Narnia books except the build-up and confrontation with paranoically conceived menaces, from an aggressive

9 David Holbrook, 'The problem Of C.S. Lewis', in Geoff Fox, Graham Hammond, Terry Jones, Frederic Smith, Kenneth Sterck (eds), *Writers, Critics and Children. Articles from Children's Literature in Education* (London: Heinemann Educational Books, 1976), pp 116–24, p. 118.
10 C.S. Lewis, *The Lion, the Witch and the Wardrobe* (1950; 2001); *Prince Caspian* (1951; 2001); *The Voyage of the Dawn Treader* (1952; 2001); *The Silver Chair* (1953; 2001); *The Horse and His Boy* (1954; 2001); *The Magician's Nephew* (1955; 2001); *The Last Battle* (1956; 2001). All (London: Collins). 11 Cristina Odone, 'In Narnia, boys are brave and bossy, while girls cook and are pure of heart', *The Observer*, 27 Nov. 2005. Accessed 3 Jan. 2006. 12 John Ezard, 'Narnia books attacked as racist and sexist', *The Guardian*, 3 June 2002. Accessed 20 Nov. 2005. Polly Toynbee, 'Narnia represents everything that is most hateful about religion', *The Guardian*, 5 Dec. 2005. Accessed 3 Feb. 2006.

posture of hate, leading towards conflict. And in this there is often an intense self-righteousness, which must surely communicate itself to children [...] the main message of the Narnia books [is]: *it is no good being half-hearted about fighting.* The most valuable thing is to fight and kill the 'enemy' and one must not be ashamed of it [...] The Last Battle [...] is full of hate.[13]

According to Polly Toynbee, 'we can do well without an Aslan [...] His divine presence is a way to avoid humans taking responsibility for everything here and now.'[14] Hatred, prejudice, violence and passivity, packaged in apparent Christianity for a young readership, are the accusations levelled against the Chronicles. This paper responds to those issues by exploring Lewis' motivation in writing the series and identifying the kind of Christianity and the fictional forms to which he subscribed.

WHY A CHILDREN'S TALE?

Lewis explained the immediate inspiration for *The Lion, the Witch and the Wardrobe* was a series of nightmares that he had been having about lions. However, on a deeper level he also explained that it was to answer to the question: 'What might Christ be like if there really were a world like Narnia and he chose to be incarnate and die and rise again in that world as he actually has done in ours'[15] The impulse, therefore, was to explore the myth of the resurrection by transposing it into an alternative world. However, the form of children's tale suited him for many other complex and interrelated reasons: because of his ability to tell a good story, because children's story was 'the best art form' for what he wanted to say,[16] and because he believed in the transformative power of the mythic and religious.

The concept of 'muscular Christianity', which exalted robust health and strenuous, manly pursuits, and that dates from the mid-nineteenth century, appealed to him and had already found expression in popular school fiction. Its proponents – among them the writers Charles Kingsley (1819–1875) and Thomas Hughes (1822–1896), author of *Tom Brown's School Days* – believed that it inspired a kind of masculine heroism that was associated with strong religious values and elevated principles. It was seen to contribute to vitalizing the British empire and to provide an antidote to the effeminacy and weakness with which it was believed Tractarianism and asceticism diluted the Anglican Church.

13 Holbrook, 'The problem of C.S. Lewis', p. 118. 14 Toynbee, *The Guardian*, 5 Dec. 2005. 15 Carpenter, *Inklings*, p. 223. 16 C.S. Lewis, 'On three ways of writing for children', in Sheila Egoff, G.T. Stubbs, and L.F. Ashley (eds), *Only Connect: readings on children's literature*, 2nd ed. (Canada: OUP, 1980), p. 208.

A ready precedent for combining Christianity and children's fiction, therefore, already had achieved considerable popularity. Lewis understood that Christianity could provide a narrative of escape from this 'vale of tears', and Justine Picardie has underlined 'Lewis' ability to evoke our need to escape, as well as to find ourselves'.[17] Furthermore, he was aware that a good children's tale could guarantee literary immortality and could cross age boundaries. He famously stated that 'a children's story which is enjoyed only by children is a bad children's story. The good ones last.'[18]

However, fantasy held more appeal than any other genre for him, and in fellow fantasy writer, friend and mentor J.R.R. Tolkien, he found a ready ally who took the forms associated with children deadly seriously.

> The whole association of fairy tale and fantasy with childhood is local and accidental. I hope everyone has read Tolkien's essay on fairy tales, which is perhaps the most important contribution to the subject that anyone has yet made [...] According to Tolkien the appeal of the fairy story lies in the fact that man there most fully exercises his function as a 'subcreator'; not, as they love to say now, making a 'comment upon life' but making, so far as possible, a subordinate world of his own. Since, in Tolkien's view this is one of man's proper functions, delight naturally arises when it is successfully performed.[19]

Lewis' views on the power of story find support among contemporary critics. For Ted Hughes, 'A simple tale, told at the right moment, transforms a person's life with the order its pattern brings to incoherent energies'.[20] Peter Hunt and Millicent Lenz identify its therapeutic value, arguing that it provides a way of 'coping with deprivation [...] repression [... and] desire'.[21] For Humphrey Carpenter, 'a children's book can be the perfect vehicle for an adult's most personal and private concerns.'[22] Carpenter has shown that Lewis had little sympathy for the '*steam* of consciousness' of the modernist movement in the arts,[23] which he described as 'detailed studies of complex human personalities'. Lewis was adamant that: 'We must not allow the novel of manners to give laws to all literature.'[24] He had, therefore, a clear sense of what constituted a good story, and how he could integrate his Christian beliefs into the form.

17 Justine Picardie, 'Fantastic Four', *The Guardian*, 7 Oct. 2005. Accessed 7 Feb. 2006. 18 Lewis, 'Writing for children', p. 210. 19 Ibid., p. 212. 20 Ted Hughes, 'Myth and education', in Fox, Hammond, Jones, Smith and Sterck (eds), *Writers, Critics and Children* (New York: Agathon, 976), pp 77–94, p. 94. 21 Peter Hunt and Millicent Lenz, *Alternative Worlds in Fantasy Fiction* (London: Continuum, 2001), pp 4–5. 22 Carpenter, *Secret Garden*, p. 37. 23 Carpenter, *Inklings*, p. 48. 24 Lewis, *Dawn Treader*, p. 65.

GENESIS

All of the books in the series were published within a relatively contained six-year period between 1950 and 1956, and some specific factors can be identified as precipitating the series' genesis. The first was Lewis' deep appreciation and knowledge of myth, which had fascinated him since he was a boy. He particularly relished the Northern myths, which he had come across at Oxford as a regular member of the Inklings literary discussion group. This group included Tolkien, who would declaim the great Icelandic and Anglo-Saxon myths in the original at these gatherings. Like Tolkien, Lewis believed in the need for myth-making, although in his case it was for a specifically Christian myth, which he understood to be a true myth. His was the myth of a dying god, 'the theme of the gospels and the Christian liturgy. Judah's lion broke the chains of sin and death and set his people free.'[25] This development also came about through his discussions with Tolkien and resulted in his re-conversion[26] – some would say his regression in 1930 - from which time he 'accepted the Christian world picture as a literal truth … and set about defending it.'[27]

'COME FARTHER UP, COME FARTHER IN'

By the time he came to write the Chronicles he had come to see how the two strands of his belief system could be combined in the same story, by use of the creative imagination. In his view, the longing for fairyland that is at the core of the human spirit is an enriching impulse. It arouses in the individual 'a longing for he knows not what. It stirs and troubles him (to his lifelong enrichment) with the dim sense of something beyond his reach and, far from dulling or emptying the actual world, gives it a new dimension of depth.'[28] That 'something beyond his reach' is the Christian eternity. When Diggory says, 'It's all in Plato, all in Plato,' at the end of *The Lion, the Witch and the Wardrobe*, we are given a broad hint as to the major theme that underlies the Chronicles. Lewis, as a scholar and a teacher, was well acquainted with the Platonic tradition, the idea of 'the shadowlands' that what we experience in our earthly existence is merely a dim reflection of a greater reality that we all strive to attain.[29] Poet Ted Hughes expresses a somewhat similar view when he observes that:

> the outer world and inner world are interdependent at every moment. We are simply the locus of their collision … life is what we are able to make of

25 Wilson, *Guardian*, 31 Dec. 2005. 26 Carpenter, *Inklings*, pp 43–4. 27 Ibid., p. 155. 28 Lewis, *Dawn Treader*, pp 214–15. 29 Paul F. Ford, *Companion to Narnia: a complete guide to the enchanting world of C.S. Lewis' The Chronicles of Narnia*, 4th ed. (San Francisco: Harper Collins, 1994), pp 315–16.

that collision and struggle ... (The) faculty that embraces both worlds simultaneously ... is the imagination ... The faculty that makes the human being out of these two worlds is called divine.[30]

The second strand was possibly precipitated by a distressing altercation with the Catholic philosopher Elizabeth Anscombe during a debate at the Socratic Club in Oxford in early 1948.[31] *Miracles*, published in 1947, was Lewis' 'most carefully thought through and judiciously written theological work'.[32] Anscombe, herself a practising Christian, demonstrated that his 'proof' of theism in this book was severely flawed. Although Lewis had studied philosophy, he was not a theologian but rather a popular Christian apologist, and for the first time someone demolished 'his "argument for the existence of God"'.[33] He was devastated and, according to his biographer A.N. Wilson, '*The Lion, the Witch and the Wardrobe* grew out of Lewis' experience of his defeat at the hands of Elizabeth Anscombe.'

FORM

Following this encounter, 'Lewis never attempted to write another piece of Christian apologetics,'[34] and instead turned to children's fiction, which united his interest in fairy stories and myth, now combined with his ability to tell a good story:

> I am not sure what made me, in a particular year of my life, feel that to only a fairy tale, but a fairy tale addressed to children, was exactly what I must write – or burst. Partly, I think that this form permits, or compels, you to leave out things I wanted to leave out. It compels you to throw all the force of the book into what was done and said. It checks what a kind but discerning critic called 'the expository demon' in me. It also imposes certain very fruitful necessities about length.
>
> If I have allowed the fantastic type of children's story to run away with this discussion, that is because it is the kind I know and love best, not because I wish to condemn any other.[35]

Having returned to Christianity with an almost fundamental zeal[36] and having had his confidence in his ability to defend Christian apologetics severely dented, the 'imaginative man' in Lewis, 'stung back into childhood' by Anscombe,[37]

30 Hughes, 'Myth and education', pp 91–2. 31 Carpenter, *Secret Garden*, p. 217; A.N. Wilson, *C.S. Lewis: a biography* (London: Norton, 1990), p. 220. 32 Wilson, p. 211. 33 C.S. Lewis, *Surprised by Joy: the shape of my early life* (London: Harvest, 1955), p. 154. 34 Ibid., pp 214–15. 35 Lewis, *Dawn Treader*, p. 213. 36 Carpenter, *Inklings*, p. 155. 37 Wilson, *Biography*,

sought and found a suitable and perhaps comforting medium for the message he wanted to convey in the form of fantasy fiction for children. This form allowed him to deal with the two matters that defined the architecture of his world, the Christian myth and mythmaking itself. The form, the audience and the exigencies of publishing relating to both meant that, of necessity, the narratives would favour story over theology and plot over character development. These, then, are the imperatives that imposed discipline on Lewis' fiction.

In contextualizing C.S. Lewis it is useful to see how he combines elements of the approaches associated with both Blyton and Tolkien. He follows Blyton in providing an adult-free world populated by two-dimensional characters, a world that has been perceived as both racist and sexist,[38] and in which growing up seems to carry pejorative connotations. Tight control of the viewpoint is maintained throughout the narrative by means particularly of an intrusive narrative voice from which it is impossible to escape, except perhaps in the comic scenes; here Lewis seems, either consciously or subconsciously, to be able to shed the didacticism that is an inevitable marker of his style, coming as it does from his own natural desire to proselytize. Both Blyton and Lewis share an unquestioning assumption around the authorial presence in directing – and being clearly heard to direct – the story.

LEWIS' CHRISTIANITY

Like Tolkien's, Lewis' Christianity is also central to the direction of the story. He too creates a believable and seductive secondary world, where the main preoccupations are with war and conflict, where 'men'– 'the Sons of Adam and the Daughters of Eve'– cause evil in that world and, therefore, must strive for its defeat. However, this world is racist and sexist: numerous examples of stereotyping are to be found in the Chronicles. Its brand of muscular Christianity and Christian allegory can be awkward and rather crude. For instance, at the climax of *The Lion, the Witch and the Wardrobe* in Chapters 14 and 15, which revolves around the central motif of the passion, death and resurrection of Aslan, Susan and Lucy, emblematic of the women at the foot of the cross, are witnesses to the event. Aslan's reappearance is accompanied by the cracking of the stone table, recalling the rending of the veil of the temple in two:

> The Stone Table was broken into two pieces by a great crack that ran down it from end to end; and there was no Aslan.[39]

p. 220.   **38** Ezard, *Guardian*, 3 June 2002; Holbrook, 'The problem of C.S. Lewis'; Toynbee, *Guardian*, 5 Dec. 2006.   **39** Lewis, *The Lion*, p. 174

The comparisons are numerous, and biblical sources easily identifiable. The episodes from *The Silver Chair*, *The Magician's Nephew* and *The Last Battle* that follow here are highly redolent of Christian mysticism, ritual and mythology and are conveyed, I would argue, in highly charged and emotionally manipulative language:

> Then the voice said again, 'if you are thirsty, come and drink' ...
> 'Are you not thirsty?' said the Lion.
> 'I'm *dying* of thirst,' said Jill.[40]
> As Adam's race has done the harm, Adam's race shall help to heal it.[41]
> 'Yes,' said Queen Lucy. 'In our world too, a Stable once had something inside it that was bigger than our whole world.'[42]

In *The Last Battle* Jill declares: 'Even if we are killed. I'd rather be killed fighting for Narnia than grow old and stupid at home'.[43] This is highly charged language, based on the rhetoric of muscular Christianity that had often been used to justify war and sacrifice. Here Lewis falls into a fundamentalist retelling of the Christian myth. Similarly, in *The Last Battle*, the least successful of the books, the use of the stable door to symbolize death, is, to my adult mind (and, as I recall, seemed also to my childish mind when I first encountered the book), clumsy and contrived. Here the highly charged, emotive symbol of the stable door, so familiar to children familiar with a more affirmative version of Christianity, is manipulated to embrace death rather than celebrate life. Aslan's escapist clarion call of 'Come farther in! Come farther up'[44] – that gives chapter 15 of *The Last Battle* its title – and the violent train crash that heralds the dawn of the 'new Narnia' glorify death rather than life and Lewis has Jewel, the Unicorn restate – yet again – the Platonic underpinnings of the Chronicles:

> I have come home at last! This is my real country! I belong here. This is the land I have been looking for all my life, though I never knew it till now. The reason why we loved the old Narnia is that it sometimes looked a little like this ... Come farther up, come farther in![45]

This writing is weak, sentimental and manipulative and illustrates the reasons why critics such as Holbrook, Pullman and Toynbee have been so critical of this aspect of the books. It insists not only on suspension of disbelief but also on a *belief* in a Christian version of heaven, and trust in an all-powerful Aslan who manipulates reality in a determinist universe. This is presaged in the title of the final chapter, 'Farewell to the Shadowlands', the chapter in which Lewis unrepentantly dons 'the skin' of a Christian apologist.

40 Lewis, *The Silver Chair*, p. 31.   **41** Lewis, *The Magician's Nephew*, p. 162.   **42** Lewis, *Last Battle*, p. 174.   **43** Ibid., pp 119-20.   **44** Ibid., p. 194.   **45** Ibid., p. 210.

The railway accident at the end of *The Last Battle*, trading on the childhood fear of loss and abandonment, can therefore be read as the last in a series of betrayals to do with a lack of faith in life, self and reality, as Lewis turns each of these on its head:

> 'There was a real railway accident,' said Aslan softly. 'Your father and mother and all of you are – as you used to call it in the Shadowlands – dead. The term is over: the holidays have begun. The dream is ended: this is the morning.'[46]

I first read the Chronicles of Narnia when I was ten years old, and I was amazed by the wardrobe and rather frightened by the White Witch, who reminded me of Hans Christian Andersen's Snow Queen. It was the White Witch, rather than Aslan, who made the biggest impression on me. The realization that there might possibly be an allegorical, didactic second level of meaning to the story was disappointing, and left me feeling somewhat betrayed by the author and somehow guilty because of feeling betrayed. With adult hindsight I see that the sense of betrayal is centred around the realization that the reader has been taken in and led down the garden path, not to tea with Mr Tumnus, but to be taught a lesson and to be convinced of an argument, without the narrator or author having had the honesty to admit that this was part of the bargain. Fantasy in its many manifestations has always run this risk, employed as it has been both in the service of polemic and allegory, and critics such as Raymond Tallis have accused it of imposing a passivity on the reader, of retaining control of the action and/or excluding the reader.[47]

GENDER AND GROWING UP

Highlighting what some have criticized as a dangerously backward philosophy in the Chronicles, this denial of life, what might be characterized as the Christian embrace of death, may be seen most clearly in Susan's final exclusion from Narnia, because she has dared to grow up. Here, the central message seems to be, do not grow up, do not pursue autonomy, do not seek to be happy in this life, but rather, in the next, and it is borne out particularly by the ending of *The Last Battle*.

> '... we're not coming back to Narnia ... He says we're getting too old.'[48]

> 'Grown up, indeed,' said the Lady Polly. 'I wish she *would* grow up. She wasted all her school time wanting to be the age she is now, and she'll waste

46 Ibid., p. 224.   47 Raymond Tallis, *In Defence of Realism* (London: Arnold, 1988).   48 Lewis, *Prince Caspian*, p. 218.

all the rest of her life trying to stay that age. Her whole idea is to race to the silliest time of one's life as quick as she can and then stop there as long as she can.'[49]

Susan, always 'a jolly sight too keen on being grown-up',[50] provides an interesting study with regard to Lewis' view of women and grown-ups: 'Critics who treat *adult* as a term of approval, instead of as a merely descriptive term, cannot be adult themselves. To be concerned about being grown up, to admire the grown up because it is grown up, to blush at the suspicion of being childish; these things are the marks of childhood and adolescence.'[51] All of this attests to the fact that Lewis was someone who found it easier to avoid the real world of adults, particularly that of adult women, preferring to engage with it on a more mythological level. Holbrook has argued that 'under cover of his apparent religious intentions and his mask of benignity', Lewis' sole aim was to convey 'to his readers a powerful unconscious message that the world is full of malignancy ... and ... that tenderness, cowardice and reticence are weak.'[52]

His attitudes and fears collide spectacularly in the depiction of the White Witch, easily the most dramatic and exciting character in the Chronicles, powerfully captured by Tilda Swinton in the 2005 film version of the story.[53]

> The witch bared her arms as she had bared them the previous night when it had been Edmund instead of Aslan. Then she began to whet her knife. It looked to the children, when the gleam of the torchlight fell on it, as if the knife were made of stone, not of steel, and it was of a strange and evil shape.
>
> At last she drew near. She stood by Aslan's head. Her face was working and twitching with passion ... Then just before she gave the blow, she stooped down and said in a quavering voice, 'And now, who has won ? ... Now I will kill you instead of him as our pact was and so the Deep Magic will be appeased ... you have given me Narnia forever, you have lost your own life and you have not saved his. In that knowledge, despair and die.'[54]

The already powerfully symbolic sacrificial scene, reminiscent of Jesus' final despair on the Cross, is overlaid with suggestions of matricide, expressed as the son's fear of, and desire to kill the mother before she emasculates him. Lewis seems to step back from the implications of this almost immediately, deflecting the evil characteristics onto the knife and indeed this may have been more subconscious than conscious on his part, but there is no denying the strength and power of the passage and the primitive anger and aggression evident in the final

49 Lewis, *Last Battle*, p. 168. **50** Ibid., p. 168. **51** Lewis, 'Writing for children', p. 210. **52** Holbrook, 'The problem of C.S. Lewis', p. 124. **53** Andrew Adamson (dir.), *The Chronicles of Narnia: The Lion, the Witch and the Wardrobe* (Walt Disney Pictures, 2005). **54** Lewis, *The Lion*, pp 168–9.

sentence quoted above: 'In that knowledge, despair and die.' Her triumphant speech reflects Lewis' almost infantile fear of annihilation and it is hard to see it as accidental that it is put into the mouth of the most powerful female character. Swinton also manages to imbue the Witch with a certain androgynous quality, rendering her all the more powerful and disturbing and making her the most complex of the characters foregrounded in both the book and the film versions. She exemplifies the qualities of the warrior more than any other character and provides the most interesting departure point for further study of Lewis' rather troubling portrayals of gender in the Chronicles.

Depictions of gender are inextricably bound up with war and violence, exemplifying the vigorous, manly Christianity so beloved of Lewis. Whether male or female, the only way for characters to prove their mettle is to be brave in battle. Jill, Lucy and Polly are brave and courageous and provide real leadership in many of the scenes in which they appear. However, their non-traditional characteristics are seen as properly belonging to boys: for example, Corin patronizes Lucy when he says that she is 'as good as a man, or at any rate as good as a boy',[55] while Queen Susan is more grown up. Elsewhere there are non-stereotypical characters, but they do not enjoy the approval of the narrator. Among them is the case of the White Witch already cited. Another example is Alberta Scrubb, Eustace's mother in *The Voyage of the Dawn Treader*, whose commitment to vegetarianism and pacifism might now be considered progressive but whom the narrator perceives as faddish;[56] and the head of the Experimental School in *The Silver Chair*, who engages in psychological discussions with her pupils, but leaves herself open to manipulation and so allows bullying to flourish.[57] Other female characters such as Caspian's wife, Rilian's mother, and the Daughter of Ramandu,[58] are never actually named and thereby are diminished.

With the introduction of Aravis Tarkheena, the main character in *The Horse and His Boy*,[59] however, there is, perhaps, some real change in female characterization. Her instincts are always good, and it is the idea of marriage to the despicable Ahoshta Tarkaan that prompts her to escape. She refuses to be pushed around, and will not accept the role of passive female, and neither will her horse Hwin. To Shasta's dismissive comment, 'Why, it's only a girl!' she bristles: 'And what business is it of yours if I am *only* a girl?'[60] However, in traditional heroic fashion, she 'became full of shame for none of my lineage ought to fear death more than a gnat'[61] and 'she never lost her head even for a moment.'[62] In contrast to Lasaraleen,[63] a female stereotype whose only interests appear to be clothes and men, Aravis has always been more interested in bows and arrows and

55 Lewis, *Horse*, p. 196.   56 Lewis, *Dawn Treader*.   57 Lewis, *Silver Chair*, p. 11.   58 Lewis, *Dawn Treader*.   59 Lewis, *Horse*, p. 39.   60 Ibid., p. 40.   61 Ibid., p. 48.   62 Ibid., p. 106. 63 Ibid., p. 106 ff.

horses and dogs and swimming, considered boys' preserve by Lewis' generation. A comparison may be drawn between Lewis' more successful female characters such as Aravis and Blyton's George, and this approach may offer one key to repositioning Lewis within a tradition of children's writing that allows for an alternative reading of the Chronicles and an understanding of their continuing popularity despite their overtly Christian message.

FUN AND FEASTING

Other reasons for their popularity may be adduced. Ian Wilson asserts that: 'It is the Lewis who plumbed the irrational depths of childhood and religion who speaks to the present generation.'[64] Their storyline is captivating and the sheer genius of turning something as mundane as a wardrobe into a magical object cannot be overestimated. The Narnia stories have lasted because Lewis' apologetics are accompanied by, and outweighed at certain points, by real heroism, humour, innocence and playfulness. A consistent and central theme is heroism, a heroism ostensibly patterned on the mythic tradition, composed of psychologically two-dimensional, self-sufficient solitary male warriors, not much given to introspection, and eternally engaged in quests of epic proportions, with gods and mortals generally locked in eternal combat.[65] In the Chronicles, Lewis was preoccupied with how one can acquit oneself with courage, honour and dignity so as to avoid the ridiculous and recover from the ignoble. This is demonstrated most clearly, not in the plethora of rather wooden foregrounded characters, but in the colourful cast of background characters that make up the rich tapestry of the stories.

It is the background rather than the foreground that is Lewis' triumph in Narnia, because it is here that the imagination is set free to play at last. Lewis' real heroes, Lucy Pevensie, the beavers, Puddleglum, Trumpkin, Mr Tumnus and Reepeecheep, are always the smallest and least realistic of characters. They are the reason that we come to love and remember Narnia and they carry its real heart. Here in the background of the tales we find 'a lamp-post in the middle of a wood';[66] 'Father Christmas ... so big, and so glad, and so real';[67] and a myriad other humorous vignettes, asides and portrayals. Justine Picardie underlines how details re-emerge into the light decades after a first reading:

> I've just rediscovered this passage, for example, close to the end of Lewis'
> final installment of the Narnia books, in *The Last Battle*: 'In Narnia your

64 Wilson, *Biography*, p. x. **65** Jane O'Hanlon, 'The hero in the twenty-first century: transgressing the heroic gender construct', in Celia Keenan and Mary Shine Thompson (eds), *Studies in Children's Literature, 1500–2000* (Dublin: Four Courts, 2004), pp 148–54. **66** Lewis, *The Lion*, p. 15. **67** Ibid., p. 117.

good clothes were never your uncomfortable ones. They knew how to make things that felt beautiful as well as looking beautiful in Narnia; and there was no such thing as starch or flannel or elastic to be had from one end of the country to the other.'[68]

It was precisely this playfulness and abundance that caused Tolkien to turn his back on the Chronicles, and they were never read at the gatherings of the Inklings, Lewis' coterie of friends and critics at Cambridge. In Lillian Smith's view, it was also this 'final quality' of C.S. Lewis' writing about Narnia, 'that above and beneath and beyond the events of the story itself there is something to which the children can lay hold: belief in the essential truth of their own imaginings.'[69] Beneath the violence, the warmongering and the Christian accretions, this other story is being told, involving another cast of characters, a story within a story, and it is this story that continues to play to today's audience of young readers, and keeps its adult readers coming back again and again.

THE COMEDIC

Children have an unerring sense of the comedic and this sense is one of the reasons for the endurance of the Chronicles. If we think of the Chronicles as two parallel stories, then these stories are linked by the comic threads with which Lewis laces the story. This description found in chapter 8 of *The Horse and His Boy*, 'In the House of the Tisroc', which deflates the Grand Vizier's grandeur, is a genuinely funny piece of writing:

> 'How well it was said by a gifted poet,' observed the Grand Vizier raising his face (in a somewhat dusty condition) from the carpet, 'that deep draughts from the fountain of reason are desirable in order to extinguish the fire of youthful love.'
> This seemed to exasperate the Prince. 'Dog,' he shouted, directing a series of well-aimed kicks at the hindquarters of the Vizier, 'do not dare to quote the poets to me. I have had maxims and verses flung at me all day and I can endure them no more.' I am afraid Aravis did not feel at all sorry for the Grand Vizier.[70]

The description of Puddleglum, the principal character in *The Silver Chair*, as being 'too full of bobance and bounce and high spirits',[71] creates a vivid pen picture for the reader.

68 Picardie, 2005; Lewis, *Last Battle*, p. 166. 69 Lillian H. Smith, 'News from Narnia', in Sheila Egoff, G.T. Stubbs and L.F. Ashley (eds), *Only Connect: readings on children's literature*, 2nd ed.; article 1st pub. 1958 (Toronto: OUP, 1980), pp 171–5. 70 Lewis, *Horse*, p. 122. 71 Lewis, *Silver Chair*, p. 88.

And who can forget Reepicheep, 'Chief Mouse', small in stature but enormous of heart:

> Reepicheep put forward his left leg, drew back his right, bowed, kissed her hand, straightened himself, twirled his whiskers, and said in his shrill, piping voice: 'My humble duty to your Majesty. And to King Edmund, too.' (Here he bowed again.) 'Nothing except your Majesties' presence was lacking to this glorious venture.'[72]

Not to mention all that lovingly described food that characters seemed to find time to eat despite every other exigency! Lillian Smith underlines the Narnia books' significance: 'We may call these books fairy tales or allegories or parables, but there is no mistake about the significance of what C.S. Lewis has to say to the trusting, believing, seeking heart of childhood.'[73] Perhaps one of the difficulties with the Chronicles is that they have been seen too much in the light of the Tolkien myth-making tradition rather than in the Blyton feasting and fun tradition, where they also belong. Surely that rather arch narrative voice, accompanying us on the adventures of 'Four let out from School' and the moral lessons to which the reader is subject from time to time are reminiscent of Blyton country, where we settled down happily and snugly to read the next adventure knowing we were in safe hands.

Lewis encourages his readers to play, to have fun and to believe that they have the power to re-imagine their own realities, even and maybe, particularly, if they do not match the reality around them. One of the fundamental attributes of a successful children's book is that it furnish its readers with access to other possible realities, and notwithstanding their Christian message, the Chronicles succeeds in doing this:

> 'Suppose we *have* only dreamed, or made up, all those things – trees and grass and sun and moon and stars and Aslan himself. Suppose we have. Then all I can say is that, in that case, the made-up things seem a good deal more important than the real ones … I'm on Aslan's side even if there isn't any Aslan to lead it. I'm going to live as like a Narnian as I can even if there isn't any Narnia.'[74]

If, as A.N. Wilson suggests, the strength of Lewis was his ability to plumb 'the irrational depths of childhood and religion' and that this is what children relate to in the Chronicles, then the parallels with Blyton become even more obvious. Both writers seem to inhabit a liminial space between permissiveness and

---

72 Lewis, *Dawn Treader*, p. 17.   73 Smith, 'News from Narnia', pp 174–5.   74 Lewis, *Dawn Treader*, p. 174.

authority, clearly exhibiting and negotiating this space by means of an intimate narrative presence:

> In Narnia C.S. Lewis seemed to have invented objects for me to long for that I never would have thought of, and yet they seemed exactly right: he had anticipated what would delight me with an unearthly kind of intimacy.[75]

So Lucy will always be walking in that snow-laden wood with Mr Tumnus, by the light of that unlikely London lamppost, and we will never be sure whether the sledge bells we hear in the background belong to Father Christmas or to the White Witch, and snow will be general all over Narnia.

---

75 Francis Spufford, 'Pillow talk', *The Guardian*, 13 Mar. 2002. Accessed 7 Feb. 2006.

Bellsybabble for the childers[1]

VALERIE COGHLAN

The retelling of the French folk-tale, 'The Cat of Beaugency' by James Joyce, was not, as far as we know, intended for publication as a children's book, although that is what subsequently happened. There are three picturebook editions of this story published in English, and illustrated editions are also originally published in German, Hungarian, Czech and Croatian. These are listed at the end of this article. The interplay between text and illustration developed to varying degrees by the artists involved, shows the characteristically visual richness of Joyce's words as they prompt much playfulness in the imaginative space between word and picture. Why this story has not greater prominence in the vast amount of literature devoted to the study of Joyce's life and work is also for speculation. Does this say something about the status of children's literature in the 'grown-up' academy? There are riches in the retelling of the tale that are worthy of consideration, and when we consider how imaginative illustrators mine the interstices in the text how truly Joycean it is becomes evident.[2]

The story that Joyce wrote was set down in a letter to his grandson, Stephen, then aged four.[3] Stephen James, the son of Joyce's son, George or Giorgio, and his wife Helen, was born on 15 February 1932. From the time of the boy's birth, Joyce was very attached to his grandson, and he wrote a poem, 'Ecce Puer' to commemorate the occasion, and in its lines to draw together the recent death of his father with the birth: 'A child is sleeping/ an old man gone …'[4] He spent a lot of time with the young boy, and Stephen was deeply fond of James Joyce whom he called 'Nonno', the Italian word for grandfather. He and his parents were in Zurich with James and Nora Joyce when Joyce died on 13 January 1941, just a month before Stephen's ninth birthday. During the time in Zurich, where the Joyce family had gone to escape the war, Stephen spent most afternoons walking with his grandfather along the Zurichsee. According to Richard Ellmann, Joyce's biographer, a couple of weeks before his death James Joyce bought Stephen a little artificial Christmas tree in a small pot. Around this time

1 'Bellsybabble for the Childers' takes the terms 'childers', used colloquially in Ireland for children, from an early draft of a portion of *Finnegans Wake* entitled 'Haveth Childers Everywhere'. 2 Joyce as an inspiration for visual artists has prompted the publication of a substantial monograph by Christa-Maria Lerm Hayes, *Joyce in Art. Visual art inspired by James Joyce* (Dublin: Lilliput, 2004). However, this volume makes no mention of *The Cat and the Devil*. 3 Richard Ellmann, *James Joyce*. 1st rev. ed. with corrections. (Oxford: OUP, 1983), pp 691–2. 4 Ibid., p. 646.

he also bought the boy three books of Greek mythology, and we also know from Ellmann that he bought the young Stephen other books of myths.[5] In Canada an edition of *The Cat and the Devil* containing a letter from Stephen J. Joyce addressed to young readers of the book was published in 1990.[6] Here, Stephen Joyce briefly explains the origins of the legend and suggests that when readers of the story of 'The Cat and the Devil' grow up they will find some of the answers to questions which they may have about the story in *Dubliners*, *A Portrait of the Artist as a Young Man* and *Ulysses*. In a postscript he tell how he would sit by 'Nonno's' bedside in the mornings of the last year of Joyce's life and how Joyce related to him stories of Ulysses.

In his letter to the four-year-old Stephen, or 'Stevie', Joyce recounted an old French story known as 'Le Chat de Beaugency' or 'The Cat of Beaugency'.[7] This is a well-known tale in France, and is one of many European stories involving a pact with the devil or other supernatural agencies to build something beyond the resources of mortals, very commonly bridges. Jacqueline Gmuca cites this as a type 1191 motif in the Aarne-Thompson classification of folk-tales.[8] Frequently the price for the devil's assistance was the soul of the first living being to cross the bridge. A trick is played on Satan by sending across a cat instead of a human in some versions of these stories. Possibly this trick was inspired by a tale of a Breton bishop, Saint Cado or Cadoc involving the handing over of a black cat to the devil while they stand on a bridge. Cats, it has been suggested, are go-betweens linking the human world and the world of the dead, or the world of magic, thus forming another bridging association. Cats, in some traditions, are psychopomps, that is, they form a conduit between the living and the dead. It is said that Tutankhamun was led into the underworld by a black cat.

The Beaugency legend is one of many in which the devil demands the traditional price for his assistance in providing a bridge over the Loire, but here, as in other similar legends, the devil is outwitted by the mayor of the town who sends over a cat as the first creature to cross the new bridge. At Beaugency this was too much for the devil who lost his temper and hurled abuse at the town's inhabitants, calling them cats, a nickname by which, as Joyce relates in *The Cat and the Devil*, the Balgetians are still known. The town of Beaugency is 150 kilometers south-west of Paris and its 26-arch bridge still stands today, despite a battle-scarred history. It was the only Loire crossing connecting Orléans and Blois left standing during the war between France and England in the fifteenth century and was, therefore, a strategic point. In June 1429, approximately 500 English soldiers retreated to the twelfth century tower at Beaugency, leaving a smaller

5 Ibid., pp 739–40. 6 James Joyce, *The Cat and the Devil* (St John's, Newfoundland: Breakwater, 1990). 7 Ellmann, pp 691–2. 8 Jacqueline L. Gmuca, 'Transmutations of folktale and school story in *A Portrait of the Artist as a Young Man*', in Betty Greenway (ed.), *Twice-told Children's Tales: the influence of childhood reading on writing for adults* (New York: Routledge, 2005), p. 210.

group to hold the bridge. On 17 June 1429 they surrendered to the French forces and the town was liberated, allowing Jeanne d'Arc to continue on her way to Orléans. On 16 September 1944 the bridge was the scene of another significant surrender when German troops capitulated to the US army.[9] Joyce's letter to Stephen was written on 10 August 1936, during a stay with friends, the Baillys, at Villers-sur-Mer in Calvados in Normandy. It was not until well after Joyce's death in 1941 that the telling by Joyce of the old story was published in book format as *The Cat and the Devil*. It was first published in the collected letters of Joyce[10] and perhaps following this, artists and publishers began to think it would be a good idea, commercially and artistically, to produce it as a book for children. Richard Erdoes, an Austrian-American, was the first artist to illustrate the story. This edition was published in 1964 by Dodd, Mead & Company, Inc., New York. The following year, 1965, British publisher Faber and Faber produced an edition with art work by the English illustrator Gerald Rose. In 1978 Paris publishers Gallimard produced a French edition illustrated by Roger Blachon, and this was published in English in 1980. This edition has been published in a number of different languages and is the best-known. This essay is mainly concerned with the three editions currently available in English, as they are most likely to be accessible to readers. A list of editions in languages other than English is appended at the end of this article.

Many scholars have discussed Joyce's knowledge of children's games, stories, nursery rhymes and the culture of childhood and his integration of this into his writing. Consider the opening lines of *A Portrait of the Artist as a Young Man*, in which Joyce not only begins the book with Stephen's infancy, but he vivifies it through the language of a very young child in the well-known lines about 'a moocow coming down along the road' to meet a 'nicens little boy named baby tuckoo'.[11]

While the linguistic playfulness of 'The Cat and the Devil' might not be altogether appreciated by a four-year-old, its absurdity would be enjoyed by an older child, as in the scene in which the people of Beaugency wake to see their new bridge, and exclaim 'O Loir, what a fine bridge', a play on the English expression, 'O Lord'; and where the text refers to the cat looking up at the Beaugency mayor, because there a cat was allowed to look at a lord mayor. This surely nudges at the expression 'a cat may look at a king'.

In *Children's Lore in Finnegans Wake*[12] Grace Eckley connects Joyce's linguistic interplay with the bricolage of childhood language and thought. Eckley cites Mabel Worthington's contention that "'... Joyce considered folk-material an expression of important, universal and ever-recurring experiences of

9 *The Rough Guide to France*, 8th ed. (London: Rough Guides, 2003), p. 513. **10** Richard Ellmann (ed.), *Letters of James Joyce* (London: Faber, 1966). **11** James Joyce, *A Portrait of the Artist as a Young Man* (London: Penguin, 1960), p. 7. **12** Grace Eckley, *Children's Lore in Finnegans Wake* (New York: Syracuse UP, 1985).

the human race".' Worthington identifies references to sixty-eight childhood rhymes in *Finnegans Wake*, in, for example, a well-known rhyme about the Norse foundations of Dublin city 'Humptydump Dublin squeaks through his norse'.[13] Jacqueline Gmuca gives examples of other instances of Joyce's familiarity with childhood reading and culture, in for example, his reference to popular boys' magazines in a story in *Dubliners*.[14]

Joyce's retelling of *The Cat and the Devil* is full of humorous embellishment. The devil is portrayed as an avid reader of newspapers and the lord mayor of Beaugency, we are told, sleeps with his knees in his mouth. These are touches that would appeal to small child, such as the ridiculous notion of an important adult sucking his knees in sleep like a baby sucks its thumb, and the young Stephen Joyce is likely to have been aware of his grandfather's fascination with newspapers, their production and transmission of news.[15] All of the illustrators whose work is discussed choose to either depict the devil reading a newspaper, or in Rose's illustrations, to show the *Beaugency Gazette* tossed on the floor as the devil dresses himself to meet the mayor. In Jan de Tusch-Lec's illustration the reader is positioned to view the back of the devil, but observes him in a mirror at the end of the room where he sits, holding a newspaper before him – perhaps *Der Spiegel*.

Joyce's devil is benign and apparently fond of animals: outwitted, he scoops up the cat, murmuring words of comfort to it, and reserves his ire for the mayor and citizens of the town. A PS at the end of the story says that the devil speaks his own language, 'Bellysbabble', but when he is angry he speaks bad French and has a strong Dublin accent (like Joyce). His words to the cat are quoted in French, and both the Erdoes and the Blachon editions translate this slightly differently. The Rose edition relies on the reader to make a translation, as does Joyce's original letter to Stephen.

The story bears hallmarks of James Joyce's writing: it is linguistically playful, and it incorporates an easily recognizable, real Irish character. Here, the central character apart from the devil, is M. Alfred Byrne, the Mayor of Beaugency, who is quite obviously based on Alfie Byrne, a famous Lord Mayor of Dublin in the 1930s and 1950s. Perhaps because they were both born in the same year, 1882, Joyce followed Byrne's career with some interest, reading about it in the *Irish Times*.[16] Byrne was a well-known figure in Dublin, and was regarded as something of a character. He was elected Lord Mayor of Dublin nine times from 1930 to 1939, and was elected again in 1954 and 1955. He was a member of parliament, representing Dublin Harbour, and following independence, was

---

13 Mabel P. Worthington, 'Nursery rhymes in *Finnegans Wake*', *Journal of American Folklore*, 70 (Jan.–Mar., 1957), 37–48, quoted in Eckley, p. 86.   14 Gmuca, 'Transmutations of folktale', p. 211.   15 For a discussion about this see Declan Kiberd, '*Ulysses*. Newspapers and modernism', in *Irish Classics* (London: Granta, 2000), pp 466–70.   16 *Letters III*, p. 346.

elected to represent several different Dublin constituencies in Dáil Éireann on different occasions, and he was a senator from 1928 to 1931. He died in 1956. Like Joyce, Byrne was sartorially aware, and in *The Cat and the Devil* Joyce refers to the devil's attention to his appearance before he calls on M. Byrne, and on the Lord's Mayor's own fondness for dressing up. It was noted in the *Irish Times*[17] that Byrne was again re-elected Lord Mayor in 1936 (just before Joyce wrote his letter to his grandson).

In her article on '*The Cat and the Devil* and *Finnegans Wake*' Janet E. Lewis notes that cats, devils, bridges and mayors are frequently invoked. She cites the 'Dom King' episode in *Finnegans Wake* in which 'the ceremonies are enhanced by "brilliant bridgeclothes" and "crimosing balkonladies", details of which draw in both bridges and the crimson of the robes'.[18] Maurice Beja cites Stuart Gilbert's observation in his diary that Joyce ' "inserted punnishly the names of 60 Mayors of Dublin (taken from the Dublin Postal directory of 1904)"' in *Haveth Childers Everywhere*.[19] Lewis also points out that '[b]ridges, obviously, are important in a book in which the heroine is a river', and that '[t]he partnership of a cat and a lord mayor was already a part of *Finnegans Wake* in the guise of Dick Whittington, thrice lord mayor of London.'[20] Marie-Dominique Garnier also associates the 'linguistic twists and threads in the letter' with 'the mainstream of Joycean fiction',[21] noting the significance of the river running through this story too, and developing the bridge motif to encompass 'two opposite ends of a linguistic spectrum, ranging from proverbs, or order-words which the letter aptly deconstructs into pass-words,[22] to the opposite end, here called "Bellsybabble"', and concludes that reading of the letter amounts to a crossing process.

Richard Erdoes, the first artist to illustrate *The Cat and the Devil*, was born in 1912 in Vienna. Following the rise of Nazi power he went to the United States where he established a successful career as an illustrator and author. In the 1950s and 1960s he contributed illustrations to newspapers and periodicals including the *New York Times*, *Time*, *Life* and *Fortune*. Following *The Cat and the Devil* he illustrated several information texts for children. These include *A Picture*

17 *Irish Times*, 11 July 1936, p. 9. **18** Janet E. Lewis, '*The Cat and the Devil* and *Finnegans Wake*', *James Joyce Quarterly* 29:4 (Summer 1992), 805. **19** Maurice Beja, *James Joyce: a literary life* (Basingstoke: Macmillan 1992), p. 120, quoting Stuart Gilbert, 'Selections from the Paris Diary of Stuart Gilbert', in Thomas F. Staley (ed.), *Joyce Studies Annual 1990* (Austin: U. of Texas P., 1990), pp 3–25. **20** Lewis, '*The Cat and the Devil* and *Finnegans Wake*', 806. **21** Marie-Dominique Garnier, 'The lapse and the lap: Joyce with Deleuze', in Laurent Milesi, *James Joyce and the Difference of Language* (Cambridge: CUP, 1983), pp 100–1. **22** Presumably she is referring here to the reference to the cats being allowed to look at a lord mayor in Beaugency, a play on the proverb that 'a cat may look at a king'. The 'pass-words' referred to in Garnier's essay are 'beneath order words, laps beneath lapses'. Garnier, p. 97, citing Gilles Deleuze and Félix Guattari, *A Thousand Plateaus: capitalism and schizophrenia* (Minneapolis: U of Minneapolis P, 1987), p. 110.

History of Ancient Rome,[23] and *Policemen Around the World*.[24] This is a witty, cartoonish look at policemen performing their duties in a variety of locations and could well be a precursor of Richard Scarry's 'Busy People' books. Later, Erdoes developed a great interest in Native American people and has written extensively about them.[25]

For Joyce's story Erdoes has chosen a medieval setting. His artwork represents a style popular in the 1950s/1960s. Pages alternate between full-colour, and a greeny-brown hue used as an infill imparts a period atmosphere. Erdoes is an accomplished artist and designer, paying attention to the layout of word and image, and his disinclination to fill all of the page with his drawings also lends a feel for the time in which the story is set. The peritext in Erdoes pictorial version of the story contributes to the tale.[26] The endpapers hint at the central characters: the viewer sees the mayor's lower half, hand clutching a bucket, a black cat peers over the swirling floral border. On the opposite page the top two-thirds of the devil's face peers inquisitively, horns and ears raised, ready for action, while his arrow-like nose points downwards, perhaps signaling from whence he came, or maybe encouraging us to turn the page. The title is on a double spread, and shows what appears to be contemporary Beaugency. Bordering the waters of the Loire stands a troupe of 'typical' French characters: postman, gendarme, two nuns in starched head-dresses, and, in a little tribute to Ludwig Bemelmans' 'Madeline' books which were popular in the early 1960s, a group of 'Madeline-like' schoolgirls. And perhaps too a teasing reference to the 'petites madeleines' of Marcel Proust whom Joyce met on 18 May 1922![27]

An introductory note tells the reader the background to the story, and advises that '[t]today any young reader who might doubt this tale may still walk or ride his bike over this very old bridge.' This is the only edition of the story in English to cite the origin of the published letter, which is given as Stuart Gilbert's *Letters of James Joyce*.[28]

Erdoes' images are full of life and humour. A satisfyingly rotund lord mayor is shown curled up in sleep, his knee in his mouth (as described in the text) and his gold chain which he always wore, even when asleep, spread out beside him. Although the size of the book is relatively small, double page spreads are used to full-effect, heightening a sense of vibrancy and theatricality, such as the scene where the cat springs at an obviously furious devil. The book closes with the devil bowing to his audience, the reader; before that, a double spread shows the

23 Richard Erdoes, *A Picture History of Ancient Rome* (New York: Macmillan, 1967). 24 Richard Erdoes, *Policemen Around the World* (New York: McGraw-Hill, 1967). 25 Anne Commine (ed.), *Something About the Author*, vol. 33 (Detroit: Gale Research Company, 1983), pp 63–4. 26 Peritext is described by G. Genette in *Paratexts: thresholds of interpretation* (J. Lewin) (Cambridge: CUP, 1987), p. 5 as the components in a text that surround the central contents, such as the covers, title page and endpapers. 27 Ellmann, *James Joyce*, pp 508–9. 28 Stuart Gilbert (ed.), *Letters of James Joyce* (New York: Viking, 1957).

cat on the verso gesturing to seven Schiaparelli-pink behorned dancing cats on the recto. All the colour pages have touches of this pink; it is the colour of M. Alfred Byrne's jerkin and the devil's hood, visually linking characters and events throughout the book. Their horns echo those of the devil, and emerging from the page gutter a pink mouse, also with horns, jumps impishly towards the cat.

At the conclusion, where Joyce tells us that the bridge is still in place, we see the sweep of the bridge leading us into a fully-bled full-colour page opening, indicating that this is now the present time. A descendant of Monsieur Alfie Byrne dangles a fishing rod over the edge of the bridge, a boy, perhaps a young Joyce or Stevie, balances precariously on the parapet, admired by the same Madeleine-like schoolgirls who appear on the title page. Erdoes delightfully depicts the devil speaking Bellysbabble which clearly references Babel: in a large speech bubble, Chinese, Arabic, Egyptian hieroglyphics and other symbols all emerge as the devil's own language. Erdoes also shows the mayor and the people of Beaugency as black cats, although Joyce did not specifically state that they were transformed, merely that the devil told them they were 'only cats'.

Gerald Rose, whose version of *The Cat and the Devil* was published in London by Faber and Faber in 1965,[29] is a well-known British illustrator. He was born in Hong Kong in 1935 and came to England to attended art college. Over a long career he has illustrated many books for children, some of which he wrote himself.[30] In 1960 he won the UK Library Association's Kate Greenaway Medal for *Old Winkle and the Seagulls*, the text of which was written by his wife, Elizabeth.[31] Possibly the resulting prominence gained by Rose led to his selection as an illustrator of the Joyce tale. Although Rose's style varies overall in his books, the artwork of these two books is broadly similar and is stylistically in tune with the 1960s when they were published. Here, his palette leans to solid, bright colour, intensified by matt pages, and his painted images are fluid and easy-looking. Again, in the manner of the 1960s when colour printing was only beginning to become more economical, every second page is fully coloured, and the intervening pages are in black and white. These show Rose's strength as a draughtsman. His line is assured and solid, and decoration embellishes his images, except for those of the devil, who is always shown more simply with jacket and trousers inked in solid black. Rose's enjoyment of Joyce's tale seems obvious in his witty illustrations, and it seems the author has met an insightful interpreter of his work. The devil bears a remarkable likeness to Joyce, and the mayor is not unlike Alfie Byrne, the real Lord Mayor of Dublin.

Like Erdoes, Rose begins with an image of the cat filled with sweets which Joyce had sent to Stevie a few days before sending his letter. But visually he

29 James Joyce, *The Cat and the Devil*, Gerald Rose illus. (London: Faber, 1965). 30 Alan Horne, *The Dictionary of 20th Century British Book Illustrators* (Woodbridge, Suffolk: the Antique Collectors' Club, 1964), p. 376. 31 Elizabeth Rose and Gerald Rose, *Old Winkle and the Seagulls* (London: Faber, 1959).

places the story much later than Erdoes and chooses some different key scenes to illustrate. He lays emphasis on the devil's sartorial style, showing him adjusting his bow-tie in a full-length looking glass, playing with Joyce's reputation as a stylish dresser. While some other illustrators have stayed with the traditional black cat, Rose's cat is white, perhaps because it shows up against the devil's black jacket, but also in recognition that in this tale the cat does not have magical powers. In the scene where the devil vilifies the Balgetiens, the cat looks as irritated as it might be expected to be, having been doused with water, while Erdoes' cat is knowing, much more a participant in the story.

Perhaps Rose has chosen as a setting the year 1904, the year in which *Ulysses* is set. Some of the characters depicted by Rose could well be those met by Leopold Bloom as he perambulated through the streets of Dublin on 16 June 1904. And, while it is fanciful, we could read the scene where the townspeople look in horror at the Joyce-like devil as he stands on the far side of the bridge, waiting for his payment, as emblematic of some contemporaneous receptions of Joyce's writing. Fashionably dressed Edwardian ladies hold up their hands in dismay and one brandishes an umbrella; an agricultural-looking man waves a digging fork, creating a direct line of vision to the devil's fork which, across the empty space of the bridge, he trails on the ground. The turn of the page shows buglers indicating that the people be silent for the arrival of M. Alfred Byrne, resplendent 'in his great scarlet robe' and wearing a top hat and holding a cat. The next four openings lead up to the dramatic moment when the cat is placed on the bridge and dowsed with water, sending it running into the devil's arms. The theatricality of the story is emphasized here by Rose who spreads the cat leaping forward across two pages, straight into the devil's arms. That this is a monochrome opening heightens the cat's rage, showing it mouth agape, spitting furiously against a washed watery grey background.

Roger Blachon's cat is also white, and he too emphasizes its annoyance as it also traverses a two-page spread, this time, unlike Rose's cat, traveling from right to left and engaging the reader less directly. Blachon is a French illustrator, born in 1941 at Romans. He was a drawing teacher before becoming an illustrator. He has illustrated children's books, comic books and specializes as an illustrator for books about sport.

Like Erdoes, Blachon uses the more traditional medieval setting of a folktale. In the Blachon edition,[32] the cat filled with sweets makes a more discreet appearance, peering out of the basket of the postman who, presumably, is bringing young Stephen his grandfather's letter. Overall it is less witty than the other versions discussed, but some amusing touches are provided such as the cat playing with the mayor's gold chain, and at the end, instead of showing the bridge in modern times he concludes with an image of the cat playing with the

32 James Joyce, *The Cat and the Devil*, Roger Blachon illus. (London: Moonlight, 1980).

tail (tale?) of the devil. His devil appears on the cover, clutching the cat and looming over the town of Beaugency. He looks rueful as well he might, for on the title page he is fully revealed clad in something that looks rather like a red baby-gro.

The other European illustrators mentioned, especially de Tusch-Lec, Saša Švolikova, and Tomiscal Torjanac have responded more fully to the fantastical elements of Joyce's retelling. De Tusch-Lec's cat is purplish-pink and his setting has a psychedelic aura. His Beaugency is a busy place, teeming with inhabitants whom he shows attempting to build a bridge. In the scene mentioned earlier in which the devil reads the newspaper, a pair of pink bedroom slippers with pompoms is visible, implying, as other artists have too, that the devil has a comfort-loving side to him, and heightening Joyce's own emphasis on the everyday aspects of a figure sometimes held in front of children as a threat.

Saša Švolikova's illustrations are more abstract and stylized, figures are set against a deep greeny-blue background, and move in a manner that suggests the influence of traditional Prague puppetry. In *Mačak I Vrag*, Tomiscal Torjanac evokes a somewhat gothic air. His devil looks villainous in a stovepipe hat and sharply pointed moustache and the mayor is a stout eighteenth century burgher.

These illustrators have expanded the traditionally medieval setting for many folk-tales in their presentations; nor have they acceded to the more western European look of the edition illustrated by Gerald Rose. Although very different and responding to a translation of Joyce's original words, each has brought something of a cosmopolitan Europe, a sense of magic realism and an obvious commitment to interpreting the work of a great modernist writer. And Joyce's telling of this modest, traditional story shows how text can be open to many interpretations, and how, in the hands of a master storyteller, a simple tale can prompt many visual constructions of meaning.

'The Cat and the Devil' was not originally intended for a wide audience, but like Joyce's stories and novels, it has traveled across the world,[33] and perhaps, as Stephen Joyce hopes in his letter, recruits readers to his grandfather's adult texts.

33 Illustrators who have produced versions of 'The Cat and the Devil', in languages other than English include: Jan de Tusch-Lec, *Die Katz und der Teufel* (German) (Frankfurt-am-Main: Insel Verlag, 1976); Péter Vladimir, *A macska és az ördög* (Hungarian) (Budapest: Ab Ovo, 1997); Saša Švoliková, *Kočka a čert* (Czech) (Prague: Argo, 1999). Tomiscal Torjanac, *Mačak i vrag* (Croatian) (Zagreb: Mozaik Kniga, 2005). Two translations of *Neko to akuma* (*The Cat and the Devil*) have been published in Japanese, the first by Maruya Sauch Yaku in 1976, and in 1981 a translation by Ando Motoo was published with the Blachon illustrations.

A French perspective on the Irishness
of Morgan Llywelyn's *Cold Places*[1]

CORALLINE DUPUY

This essay deals with a non-native reader's reception of the Irish references to landscape, history and myth contained in Llywelyn's novel. The issues addressed in this essay are the following: what makes the novel Irish? Does its Irishness make it difficult to read for readers unacquainted with the landscapes and myths mentioned in the story? Llywelyn's Celtic roots are intrinsic to her fiction. The author, although born in New York, claims a stronger connection with Ireland through her Irish parents and her childhood (half spent in Ireland) than with her birth-country. Llywelyn's fascination for Celtic myths and history is also spurred by her Welsh lineage. In the context of her extensive literary output, the novel *Cold Places* might seem to be set apart from Llywelyn's other sagas about ancient or recent Irish history. Indeed, the time setting is a contemporary one, and the plot focuses on a young teenager's difficult transition into adulthood. What then makes this novel an Irish novel for teenagers? This essay will examine how the novelist has made *Cold Places* a more accessible work for non-native readers by avoiding references to specific historical facts and by focusing on the personal development of her young protagonist instead. Llywelyn's rich novel narrates the coming-of-age adventures of fifteen-year-old David McHugh when the latter is transplanted from Dublin to County Cork for the summer break. What the non-native reader might find intriguing is the fact that the plotline about David's painful transition into young adulthood is subtly interwoven with another plotline that revolves around the meaning of history and its impact. Llywelyn's novel evokes the pains of growing up and dealing with family breakdown, while making noteworthy points about Irish topography and history. My aim is to explore a non-Irish reader's understanding of the meaning of topography in *Cold Places* in relation to the representation of personal and national history.

In children's fiction, a genre that focuses regularly on a given character's personal growth and interaction with his or her surroundings, the significance of locations cannot be underestimated. The device of the protagonist's move from the primary world into the secondary world is frequently used in seminal works of literature for children, from Lewis Carroll's *Alice's Adventures in Wonderland*[2]

---

1 Morgan Llywelyn, *Cold Places* (Dublin: Poolbeg, 1995).

and J.M. Barrie's *Peter Pan*[3] to Philip Pullman's *Northern Lights*,[4] to quote but a few works considered central to the canon and appreciated in many languages by readers of numerous nationalities and backgrounds.

In Lewis Carroll's fantasy, Alice plunges after the White Rabbit into Wonderland, where she muses about death and her identity, faces threats, rude behaviour and cryptic pieces of advice[5] before eventually outgrowing the madness of Wonderland. Wonderland ceases to exist when Alice exclaims: 'You're nothing but a pack of cards!' (161), thereby displaying her recognition of and subsequent control over the fantasy-world of her dreams.

In Barrie's *Peter Pan* (released as a play in 1904, later published as a novel in 1911), the Darling children move from the family house into Neverland. Discovering the existence of The Island Come True and experiencing life on it forms the main part of the novel: 'Thus sharply did the terrified three learn the difference between an island of make-believe and the same island come true'.[6] They eventually return home, together with the Lost Boys. Peter is the only child who never leaves the Island because he refuses to grow up and to eventually become a man. Barrie's novel makes a clear link between personal maturation and the desire and ability to dwell on the Island Come True.

More recently, Pullman's *Northern Lights* (1995) narrates Lyra Belacqua's adventures, starting in Oxford, then moving northward to Bolvangar and then to Svalbard. Each location in this geographical trinity stands for a different stage of Lyra's development[7] and the progress of her journey runs parallel with the emergence of new and increasingly socially eccentric helpers on Lyra's path (the Gyptians, the witches, the Texan adventurer Lee Scoresby, and the armoured bear Iorek Byrnison). At the end of the narrative, her journey does not reach an end. Instead, she has to leave all her protectors behind and continue on with her daemon Pan. Eloquently, the novel concludes on the following sentence: 'So Lyra and her daemon turned away from the world they were born in, and looked towards the sun, and walked into the sky' (*Northern Lights*, 399). In the second novel in the trilogy, *The Subtle Knife*,[8] the plot focuses even more on geographical settings and revolves around Will Parry's growing ability to move between worlds.

These various examples demonstrate how the locations of a story for children or teenagers not only bring a richly significant background for plot development, but can also be woven into the narrative as an intrinsic part of the storyline.

2 Lewis Carroll, *Alice's Adventures in Wonderland*, 1st pub. 1865. Ed. Martin Gardner (London: Blond, 1960).   3 James Matthew Barrie, *Peter Pan*, 1st pub. 1911 (London: Penguin, 1995). 4 Philip Pullman, *Northern Lights* (London: Scholastic, 1995).   5 'You must be [mad] or you wouldn't have come here', the Cheshire Cat tells Alice (89).   6 Barrie, *Peter Pan*, p. 49.   7 The Master of Jordan College informs her: 'the part of your life that belongs to Jordan College is coming to an end' (70). Lyra's destiny is tied up with her journey.   8 Philip Pullman, *The Subtle Knife* (London: Scholastic, 1997).

Many of Llywelyn's novels are historical ones (such as *1949*, where the title clearly indicates emphasis on the events of the past). Her 1995 work, *Cold Places*, stands out by blending the paradigms of historical novel and teenage fiction. Indeed, the novelist devotes equal attention and details to the coming-of-age plot and to her engaging reflection on Ireland's turbulent past. This characteristic makes the novel her most approachable work for a non-native reader.

The three main locations of the novel are Dublin, Co. Cork, and an ancient ring fort. These places and their succession in the narrative stand for David's life path. Like many other young characters in children's fiction, David must be removed from his familiar environment in order to progress, in accordance with Bettelheim's theory that 'only by going out into the world can the fairy tale hero (child) find himself there; and as he does, he will also find the other with whom he will be able to live happily ever after'.[9] Readers of children's fiction are well-acquainted with this displacement device.

The novel begins in Dublin. This first location is quickly abandoned after a few pages. Yet its significance is substantial. Life at the McHughs' household in Dublin is suffocating and dominated by Arthur McHugh's academic career. Tellingly, he first appears 'glancing up from some papers he was grading at the table by the window' (1). Clearly an absentee figure in his family on account of his research ('That book! It was taking over their lives' [2]), he arranges his archaeological research trip to Co. Cork as a family holiday, thereby dangerously blending the realms of the professional and familial. The financial situation is strained. David's father declares: 'I'm up to my ears in debt.' (24) Communication between Alice McHugh and her husband is blatantly absent: 'She did not understand him [David] any better than she understood her husband … Now all the romance in her life was on the telly, while her husband found his in old ruins.' (3) When verbal exchanges do take place between them, the reader shares David's frustration at what is being omitted because of his presence: '"You insisted on coming because …" He stopped, glanced at his son as if he had just remembered the boy was in his room.' (24) Speech utterances are counterproductive and stunted by the underlying conflict between adults. David therefore finds himself excluded from any meaningful verbal communication with his parents. The hero's life in Dublin is strained and the difficulties he encounters in his daily life, such as warring parents and communication breakdowns, are frequent themes of coming-of-age stories.

Dublin is also David's social scene, and the place for interaction with male friends such as Paddy, with whom he indulges in shared daydreams about the heroes of recent Irish history: 'David thought about … heroes and Easter Rising and great adventures. There sure as hell weren't going to be any great adventures

---

9 Bruno Bettelheim, *The Uses of Enchantment: the meaning and importance of fairy tales*, 1st pub. 1975 (New York: Random House, 1989), p. 11.

in Bally-Go-Backwards.' (5) In this specific case, the reference to an isolated place with the expression 'Bally-Go-Backwards' – a reference to the fact that many Irish place names, especially rural ones, contain the prefix 'Bally', an Anglicization of 'Baile', the Irish word for town – might be completely lost on a non-native reader. It is one of the occasions when any future translator will have to decide between either keeping the expression as it is in the text (and then adding an explanatory footnote) or finding an equivalent in the destination language.

This is one of many instances where Llywelyn deftly blends specifically Irish references with widespread sources of teenager angst. The description of David's parents incessantly feuding is particularly effective and skilfully renders the oppressive atmosphere in their Dublin house at the stroke of a few sentences:

> 'Your wages.' The words were sheathed in ice. There was going to be an argument, David could feel it. There were too many arguments. Too many raised voices, slammed doors, frosty silences. The frosty silences were the worst, they made him feel helpless ... Through the open front door he could hear them quarrelling. Then an interior door slammed, followed by a silence as heavy as stone. (11)

The rural setting of Co. Cork provides a vivid visual contrast with the urban landscape of Dublin: 'They drove for miles along one narrow, winding road and then another, among heathered hills where great rocks broke through the surface of the land' (9). The novel articulates a familiar dichotomy between the artifices of urban settings and the authenticity of more modest rural scenery. The cottage rented by the McHughs exemplifies this opposition: 'The cottage was shabby and dismal, though its rundown appearance was partially disguised by a riot of climbing roses.' (10) The marriage of the McHughs comes to an end during their stay in the countryside. In this rural setting, silences become more frequent: 'By the heaviness of the air he knew they had been arguing again.' (128) Conversations, when they do take place, are more genuine and therefore more confrontational. Alice McHugh angrily confronts her husband's policy of retreat: 'There's never a good time or place, is there? You just don't want to face this.' (93) The change of location accentuates rather than resolves the diffi-culties.

The pattern of pitting opposites against each other is again used when intro-ducing the other family unit of the plot, the Doyles. David meets and befriends Molly Doyle, a local girl living on a nearby farm with her widowed father, Liam. Although the Doyles' family is incomplete, the Doyle household embodies more authentic family values. On the other hand, David's family disintegrates further when they find themselves in the isolated landscape: 'Home for now was that shabby cottage and his parents bickering ... When he reached the cottage his mother was in her bedroom with the door shut. His father was still in Cork.' (52) As a consequence, the Doyles provide David with a substitute family: 'Being with them was like summer. His parents were winter.' (57) David is cut off from male friends. Molly Doyle represents a formative influence; she helps David to reach his potential and pushes him to grow up and to investigate the cold places. So far, the novelist has succeeded in creating for non-native readers a riveting atmosphere set in an exotic country, while simultaneously presenting them with familiar topics of splitting families and parental substitutes.

The next location, the ring fort, is what might constitute the only obstacle for the enjoyment of the novel by a non-Irish reader. The place is crucial for the plot development and the personal progress of the main character. Some knowledge of Celtic mythology is necessary in order to fully comprehend the significance of the ring fort in the narrative, and this is where non-native readers are at a disadvantage. In the novel, the ring fort is a magical place where histories elide and where a powerful forgotten force lies dormant until David awakens it. In Celtic mythology, a stone circle represents a magical barrier. For instance, Cuchulainn uses magical letters on a wooden ring to stop an army from invading Ulster. The Earth is a spiritual centre in numerous mythologies around the world. In Celtic culture, it has a dual meaning. As in Latin, there are two words for 'earth' in the Gaelic language. They are *talamh* (earth as one of the elements) and *tír* (the geographical Earth). In Celtic myths, druids have control over earth as an element.[10] Celtic mythology regularly features one female character who is the embodiment of this element, such as the myth of Lug the warrior, where earth is represented by the female character Tailtiu, Lug's nurse. Whereas most Irish children are acquainted with the folk tales and myths about the Celtic deities, some research would be necessary for the non-Irish neophyte to learn about those.

However, the psychological significance of the earth and what lies beneath is easily accessible for all. In psychological terms, the earth and its hidden depths are an apt metaphor for the human psyche, what lies above the surface being the consciousness, what lies beneath (monsters, demons) standing for the unconscious. As a consequence, the earth becomes a symbol for the human consciousness and its inner conflicts.[11] This key concept also applies to David, the teenage only son of a disintegrating family. The novel traces how his development is brought about by his encounter with the cold places. David's first contact with the cold places is physically traumatic: 'The boy had come to an abrupt between the two pillar stones that marked the entrance. His face was drained of colour and skin had drawn so tight across his cheekbones that it looked like a skull. Gooseflesh pimpled his bare arms.' (18)

10 Jean Chevalier and Alain Gheerbrant (eds), *Dictionnaire des symboles*, 1969 (Paris: Laffont Jupiter, 1995), p. 942.   11 Seminal works by Paul Diel have focused on the symbolical richness of the earth in analytical terms.

The novel follows David on his life-path toward what in Jungian terms is called individuation. The term individuation describes the emotional state of a person who has reached maturity and who has become acquainted with all aspects of his or her personality, even and especially the dark ones. According to Jung, the development of one's personality is 'an act of courage flung in the face of life, the absolute affirmation of all that constitutes the individual, the most successful adaptation to the universal conditions of existence coupled with the greatest possible freedom for self-determination.'[12] This theme will resonate powerfully in a teenage audience.

David at the beginning is the epitome of the change-reluctant teenager. His personal growth is stunted and he is unable to grow up and to embrace change: 'New friends. The very idea of having to make new friends made David uncomfortable. He liked things the way they were, with his old friends.' (4) Leaving Dublin and his familiar surroundings is experienced as a trauma: 'He stared out the window and watched the familiar neighbourhood slide away. Going ... going ... gone.' (6) Llywelyn's use of direct reported speech facilitates the reader's identification with David's turmoil

The metaphor of the title of the novel becomes all-pervasive and multi-layered. Even before David discovers the ring fort, his life at home in Dublin is already suffused with an overwhelming lack of warmth in the family conversations: 'She shot a meaningful look at her husband. There had been a lot of meaningful looks lately. There were shadowy undercurrents in the house, David could sense them.' (2) While there are numerous verbal exchanges between Alice and Arthur McHugh, they cannot communicate and they skirt around the actual issues: 'Mrs. McHugh kept arguing. Listening to the two of them, David became convinced that the quarrel wasn't really about him at all, but about other issues.' (23) Robert Dunbar sees the cold places as 'a metaphor for many suppressed traumas and emotions'.[13] Marital breakdown will be a familiar topic for teenager readers.

Jungian critic and folklorist Mary Louise von Franz defines the beginning of the journey into the unconscious as shrouded in uncertainty: 'The centre of interest has shifted from the outer world to the inner, but the inner world is still completely unintelligible. At this stage, the unconscious seems senseless and bewildering.'[14] This analysis is especially applicable to a teenager's hesitating steps into maturity when his parents' relationship is failing. The breakdown of the McHugh marriage takes place simultaneously with David's encounter with the eponymous cold places. As a consequence, David has to wage two battles. He must learn what the cold places are and what they might unleash while also

12 Carl Gustav Jung, *The Development of Personality*, 1st pub. 1912. Trans. R.F.C. Hull (London: Routledge, 1964), p. 171.   13 Robert Dunbar, 'My top fifty Irish children's novels', *Inis* (10): Winter 2004.   14 Marie-Louise von Franz, *An Introduction to the Interpretation of Fairy Tales*, 1st pub. 1970 (Dallas: Spring, 1982), p. 87.

dealing with his dysfunctional parents and their inability to communicate and to provide him with a stable family environment: 'The world was falling apart and he could not go to his parents for comfort because they were part of the problem.' (134) Despite depicting Arthur and Alice McHugh as a sterile and destructive couple, the novel suggests that David is able to be receptive to the power coming from the ring fort on account of his raw emotions. Ironically, his parents' unravelling relationship forces him to mature, in keeping with Jung's claim that 'Without necessity nothing budges bulges, the human personality least of all.'[15]

The cold places and what they contain force David to come face to face with the uncanny and the unconscious. In his influential study about the notion of *unheimlich*, Sigmund Freud defines the uncanny as 'something which should have remained hidden but has come to light.'[16] The fight David must win pitches him against 'a monster that hated all things warm and living and sucked the life out of them. If he surrendered he would be swallowed up and become part of the nothingness.' (33–4) The Ice Age entity that David and Molly struggle to maintain in its subterranean lair is an arresting embodiment of many issues the teenager is facing. The spirit of the Ice is a powerful symbol whose irruption in the novel disrupts the distinction between dreams and waking life, nightmares and reality: 'The cold was intolerable. When he tried to scream he could only cough as the wind rushed down his throat. It sucked the air from his lungs and turned his warm breath to frost. *This is a nightmare!* he thought, but he knew it was no nightmare. It was something worse – reality.' (47) Encountering this spirit provides David with an uncanny experience, according to Freud's definition: 'an uncanny effect is often and easily produced when the distinction between imagination and reality is effaced, as when something that we have hitherto regarded as imaginary appears before us in reality, or when a symbol takes over the full functions of the thing it symbolizes.'[17] Facing and eventually overcoming this threatening element enables David to grow up and to develop as an autonomous person. Crossing the threshold represented by the stone circle becomes a metaphor for personal growth. In his study of the allegorical dimension of fairy tales, J.C. Cooper claims that recognizing thresholds constitutes one of the steps towards integration and personal fulfilment. He defines the threshold as the place where 'the natural and the supernatural meet and the change has to be made from the known, familiar, profane world, to the unknown, inner and sacred space'.[18] *Cold Places* features an astute blend of psychological landmarks for a teenager with specific Irish settings.

At the end of the narrative, David has realized and accepted that his parents'

15 Jung, *The Development of Personality*, p. 173. 16 Sigmund Freud, *The Uncanny*, 1st pub. 1919. Trans. James Strachey (London: Hogarth, 1971), p. 242. 17 Ibid., p. 244. 18 J.C. Cooper, *Fairy Tales: allegories of the inner life* (Wellingborough: Aquarian, 1983), p. 140.

marriage is defunct: 'As surely as he recognized cold places, David knew this was the end of his parents' being together. Something had died which would not come back to life no matter how he wished otherwise.' (133) He has also gained an understanding of other people's limitations that he did not have before: 'It occurred to David that his father was reluctant to admit a country girl might know something a university professor did not. Once, he remembered, he had thought his father knew everything.' (31) In the wake of the loss of his parents' god-like status, David has become autonomous and responsible: 'If there were stones elsewhere, it would mean more than one group of ancient people had rituals for controlling the weather ... He was in a hurry for the future.' (143) Tellingly, David now views the changes that life brings as a bonus: 'Change would come to all of them.' (142) David now looks forward to the future and knows what his ability means and how he can use it. At the end of the protagonist's journey of self-discovery and development, the previously daunting future has ceased to be an object of fear: 'The marvellous, mysterious Unknown, that had reached out and touched him of all people. He *would* not be afraid.' (139) Through the example of David, the novelist conveys a strong message about the necessity of being an active agent in one's life instead of submitting to external forces: 'As soon as he decided to do something, David felt better. He was no less afraid, but he did not feel so much like a victim.' (76)

If one examines what *Cold Places* brings to Irish children's fiction, the strategic cleverness displayed by the novelist is evident. Llywelyn deftly includes an intriguing historical dimension in her novel without taking the reader's attention away from her protagonist's predicament. The novel makes it clear that the obstacles David has to overcome are to be found both at home and in the mysterious stone circle Molly Doyle leads him to. The novelist's deliberate choice not to get too involved in historical descriptions enables her to blend a coming-of-age plotline with an intriguing reflection on the richness of Ireland's mythical past. *Cold Places* represents a successful attempt to negotiate a more subtle way to use historical elements to test present predicaments. Robert Dunbar has pointed out that one of the dangers facing writers of historical fiction is that 'too many facts and figures can easily drown the narrative'.[19] Llywelyn's novel reveals her awareness of this possibility. Her inventive story eludes this difficulty by incorporating a riveting fantastical element, the spirit of the ice, and by leaving the ending open: 'It would take a while yet, but the Age of Ice would gather its allies and return to claim its kingdom. Meanwhile the spirit in the earth waited. It had time. All the time in the world.' (144) Non-native readers will not only derive entertainment from her novel, but also *dépaysement*; an experience of being thrown into an alien world, the feeling of leaving their country and of finding themselves *sans pays* during the time they

19 Robert Dunbar, 'My top fifty Irish children's novels'.

read the novel and immerse themselves into the universal themes dealt with by the author.

Llywelyn's work belongs to an emerging phase of the evolution of Irish children's fiction; we are now witnessing the emergence of works to which readers of other nationalities can relate. In her 2005 review of contemporary children's fiction written in Ireland, Áine Nic Gabhann notes that: 'The primary preoccupation of the historical novel [produced for children] up to about the year 2000 was identity, often defined in a narrow, insular way. In more recent years, however, a broader perspective has been introduced which doesn't necessarily concern itself with "Irishness". Rather, identity is being portrayed in more global terms.'[20] This emerging phase is a welcome development in terms of the accessibility for non-Irish readers, and also an exciting literary junction for the multicultural society that Ireland is becoming.

20 Áine Nic Gabhann, 'Hardly plotting society: Irish literature', *Inis*, 11 (Spring 2005), 15–19, 16.

A sense of place? The Irishness of Irish children's literature in translation

EMER O'SULLIVAN

The major change brought about by the blossoming of publishing in Ireland in the 1980s was that a domestically produced children's literature could, for the first time, explore Irishness[1] on its own terms without having to cater for an external audience. Literature primarily for a non-domestic market will, explicitly or otherwise, address issues of national identity and reproduce autostereotypes and heterostereotypes differently from that produced for the home market. Kenneth Reddin famously described the stage-Irish children's literature produced to conform to images demanded by the British and American market in the 1940s: 'Pigs in the kitchen and little red hens and tinkers splitting skulls down bohereens',[2] and this was echoed by Tony Hickey at the beginning of the 1980s when he complained about overseas publishers tending 'to want only their notions of Irishness, the land of leprechauns'.[3]

The negotiation and celebration of Irishness or Irishnesses, in home-grown children's literature and in its accompanying critical assessment, have passed through various stages since the huge increase in the quantity of writing and publishing for the young in the 1980s.[4] The mid-1990s saw a phase of identity-fatigue; the tendency of publishers simply to satisfy the demand for Irish books for Irish children without sufficient concern for standards was criticized as was

1 Issues of identity politics, past and present, and contemporary constructions of Irishness that range from the shamrock-laden webpage 'irishidentity.com' to the 'reinvention' of the country of Ireland as a result of the new era of economic boom and European integration cannot be comprehensively addressed within the confines of this piece. See, for recent discussions, Fintan O'Toole, *The Lie of the Land: Irish identities* (London: Verso, 1998) and Peadar Kirby, Luke Gibbons and Michael Cronin (eds), *Reinventing Ireland. Culture, society and the global economy* (London: Pluto Press, 2002). 2 Kenneth Reddin, 'Children's books in Ireland. Were we all brought up behind a half-door?' *Irish Library Bulletin*, 7 (1946), 74. 3 Tony Hickey, '… And after Lynch?', in *Loughborough '81. Conference Proceedings 14th. Loughborough International Conference on Children's Literature, Dublin 1981* (Dublin: Dublin Public Libraries, 1982), p. 36. 4 For an account of the background to these changes and the subsequent development, see Valerie Coghlan, 'Ireland', in Peter Hunt (ed.), *International Companion Encyclopedia of Children's Literature*, rev. ed. (London, New York: Routledge, 2004), pp 1099–1103; Robert Dunbar, 'Rarely pure and never simple. The world of Irish children's literature', *The Lion and the Unicorn*, 21:3 (1997), 309–21; and Emer O'Sullivan, 'The development of modern children's literature in late twentieth-century Ireland', *Signal*, 81 (1996), 189–211.

the insular tendency to write mainly about domestic issues. Some authors notably transcended the local and the national to tackle non-Irish subjects, especially in historical novels, and were widely praised for doing so. Eilís Dillon's final novel *The Children of Bach* (1993) and Mark O'Sullivan's *Angels without Wings* (1997), for instance, address the Second World War and the Holocaust; other examples of a broadening of the repertoire are Aubrey Flegg's *The Cinnamon Tree: a novel set in Africa* (2000) and his acclaimed Louise trilogy: *Wings over Delft* (2003), set in seventeenth-century Netherlands, *The Rainbow Bridge* (2004) which takes the reader to revolutionary France at the end of the eighteenth century and, set in Austria up to the Anschluss of 1939 and following its protagonist into the Nazi concentration camps of Theresienstadt and Auschwitz, *In the Claws of the Eagle* (2006).

The most recent phase in criticism is one that addresses with concern the decline in Irish children's book publishing. Reflecting why two of the seven publishing houses that regularly issued books for young readers in the 1990s have now ceased to operate and the output of three others has fallen considerably, Valerie Coghlan highlights the paradox of how the very strength of the Irish market in the 1990s and the availability of Irish authors led to UK publishing conglomerates setting up publishing divisions in Ireland.[5] That this development clearly brought about a qualitative change in the output of writers such as Maeve Friel, Eoin Colfer and Marie-Louise Fitzpatrick is shown by Celia Keenan who, looking closely at their work, identifies the elimination of culturally specific references, loss of country and loss of culture after their publishing migration. As a result, 'the local has ceded to the global'.[6]

The focus of interest in this article is on what happens to the local quality of Irish children's literature in translation. I would like to explore whether the sense of place and rootedness in a specific culture evident in some contemporary Irish children's books is palpable in their translations and, to this end, will look at selected examples from the work of Siobhán Parkinson, Eoin Colfer and Roddy Doyle and their German editions. German literature is a generally receptive one: between a quarter and a third of children's books produced annually are translations. Every fifth German children's book is a translation from American, British, Canadian, Australian, Irish or other English, and proportionately more Irish children's books are therefore translated into German than into any other language.[7] I will start by looking briefly at the German image of Ireland and ask to what extent the degree of specific cultural reference influences the selection

5 See Coghlan, 'Ireland', p. 1099.   6 Celia Keenan, 'Divisions in the world of Irish publishing for children: re-colonization or globalization?', in Mary Shine Thompson and Valerie Coghlan (eds), *Divided Worlds: studies in children's literature* (Dublin: Four Courts, 2007), p. 202.   7 For an account of the languages into which Irish children's books are translated, see Emer O'Sullivan, 'Irish Children's Books in Translation', in Valerie Coghlan and Celia Keenan (eds), *The Big Guide 2: Irish children's books* (Dublin: CBI, 2000), pp 128–35.

of literature for translation and its subsequent marketing. Is a book is translated because it is (or isn't) recognizably Irish or because it does or does not conform to an image of Ireland in the target culture? Is the 'Irishness' of the text or the nationality of the author used as a marketing factor? Turning my attention to actual translations to ask how Irishness is represented in texts in the German language, a second step will focus on culturally specific elements such as locations, references to sport or literature, social and religious conventions or humour, some of which may need to be explained to a target audience. The final section will address one of the major challenges for the translator, the Irish voices in children's literature. Here I will ask how German translators negotiate Irish vernacular speech patterns, borrowings from the Irish language and the influence of its grammar and other characteristic features of Hiberno-English. Examining how the idioms and varieties, the differences between rural, urban, mid-Atlantic and the other voices in Irish children's literature are represented in a foreign language, I will ask whether there is any audible difference between Colfer's Benny Shaw and Rowling's Harry Potter in their German guises.

THE GERMAN IMAGE OF IRELAND AS A FACTOR IN TRANSLATION

One single book had a greater influence on the German image of Ireland than all the Bord Fáilte campaigns rolled into one: Heinrich Böll's *Irisches Tagebuch* (*Irish Diary*). Published in 1957, it has sold over a million copies and has not been out of print since. This hymn to Ireland unleashed an *Irlandwelle*, a wave of young Germans with the Diary tucked under their arms, searching for their own identity in the West of Ireland.[8] Böll tapped into images of Ireland and the Celts that had been around at least since the Ossian affair,[9] but he gave them new currency and added some of his own. His image was an idyllic one of the Irish West, an innocent paradise forever lost to post-Nazi Germany, a substitute homeland uncontaminated by *Blut und Boden* (blood and soil) ideology. Key elements were nature, unspoilt by industrialization, time, of which there was always enough, the natives, red-haired, easy-going, non-materialistic, religious and fond of the drink, and imagination. Ireland, for Böll, was *the* country of storytellers, fairytales and legends.[10]

8 See Eoin Bourke, *Das Irlandbild der Deutschen. Deutschsprachige Autoren über Irland* (Tübingen: Deutsch-Irischer Freundeskreis in Baden-Württemberg, 1991), p. 14. 9 In 1760 the Scottish poet James MacPherson published what he claimed was a translation of poems from an ancient manuscript in Scottish Gaelic, supposedly written by Ossian. They were enthusiastically received and widely translated throughout Europe, and Ossian was hailed as the Celtic equivalent of Homer. The controversy over the authenticity of the poems continued well into the twentieth century. 10 A comprehensive account of the image of Ireland in Germany and in German

Heinrich Böll and his wife Annemarie translated Eilís Dillon's *The Island of Horses* 'out of affection for Ireland', as it says on the cover of the first German edition of 1964[11] and it has remained in print ever since. Before the 1990s Patricia Lynch and Eilís Dillon, fifteen of whose children's books have been translated into German, were the only Irish children's authors to have received any kind of recognition in Germany. Four novels by Lynch had been translated in the 1950s and 1960s,[12] some significantly shortened in the process and marketed to fit the predominant image of Ireland at that time. The 1990s saw the publication of a fresh, unabridged translation of two of these, together with first translations of two further titles, but they were not commercially successful. Lynch's Irishness is constantly emphasized in the peritexts of the German translations, both old and recent. The short blurb on the new translation of *King of the Tinkers* in 1993 proclaims:

> *Der König der Tinker* ist eines von mehr als vierzig Kinder- und Jugendbüchern der <u>irischen</u> Schriftstellerin Patricia Lynch. Ihre Bücher [zählen] zu den Klassikern der <u>irischen</u> Literatur [...] Patricia Lynch versteht es, in ihren Geschichten die Realität mit den uralten Sagen und Legenden <u>Irlands</u> zu verbinden.[13]

> [*The King of the Tinkers* is one of more than 40 children's books by the *Irish* author Patricia Lynch. Her books are regarded as classics of *Irish* literature. In her stories, Patricia Lynch blends reality with the ancient sagas and legends of *Ireland* (my translation and my emphasis)].

Contemporary Irish children's literature was presented to the international publishing world when Ireland was the Focal Theme of the Frankfurt Book Fair in 1996, and the O'Brien Press and the Wolfhound Press especially were subsequently able to position themselves in the international market. Among the most successful representatives of contemporary Irish children's literature in Germany are Martin Waddell and Sam McBratney with their picturebooks; Joan Lingard, whose *Kevin and Sadie* series is used in schools; Marita Conlon-McKenna with her successful *Children of the Famine* trilogy; Eoin Colfer, whose best-selling *Artemis Fowl* novels do very well; and Darren Shan, whose horror novels have a fan following. All of Mark O'Sullivan's books have been translated

children's literature, as well as of the influence of this image on the selection and translation of Irish literature, can be found in Emer O'Sullivan, 'German and Irish children's literature: a comparative perspective', in Susan Tebbutt and Joachim Fischer (eds), *Intercultural Connections within German and Irish Children's Literature*. Irish-German Studies II (Trier: WVT, 2008). 11 'Aus Sympathie für Irland'. Eilis Dillon, *Die Insel der Pferde*, tr. Annemarie und Heinrich Böll (Freiburg i. Br., Basel, Wien: Herder, 1964) [*The Island of Horses*, 1956]. 12 *Fiddler's Quest, Brogeen Follows the Magic Tune, Brogeen and the Green Shoes* and *The Mad O'Haras*. 13 Patricia Lynch, *Der König der Tinker*, trans. Christiane Jung (Hamburg: Hille, 1993).

into German; Roddy Doyle's *Giggler* stories have been well received; two of Aubrey Flegg's novels have appeared in German; and Siobhán Parkinson finally had her German debut in 2000: just two of her books, have been translated to date.[14] While the word 'Ireland' or 'Irish' could appear three times in a short blurb on a Lynch translation, the reader is not likely to find it on other recently translated Irish children's books, least of all perhaps in publicity material for *Artemis Fowl*, but even on the blurbs of Colfer's locally flavoured *Benny* novels, no reference is made to the nationality of protagonist or author. Andreas Steinhöfel, himself an acclaimed children's author, certainly did not translate Roddy Doyle 'out of affection for Ireland'. In fact the whole marketing of contemporary Irish children's books plays down the Irish dimension entirely; the nationality of the author and the setting of the story usually remain unnamed.[15] This trend towards de-emphasizing the local dimension is not exclusive to Irish books. In fact it corresponds to what Martina Seifert observed with regard to the reception of contemporary Canadian children's literature in Germany:

> Canadian children's literature is received within the general context of English-language children's literature imported from Britain or the USA, the dominant feature of which is that everything is imported that sells and is not too culture-specific. While in the 1950s and 1960s imported children's literature was generally of interest as a carrier of ethno-cultural information, publishers now privilege stories with few or no cultural markers.[16]

Even if not marketed as specifically Irish, most of the source texts or original texts mentioned above are encoded as products of a specific socio-cultural context. The question I would now like to ask is: has the word 'Irish' as an explicit identifier just disappeared from the covers, or has Irishness also disappeared from between them? What happens to specific social and cultural signifiers in German translations?

14 See O'Sullivan, 'Irish children's books in translation' (2000) for more details, and the extensive chapter on Irish children's literature in German translation by Martina Seifert in Gina Weinkauff and Martina Seifert, *Ent-Fernungen. Fremdwahrnehmung und Kulturtransfer in der deutschsprachigen Kinder- und Jugendliteratur seit 1945*. 2 vols (Munich, 2000), pp 897–937. 15 An exception is the blurb on the German translation of Siobhán Parkinson's *Four Kids, Three Cats, Two Cows, One Witch (Maybe)* (Dublin: O'Brien, 1997), possibly due to its rural and island setting and the storytelling motif. The German title, *Die Geschichteninsel. Das Geheimnis von Lady Island*, tr. Michael Jokisch (Stuttgart: Thienemann, 2000), translates back into English as 'The Story Island. The Secret of Lady Island'. 16 Martina Seifert, 'The image trap: the translation of English-Canadian children's literature into German', in Emer O'Sullivan, Kimberley Reynolds and Rolf Romøren (eds), *Children's Literature Global and Local: social and aesthetic perspectives* (Oslo: Novus, 2005), p. 236.

CULTURALLY SPECIFIC ELEMENTS IN TRANSLATION

In Siobhán Parkinson's dual diary novel *Sisters … No Way!* two very different Dublin step-sisters-to-be give their respective views of affairs in their own distinctive voices. The culture of the setting is not made thematic in the novel; it is what linguists call the unmarked form. An external audience doesn't have to be catered for and Parkinson has always emphasized that her Irish settings are not an end to themselves; rather, she is only interested in what happens within them. The everyday life of the girls is, nonetheless, steeped in a specific culture, elements of which can prove difficult for a translator transposing the novel into a different context. The following is an example from would-be worldly-wise Cindy's diary:

> Anyway we had just got in, with a stick of French bread and two chocolate croissants from the French bakery – bakeries in our area are open on Sundays now, very continental, don't you know – and the *Sunday Tribune*.[17]

What does 'continental' mean to the uninitiated? With connotations of European stylishness and sophistication, the adjective in Irish (in contrast to British) usage is usually positive; it is a lifestyle to which middle-class Dubliners have variously aspired. Cindy, in this passage, is having her cake (or her croissant) and eating it, sending up those very aspirations by mimicking the posh voice ('don't you know') while obviously savouring their benefits at the same time. In the German translation by Janka Panskus, whose title, *Schwestern wider Willen*, can be retranslated as *Reluctant Sisters*, this passage reads:

> Auf jeden Fall waren wir also gerade heimgekommen, mit einem Baguette und zwei Schokocroissants aus der französischen Bäckerei – in unserem Viertel haben die Bäckereien nun auch immer sonntags geöffnet, sehr kontinental, nicht – und mit der *Sunday Tribune*[18]

The translation is very close to the original – a translation back into English could produce the original text. In the translation of 'very continental, don't you know', 'sehr kontinental, nicht', the posh register of the tag question is mimicked well; however, the literal 'kontinental' for the Hiberno-English 'continental' signifies no more than land mass in German; it is used predominantly in geographical discourse. Exactly what land mass is referred to here (continental Europeans don't see themselves as 'continental') or what it could possibly have

---

17 Siobhán Parkinson, *Sisters … No Way!* (Dublin: O'Brien, 1996), p. 17.   18 Siobhán Parkinson, *Schwestern wider Willen. Cindys Tagebuch. Ashlings Tagebuch*, tr. Janka Panskus (Munich: Omnibus, 2000), p. 21.

to do with a Dublin bakery is unclear. The connotations are missing so the passage, in its literal translation, actually leaves a German reader confused.

Schools and religion are topics in the next example from Cindy's diary:

> The daughters go to a mixed school, one of those Protestant places where you have to pay fees and play hockey. Maybe their father is a Protestant, though I don't think Magee is a very Protestant name. A Protestant father would be quite exotic ...[19]

What a mixed school is needs no explanation in Ireland. It does not mean mixed species, ethnic groups or denominations but, infinitely more dangerous, co-education. In Ireland single-sex schools are still the unmarked form, while in Germany it is the other way around. The association of mixed schools with Protestantism, indeed the term 'Protestant' itself with all its connotations, the fact that some names 'sound' either Protestant or Catholic or why it might be exotic for the girls to have a Protestant father, obviously doesn't have to be explained to Irish readers who are familiar with the social nuances which are part and parcel of the different Irish denominations. But what do Germans make of it?

> Die Töchter gehen auf eine gemischte Schule, eine dieser protestantischen, wo man Schulgebühren zahlen muss und Hockey spielt. Vielleicht ist ihr Vater protestantisch, obwohl Magee nicht wie ein protestantischer Name klingt. Ein protestantischer Vater wäre ziemlich exotisch.[20]

Here, too, we have a fairly literal translation with the translator staying very close to the source text. A 'mixed school' is translated literally as just that. With co-education the unmarked form in Germany, a possible association with the term 'gemischte Schule' (mixed school) could be 'mixed aptitudes', a school which integrates children with special needs. By choosing the uncommon but known term 'protestantisch' – Protestants in Germany are generally referred to as 'evangelisch' – the translator marks the context as different and prevents an automatic reading of the text as if it were in a German setting.[21]

By generally not mediating socio-cultural difference, this translation often leads German readers in a different direction from the one intended in the source text or leaves them simply confused. The examples illustrate how a literal, non-mediating translation can generate elements in a target text whose cultural connotations either cannot be fully understood or else are positively misunder-

---

19 Parkinson, *Sisters* (1996), p. 19. **20** Parkinson, *Schwestern wider Willen* (2000), p. 24. **21** German readers whom I asked said that they associated the word 'protestantisch' with Ireland; mainly from news coverage of Northern Ireland, which always uses this term, and some said they knew it from Joan Lingard's *Kevin and Sadie* novels.

stood. German readers are exposed to the mild exoticism of an Irish setting
without being aided to decode the elements. Even for an interculturally
competent reader, much remains obscure.

While little was clarified in the translation of Parkinson's novel, we find some
very selective explanations in the translations of Eoin Colfer's *Benny* books.
These are about a boy hurler from Wexford who faces the challenge of coming
to terms with cultural otherness and being a cultural other himself in Tunisia in
Benny and Omar,[22] and about his relationship with the tomboy Babe in *Benny and
Babe*.[23] The books are rightly acclaimed for what a reviewer in *Children's Books
in Ireland* called their 'unabashed Irishness'.[24] In each of the *Benny* novels we
find exactly one paratextual explanation by the translator, Ute Mihr. In *Benny
und Omar* a footnote on the first page tells us that hurling is a team game quite
like hockey, and very widespread in Ireland.[25] This is an accurate gloss, even if a
bit on the economical side for such an exotic game from a German perspective,
and on the next page 'sliotar' (the small, hard ball used in Irish field games of
hurling and camogie) is left unexplained. In the sequel, *Benny and Babe*, hurling
features just as largely but the translator obviously presumes that the reader read
the brief footnote in the previous volume. The only note in this novel explains
what 'German bait' is – 'Kunstköder', a fake bait made of plastic or metal.[26]
References to the locations and names Croke Park (the largest Gaelic games
stadium in Ireland), Lansdowne Road (its rugby equivalent) and Cidona (a non-
alcoholic apple drink), for instance, are not explained.

THE HIBERNO-ENGLISH IDIOM IN
IRISH CHILDREN'S LITERATURE

A central feature of *Benny and Omar* is Colfer's use of different varieties of
English. Benny's mother is characterized by her correct received pronunciation;
Benny himself uses a Wexford variety; the with-it American teachers in the
Tunisian compound speak politically correct US English; Scottish pupils are
linguistically identifiable as such; and Omar, the Tunisian boy, communicates
with Benny, often to great poignant and poetic effect, in media Esperanto, the
language of television, spiked with Arabic words. Omar calls half-time during
their football game 'the commercial break' and explains his family situation using

22 Eoin Colfer, *Benny and Omar* (Dublin: O'Brien, 1998). 23 Ibid. 24 Judith Ridge, 'A taste
of Australian children's literature' *Children's Books in Ireland*, 27 (2001), 20. 25 Eoin Colfer,
Benny und Omar, tr. Ute Mihr (Weinheim: Beltz und Gelberg, 2001), p. 7. As an unknown sport,
hurling generally puzzles German commentators. In reviews of Ken Loach's film, *The Wind That
Shakes the Barley* (2006), most German reviews write about a fatal scene during a forbidden
hockey match. Why hockey should have been forbidden in Ireland isn't quite clear. 26 Eoin
Colfer, *Benny und Babe*, tr. Ute Mihr (Weinheim: Beltz und Gelberg, 2002).

the Simpsons as an analogy. He is Bart, he tells Benny, but 'No Homer. No Marge. Homer, Marge: Thomas the Tank Engine – boom … Lisa: Casualty, Chicago Hope'.[27] It hardly needs to be paraphrased: his parents were killed by a train, and his little sister is in hospital. *Benny and Omar* is a truly polyglot novel. What is striking is not just the variety of regional and social idioms; the narrative discourse of the novel, often conflated with Benny's in free indirect discourse, is itself cast in the Hiberno-English idiom. In contrast to the use of non-standard forms in, say, the novels of Charles Dickens, in which the distance between the narrator's Standard English and elaborate code on the one hand, and the regional and non-standard varieties represented in dialogue which usually served to heighten the comic effect on the other, there is little distance between the narrative voice of the *Benny* novels and the spoken Hiberno-English of some of the characters.

What becomes of all this in German translation? In order to answer this question, I will take a close look at three passages from recent Irish novels that variously illustrate phonetic, lexical and grammatical characteristics of Hiberno-English, and then I will move on to ask how they are transported into German.

Passage 1:
'Right you be, so, I'll come […]. I'll carry them yokes for you. Whatever they are.'[28]

The character speaking here is Kevin, the local from Tranarone, in Siobhán Parkinson's *Four Kids, Three Cats, Two Cows, One Witch (Maybe)*, whose idiom differs clearly from that of the young Dublin holiday-makers, marking his rural origin with the concomitant connotations of status. Various characteristics of the Hiberno-English colloquial idiom are evident in his usage: the ungrammatical verb form 'you be' in 'Right you be, so', and the marked use of the adverbial 'so', the ungrammatical article 'them' and 'yoke', an Irish term for 'contraption' not to be found in most English dictionaries.

Passage 2:
'Howza goin' there?'
The man glared at him through slitted eyes. Other children might have been scared by the guard's snarling visage, but Benny Shaw had yet to meet an adult that could catch him.
'Howza goin?' repeated Benny gamely.
'English only,' grunted the guard.
'Huh?' 'English. I speak just English.'
'Yeah. I'm just after asking you how's the form?'

27 Colfer, *Benny and Omar*, p. 83.   28 Parkinson, *Four Kids*, p. 30.

The man enunciated carefully. 'Een-gel-ish only.'

Benny retreated, never suspecting that his strong Wexford accent could be the culprit. He gave the guard a scowl and journeyed on.[29]

'Howza goin''. The Tunisian response to this contraction and to Benny's accent in Eoin Colfer's *Benny and Omar* reveals how, contrary to what he may think, Benny's specific English may not be the global *lingua franca* he takes it for. His language usage importantly creates a sense of his cultural and local rootedness in the novel. As Celia Keenan writes: 'In *Benny and Omar* that local emphasis was essential to its universal theme because the reader could only understand Benny's deracination in Tunisia in light of the meaning of home for him.'[30]

Passage 3:
'I love the sound of that. I'm in the Creative department, actually. Except I'll have to work on pronouncing "I'm". You have to say it the way Sinéad O'Connor does. It has to sound like a cross between "Oi'm" and "Aahm", not easy.'[31]

Phonetics and the status of the specific Irish pronunciation of 'I'm' between Dublinese 'Oi'm' and the rock-star mid-Atlantic 'Aahm' are an issue when Cindy, the cynical step-sister in Siobhán Parkinson's *Sisters ... No Way!*, fantasizes about her future in advertising.

Passages such as these, which feature non-standard varieties of language, present a serious challenge to a translator. Three strategies or options used by such translators are identified by David Horton in his article on German translations of Roddy Doyle.[32] In the first, the translator neutralizes non-standard forms into standard modes. In the second strategy, he or she converts non-standard forms into a broadly comparable target language form such as when, in a German version of *The Adventures of Huckleberry Finn,* Nigger Jim speaks in broad Bavarian. While, in contrast to the first one, this strategy marks linguistic difference, the dangers of misrepresentation are obvious as no dialect form can have a historical and socio-cultural equivalent in another language.[33] In between these two extremes is the third, most frequently used strategy: the translator indicates a significant deviation from standard norms without attempting to suggest an identifiable language variety.[34]

29 Colfer, *Benny and Omar*, p. 26. 30 Keenan, 'Divisions' (2007), p. 200. 31 Ibid. 32 David Horton, 'Non-standard language in translation: Roddy goes to Germany', *German Life and Letters*, 51:3 (1998), 418. 33 This aspect is analyzed in Raphael Berthele, 'Translating African-American vernacular English into German: the problem of "Jim" in Mark Twain's *Huckleberry Finn*', *Journal of Sociolinguistics*, 4 (2000), 588-613. 34 A further strategy, not mentioned by Horton and discredited today but observable in older translations, was to produce an idiom characterized by deficit for dialect speakers such as Twain's Jim.

When a non-standard form or a variety is neutralized into a standard mode in translation, not only is a pragmatic dimension of the text violated, issues of linguistic and cultural domination and the manipulative power of translation are also at stake. The acclaimed translator Hans-Christian Oeser, winner of the Aristeion Prize for his German translation of Patrick McCabe's *The Butcher Boy*, writes:

> If the Irish use of English in literature originating from the island of Ireland is levelled in translation to the extent that, in its Other, Standard English and Irish English become indistinguishable, a recolonialization of the mind has taken place, if not by design, then by default … As Tejaswini Niranjana[35] has pointed out, translation is the site in which the unequal and asymmetrical power relations prevalent in language and language use are prone to be perpetuated. Thus, by submerging its intralingual differences, the postcolonial text is easily amalgamated into a target culture sharing a dominant position with that of the colonizing language overlying it.[36]

In translation of Irish children's books into German, this type of neutralization of Irish English into Standard English is by far the most common strategy. In their German guises, the Hiberno-English spoken by Benny Shaw is totally indistinguishable from the Standard English spoken by Harry Potter. How this is actually brought about in translation will be illustrated by returning to the three examples listed above. Passage 1, from Parkinson's *Four Kids…*, is translated as follows:

Passage 1 (German):
Also gut. Ich bin dabei … Ich trage diese Dinger für dich. Was auch immer das ist.[37]

[My retranslation: Ok, count me in. I'll carry these things for you. Whatever it is.]

35 Tejaswini Niranjana, *Siting Translation. History, post-structuralism, and the colonial context* (Berkeley: U. California P., 1992). 36 Hans-Christian Oeser, unpublished manuscript. Oeser goes on to reflect on the problem of rendering the specific variety in another language: 'But what is to be done? Many words and phrases have no equivalent in any other language that would truly reflect the semantic, cultural and psychological value they have within the system of the source language, Hiberno-English. Even if one were to come upon a word in German that would approximate that value, one would run the risk of rendering something specifically Irish merely quaint, since its underlying substratum is absent from the target language.' Oeser himself has reflected intelligently on the difficulties of rendering Hiberno-English into German and has used devices and strategies in his work to that end, including the attempt, when translating expressions and turns of phrases in English which have been taken from the Irish, to 're-gaelicize' them in order to achieve a linguistic distance between the standard variety and the phrase used. 37 Parkinson, *Die Geschichteninsel* (2000), p. 33.

The German of the translation is absolutely standard, the register informal. There is no intralingual difference between Kevin's idiom in this passage and that of the Dubliners in others, and none of them have any specific non-standard linguistic features in German. When, in the source text, Kevin exaggerates his accent to make fun of Beverley's poshness, placing himself in a position of feigned deference: 'Did ye bring a taypot? ... Or ... [m]aybe it's a samovar you like your tay made in, Madam',[38] the German text imitates the mock-respectful register successfully, and it declares in a meta-comment that Kevin exaggerated his local accent, but it doesn't actually *show* any linguistic difference.

> **Passage 2 (German):**
> 'Na, wie geht's?'
> Der Mann starrte ihn an. [...].
> 'Wie geht's?' wiederholte er mutig.
> 'Nur Englisch,' grunzte der Mann.
> 'Hä?'
> 'Englisch. Ich spreche nur englisch.'
> 'Ja. Ich versuche nur, Sie zu fragen, wie Sie heute drauf sind?'
> 'N-U-R ENG-LISCH,' sagte der Mann und betonte sorgfältig jede Silbe.
> Benny wich zurück. Es kam ihn nicht in den Sinn, dass sein ausgeprägter Wexford-Akzent schuld an dem Missverständnis sein könnte. Er warf dem Wachmann einen bösen Blick zu und trollte sich.[39]

> [My retranslation:
> 'Well, how are you?'
> The man stared at him [...]
> 'How are you?' he repeated bravely.
> 'English only', the man grunted.
> 'Huh?'
> 'English. I only speak English.'
> 'Yes. I'm only trying to ask you how's the form today.'
> 'ENG-LISH ON-LY,' said the man, carefully enunciating every syllable.
> Benny retreated. He didn't imagine that his strong Wexford accent could have caused the misunderstanding. He gave the guard a dirty look and went on his way.]

'Wie geht's', Benny's question in the first line of this passage from *Benny and Omar*, is standard informal German for 'How are you', so the whole point of the passage – the Tunisian's difficulty understanding Benny's 'Howza goin' there?' in the source text – is undermined. From the perspective of the German text

---

38 Parkinson, *Four Kids*, p. 37.   39 Colfer, *Benny und Omar*, p. 32.

there is no reason why there should be any comprehension difficulties. One general anomaly of translation is that many translated texts sustain the idea that the language being spoken in their fictional world is actually that of the source text and hence different from the one the reader is reading. If, in a Spanish source text, the Spanish language of the characters is mentioned, the mention is usually transported in translation; in a Russian or Greek target text the Russian or Greek speakers will still refer to their own language as Spanish. In Colfer's case we have characters who are speaking in German about the fact that it is English they are speaking. The narrator tells us that Benny is speaking English with a Wexford accent, but Benny's words which we read are in standard German. And just as the specific Irish or Wexford dimension of Benny's speech is lost, so also is the specific Arabic pronunciation of the word 'English' (there is an emphasis in the translation but no phonetic difference), thus seriously reducing the heteroglossia of a novel in which each individual character is defined by his or her distinct use of language.

This heteroglossia is even more pronounced in a scene between Benny and Samir Assad, the school director who had gone to college in Edinburgh and who speaks English with a Scottish accent. The following exchange involves intralingual translation[40] – within the English language:

> The director remembered who he was talking to. '*Ezzah!* Why am I talking to you? You're just a wee bairn.'
> 'Bairn?'
> 'Baby.'
> 'Arabic?'
> 'Scottish.'
> 'Oh.'[41]

The German translation capitulates entirely in the face of this metalinguistic passage and deletes everything between 'Why am I talking to you?' and 'Oh.'[42]

Passage 3 (German):
Das klingt doch ganz gut, oder? Ich bin im kreativen Bereich tätig. Allerdings muss ich noch daran arbeiten, dass ich das auch im richtigen Ton rüberbringe, so wie Sinéad O'Connor zum Beispiel. Das ist nicht so einfach.[43]

---

40 Roman Jakobson differentiates between three different ways of interpreting a verbal sign in translation, intralingual translation (within a language), interlingual translation (between languages) and intersemiotic translation (between verbal and nonverbal sign system). See Roman Jakobson 'Linguistic aspects of translation', in A. Brower (ed.), *On Translation* (Cambridge, MA: Harvard UP, 1959), pp 232–9.   41 Colfer, *Benny and Omar*, p. 143.   42 See Colfer, *Benny und Omar*, p. 175.   43 Parkinson, *Schwestern*, p. 14.

[My retranslation: 'That sounds good, doesn't it. I'm in the Creative
department. But I have to work on saying it in the right tone of voice, like
Sinéad O'Connor, for instance. It isn't that easy.']

Here the challenge of trying to translate Sinéad O'Connor's pronunciation of
'I'm' was apparently too much for the translator, and it is not clear from the
translation whether she didn't understand what was being said or whether she
felt she couldn't render it into German. The translation leaves out the specific
pronunciation of 'I'm'; instead Cindy wants to be able to say she works in the
Creative department in the same tone of voice that Sinéad O'Connor would use,
rather than her wanting to imitate a specific Irish vowel sound.

The three passages in German translation discussed here share a common
strategy: they eliminate linguistic difference. In them, everyone speaks exactly
the same language. Differences in the source texts between Standard English,
Hiberno-English and other forms are indistinguishable in the German versions;
everyone is speaking the German equivalent to Standard English; a linguistic
recolonialization has taken place. This is the dominant strategy in German translations of Irish children's literature.

MAKING LINGUISTIC DIFFERENCE EXPLICIT

A contrast to linguistic recolonialization can be found in the rare translations of
books which render linguistic difference palpable by making it explicit. This is a
feature of Roddy Doyle's *Giggler* books – *The Giggler Treatment*, *Rover Saves
Christmas* and *The Meanwhile Adventures* and their German translations. These
zany, scatological novels involving a Dublin dog, his family and their friends are
full of playful postmodern elements: narrative interruptions, asides, multiple
endings and such.[44] While the full range of expletives and the more extreme
non-standard syntax forms in his adult novels, particularly his uncompromising
use of urban, working-class Dublinese in the *Barrytown* trilogy, are not to be
found in Doyle's children's books, they do contain phonetic deviation and slang
expressions to mark the specifically Hiberno-English variety. They are produced
for the non-domestic market but, rather than exchanging the local for the global

---

44 A running gag in *Rover saves Christmas* involves chapters with competing commercial breaks
for toothpaste, ultimately evolving into a regular Battle of the Paste and even featuring in a intertextual pastiche of the end of James Joyce's story from *Dubliners*, 'The Dead': 'The sugar was
general all over Ireland. It was falling on every part of the dark central plain, on the treeless hills,
falling softly upon the Bog of Allan. It was falling, too, on the baldy heads of little Irish men and
women and on the mad cows that use new, improved Mintofresh.' Roddy Doyle, *Rover Saves
Christmas* (New York: Scholastic, 2001), p. 136. Doyle, *The Giggler Treatment* (New York:
Scholastic, 2000).

like the authors discussed by Celia Keenan above, they celebrate it and mediate it to a non-Irish and non-British readership through a series of intralingual translations, explanations and glossaries.[45]

The first of a series of humorous interlingual translations in a grey underlaid 'Warning' box turns up on the second page of the *The Giggler Treatment*; Mister Mack has just been introduced as a biscuit tester in a biscuit factory. It is performed as a mock dialogue between the narrator and the implied reader, a speaker of American-English.

WARNING!
You think you know what biscuits are. They are the things you put butter on, the breakfasty things you get with eggs. That's what you think they are. And you're right. But not if you live in Ireland, like I do. In Ireland, what you call 'cookies', we call 'biscuits'. Mister Mack is a biscuit tester, but if he lived where you live, it is cookies he'd be testing. This is very useful information. Think about it. You might be in Ireland some day, and you might run into a shop (that's a 'store') wanting to shout, 'Quick! Quick! My cookie is bleeding! Give me a Band-Aid!' But now that you're reading this book, you know that you should shout, 'Quick, Quick! My biscuit is bleeding! Give me a plaster!'[46]

The narrator goes on to tell the reader that any other words which may not be familiar are explained in the glossary at the back of the book. In the glossaries we find such Hibernicisms as 'me head',[47] 'babby', 'Paddy last' and 'yis'.[48] These various mock-serious explanations are not stage-Irish, there is no exoticism involved, the books are a self-confident, funny assertion of cultural difference in language that wants to make itself seen and heard.

As language itself is made thematic in the books, the German translator is challenged to find ways of representing linguistic difference for his implied German reader.[49] Andreas Steinhöfel[50] has to produce an intralingual translation

45 Two different editions of the *Giggler* novels were issued by Scholastic Press, one in New York and the other in London; the cultural mediation features in the American editions only, on which the German translations are based. None of the excerpts discussed here feature in the British editions. **46** Doyle, *Giggler*, p. 6. **47** 'ME HEAD – my head. We often say "me" instead of "my" in Ireland. Example: IRISH PERSON 1: What's that thing on top of your shoulders? IRISH PERSON 2: Me head!' Doyle, *Giggler* (2000), p. 110. **48** 'YIS – "you", if you are talking to more than one person. So, for example, if the Pope meets the President of the United States and his wife, he will probably say, "It's nice to meet yis."' Doyle, *Rover* (2001), p. 157. **49** See for an comprehensive account of the narrative communication in translations that includes such agents as the implied reader of the translation and the narrator of the translation, Emer O'Sullivan, 'Narratology meets translation studies, or, The voice of the translator in children's literature', *Meta*, 48:1–2 (2003), 197–207. **50** Andreas Steinhöfel, whose name is featured on the front cover of the German *Rover* editions, a real accolade for translators, is not only one of of interlingual translations into a target language in which the difference made thematic in the source text is rarely significant. There are no German equivalents for the differences between American and Irish English, so a story about the synonyms for plaster in German doesn't make interesting reading, and the biscuit/cookie contrast is simply laboured in translation. But there are passages in the translation when Steinhöfel comes into his own. We find a baby in the German text who is referred to as 'Bahbie', as if it were a proper name, phonetically similar to the Irish 'Babby' in the source text. He also tries to make something special out of the Hibernicism 'Eejit', a litmus test for all translators of Irish literature, most of whom resort to using the standard form 'Idiot'. In *Rover Saves Christmas* a further 'Warning!' box contains a humorous and convoluted account of how the teacher, Mr O'Malley, got the name 'Mister Eejit'.[51] In his translation Steinhöfel introduces a German neologism 'Iddie', as follows:

> ACHTUNG!
> Ihr fragt euch vermutlich was *Iddie* für ein Name sein soll. Ihr kennt viele irische Namen, Murphy und Kelly und Doyle und Jeltzin zum Beispiel, aber von einem Iddie habt ihr noch nie gehört. Doch bei uns in Irland benutzen wir das Wort *Iddie* praktisch andauernd. Es bedeutet *Idiot* oder *Trottel*. Also wurde Jimmys und Robbies Lehrer, wenn er anderswo lebte, *Mister Trottel* gerufen werden. Deshalb bleibt er in Irland, weil er dann doch den Namen *Iddie* vorzieht. Abgesehen davon ist er alles andere als ein Iddie.[52]

> [My retranslation: You are probably asking yourselves what kind of name *Iddie* is supposed to be. You know lots of Irish names like Murphy and Kelly and Doyle and Jeltzin for instance, but you've never heard of an *Iddie*. But here in Ireland we use the word *Iddie* more or less all the time. It means idiot or dimwit. So if Jimmy and Robbie's teacher lived somewhere else he would be called Mister Dimwit. That's why he stays in Ireland because he prefers the name *Iddie*. Apart from that he isn't really an Iddie.]

These metalinguistic commentaries, playfully integrated into the narrative text, can make difference in language visible, because they make it thematic and celebrate it. They direct the readers' awareness to the specific character of the language being used and, in the hands of a good translator, can give readers of a target text a sense of the difference between, say, Hiberno-English and Standard English or American.

This type of translation is not to everyone's taste. Many prefer what Lawrence

the most talented young contemporary German authors for children, he is also one of the best translators, with novels by Jerry Spinelli and Melvin Burgess to his credit. One of his first translations was Margit Cruickshank's *S.K.U.N.K.* in 1993.   **51** Doyle, *Rover Saves Christmas* (2001), p. 16.   **52** Doyle, *Rover Rettet Weihnachten* (2002), p. 14.

Venuti and other translation scholars refer to as a 'domesticating' translation,[53] one which is idiomatic and fluent, which conforms to the norms of target language usage and does not challenge the reader's expectations of how language is used. A 'foreignizing' translation, on the other hand, is more oriented towards the target text and language, and often subverts ideas of what fluent discourse is in an attempt to simulate for the reader the experience of reading a foreign text written in a foreign language. Foreignizing translations are generally scarce and hardly ever found in children's literature. Steinhöfel's translation reads in parts like a foreignizing one, but here it is more a case of Doyle's source text having demanded such a strategy than it is of the translator having chosen to foreignize it. One reviewer of the German translation of *The Meanwhile Adventures, Mister Macks Missgeschick*,[54] was not enthusiastic:

> Es hilft auch nicht wirklich, ständig mit Begriffen und Ausdrücken der irischen Alltagssprache – natürlich in Übersetzung – bombardiert zu werden, aber es macht die Geschichte ungemein interessant. Wer will, kann sie im angehängten Glossar nachschlagen, aber der Erzähler ist so freundlich, sie auch im Erzähltext zu erklären.[55]

> [My translation: It's not really a great help to be bombarded with terms and phrases from everyday English as it's spoken in Ireland – in translated form of course, but it makes the story really interesting. If you want to, you can look them up in the glossary, but the narrator is good enough to explain them in the narrative as well.]

The book obviously does not appeal to this particular reader who even attempts to parody Doyle in his review ('really interesting'), but that he can remark on the fact that he has read, in a German text, everyday English as it is spoken in Ireland, is a tribute to the joint metalinguistic gymnastics of Doyle and his translator Steinhöfel: they succeeded in making a German text unmistakably Irish.

53 See Lawrence Venuti, *The Translator's Invisibility. A history of translation* (London, New York: Routledge,1995). **54** Roddy Doyle, *The Meanwhile Adventures* (New York: Scholastic, 2004); Doyle, *Mister Macks Missgeschicke*, tr. Andreas Steinhöfel (Munich: Omnibus, 2005). **55** Micheal Matzer, review of Roddy Doyle, *Mister Macks Missgeschicke*, *Buchworm.Info Onlinemagazine*, 15.10.2005 http://www.buchwurm.info/book/anzeigen.php?id_book=1851 (accessed 20 Jan. 2007).

Padraic Colum, the *Horn Book*, and the Irish in American children's literature in the early twentieth century

AEDÍN CLEMENTS

America's first children's literature reviewing periodical, the *Horn Book Magazine,* has been published since 1924. A survey of its first thirty years of publication reveals that Padraic Colum (1881–1972) is the Irish writer most frequently mentioned, reviewed and quoted. Edited for many years by Massachusetts bookseller Bertha Mahony, the *Horn Book* promoted what it termed 'good books', and so ignores much popular fiction. That said, it offers valuable insight into the reception of Irish children's literature in America. This magazine was first published when Ireland was a newly independent country. Americans perceived Ireland up to that time mainly as a source of poverty-stricken immigrants, but many were now beginning to form ideas on what Irish culture was. Colum's influence in American children's literature was occurring at a time when Americans' views of Ireland were evolving from the relatively negative stereotypes of the nineteenth century to a more positive, if still romantic, view that developed in the early twentieth century. Padraic Colum certainly influenced the readers of children's literature, particularly in their appreciation of Ireland's storytelling culture. He also shaped Americans' expectations in Irish children's literature.

In nineteenth-century America, the Irish were popularly associated with a number of negative stereotypes, ranging from indolent, poor people to sly, politically corrupt operators. Even though some Irish immigrants rose to the top of their professions, for example Francis O'Neill (1848–1936), chief of the Chicago police, and John Boyle O'Reilly (1844–1890), editor of the *Boston Pilot,* there was strong prejudice against the Irish. This prejudice has been explained variously in terms of alarm at the sheer numbers of poor Irish, dislike of Catholicism, and the fear caused by violence among Irish immigrants.[1] Furthermore, in the 1800s, the Irish were one of the fastest-growing ethnic groups in America. In 1890 almost six million residents were born in Ireland or had Irish-born parents, a number exceeded only by German immigrants in that census.[2] Cities such as

1 Kevin Kenny, 'Race, violence, and anti-Irish sentiment in the nineteenth century', in J.J. Lee and Marion Casey (eds), *Making the Irish American: history and heritage of the Irish in the United States* (New York, 2006). 2 United States of America, *Report on Population of the United States at the Eleventh Census: 1890* (Washington, 1895), pp 607 and 684.

Chicago and New York were seeing increasing numbers of Irish move up the social and economic ladder.

Nevertheless, Irish characters are surprisingly scarce in American children's literature of the nineteenth and early twentieth centuries. Where they appear they are usually limited to a narrow range of minor roles. The Irish characters found in this 'Golden Age of Children's Literature' are mainly immigrants or Irish-Americans – there is little literature depicting Ireland and its inhabitants. At the same time, some Irish authors were popular in nineteenth century America; Maria Edgeworth's stories are praised in Lydia Maria Child's *Mother's Book* (1831), albeit with the caveat that 'they contain nothing opposed to religion, but there is an entire absence of its life-giving spirit'.[3] Frances Browne's *Granny's Wonderful Chair* (1857) was published a number of times in America; Captain Thomas Mayne Reid's many stories for boys were published and circulated in handsome volumes.[4] Compared to those authors, whose settings and characters have little of Ireland in them, Mary Anne Sadlier (1820–1903), an immigrant from Cavan who lived in Montreal and New York, wrote many stories for and about Irish Catholic immigrants, some for children, such as *Willy Burke; or, The Irish Orphan in America* (1850), which had the express purpose of encouraging young readers to hold on to the Catholic faith. Charles Fanning records that 7,000 copies of *Willy Burke* were sold within three weeks.[5]

Very few central characters in American children's books of the late nineteenth century are Irish, one of the few being Andy Burke who achieves the American Dream by goodness and hard work in Horatio Alger's *Only an Irish Boy: the story of Andy Burke's fortunes* (c.1894).[6] A survey of the *St Nicholas Magazine* from its inception in 1873 to the early twentieth century finds a tiny proportion of Irish characters. Where they occur they are usually limited to a narrow range of minor roles, frequently funny, simple and superstitious. A typical example, found in a serialized boys' story by Rossiter Johnson, has the family's cook, Biddy, provide drama and comedy when she assumes that a nailed-up garage door is bewitched. The tale also includes the 'Dublin boys' from the other side of town, as the rivals of the story's heroes.[7]

While American Irish were gradually gaining respect, children's literature confined the immigrant Irish to marginal roles and ignored the existence of the Irish in Ireland. Irish characters lived in America, not Ireland, and their Irishness was defined and indicated by such characteristics as colourful language and dialect, superstition, simplicity, and occasionally the ability to manage horses and

3 Lydia Maria Child, *The Mother's Book* (Boston, 1830), p. 100. 4 Rolf Loeber and Magda Loeber, *A Guide to Irish Fiction, 1650–1900* (Dublin: Four Courts, 2006), pp 1093–1107. 5 Charles Fanning, *The Irish Voice in America: 250 years of Irish fiction* (Lexington: UP of Kentucky, 2000), pp 118–20. 6 Loebers, *Guide*, p. 81. 7 Rossiter Johnson, 'Phaeton Rogers', *St Nicholas Magazine*, 8:5 (1881); also pub. separately: Rossiter Johnson, *Phaeton Rogers: a novel of boy life* (New York, 1881).

other animals. The minor roles held by Irish characters included maids, carriage drivers, and sometimes boys from the poorer end of town, but the protagonists were usually Americans of British descent. Even exceptions such as Sophie Swett's stories, which figure admirable Irish immigrant protagonists, use both animals and dialect to convey the comedy and simplicity of her characters. The use of 'eye dialect', words misspelled to suggest dialect and pronunciation far from standard English, serves more to place the fictitious character in an inferior category, where the reader can enjoy a sense of superior amusement, than to accurately convey the speech of the character. For instance Swett's Mrs Bridget O'Flanigan, a generous market woman, more a stage Irishwoman than a believable character, speaks in the following manner: 'Kape off, will yees, now, or the murtherin' baste will bit yees! Sure, an' has n't a dacint widdy woman a right to kape a goose if she plazes? – bad 'cess til the rashkil that sint him til me! But, sure, it's not long I'll be wrinin' the oogly neck av him, if ye kape off an' give me tha chance!'[8]

In the twentieth century, Ireland begins to appear in children's fiction as a country with its own geography, a rich culture of myth and folktale, and characters rather than stereotypes. The colourful language has changed in perception from the mark of an uneducated and simple people to the rich language of storytellers and poets. Seumas MacManus (1869–1960) told folktales and spoke of Irish storytelling in lecture tours and in storytelling events such as at New York Public Library.[9] His *Donegal Fairy Stories* (1900) is dedicated to the 'memory of those Gaelic shanachies who have kept alive … the fine ancient tales of our race, from age to age and from generation to generation.'[10] American author, Ruth Sawyer, told stories learned on her trips to Ireland to audiences in New York, and influenced many teachers and librarians with her enthusiasm for Irish folklore.[11] Padraic Colum, Ella Young, Anne Casserly, W.G. Dowsley, and Arthur Mason, wrote books for children that had been warmly reviewed or excerpted in the *Horn Book* by 1930.[12] Anne Casserly's fictitious animals have names such as Girry Lee, the Hare and Coppal Ru, the Red Horse, thus introducing the dimension of an Irish language.[13] These developments in children's literature coincide with Ireland's new image as a nation that had fought for independence, achieved prominence in the consciousness of Americans especially from 1916 on, and was making its mark with the literature of the Irish Revival.

8 Sophie Swett, 'A Queer Valentine', *St Nicholas Magazine*, 10:4 (1883), 243. 9 Among correspondence from Seumas MacManus in the Cavanaugh Files in the Archives of the University of Notre Dame are some fliers and descriptions of his lectures. 10 Seumas MacManus, *Donegal Fairy Stories* (New York: McClure, Phillips & Co., 1900). 11 Betsy Hearne, 'Ruth Sawyer: a woman's journey from folklore to children's literature', *The Lion and the Unicorn*, 24:2 (2000), 279-307. 12 *Horn Book*, Nov. 1924, Nov., 1926, May 1927, Nov. 1927, Nov. 1928, Nov. 1929. 13 'Fairy creatures of the wood', *Horn Book*, Nov. 1929, pp 44–8.

For educators, writers, reviewers and publishers of children's books in the 1920s, Padraic Colum was an ambassador for Ireland's Literary Revival. He arrived in the United States in 1914, at the age of 33, and lived there for most of his life, writing and teaching along with his wife, Mary. He had already established his reputation as an important writer of the Irish Revival. His play, *The Land* (1905), was one of the early successes of the new Abbey Theatre, and his poetry collection, *Wild Earth* (1907), caused a stir when it was published.[14] A few years ago, a poll of *Irish Times* and *Poetry Ireland* readers found that Colum's 'An Old Woman of the Roads' follows poems by Yeats, Kavanagh and Heaney in the top 14 of this 'favourite Irish poems of all time' list.[15] Another of Colum's poems listed in that poll, the haunting 'She Moved Through the Fair', has maintained its popularity over the generations. He continued to write plays and poetry all his life, in addition to fiction and biography.

His contribution to children's literature, which includes retellings of Homer and of Norse and Hawaiian myth and legend, ensured that he was seen, not primarily as an Irishman, but as a storyteller and writer. *The Children's Homer* (1918) and *The Children of Odin* (1921) are illustrated by Willy Pogány, adding substantially to the attractiveness and drama of the books. It was Willy Pogány who first suggested an Irish folklore book to Colum, and *The King of Ireland's Son* (1916), illustrated by Pogány and published by Holt, led immediately to an agreement with Macmillan where Colum was paid an annual allowance for writing children's books.[16] The Hawaiian stories, published initially in two volumes, *At the Gateways of Day* (1924) and *The Bright Islands* (1925), were written at the request of the Hawaiian legislature. According to biographer Zack Bowen, 'the recognition that was afforded his work by the request from the Hawaiian Legislature gave him new stature in the world of children's literature'.[17]

Colum's contribution to American children's literature includes educating his readers in an appreciation of storytelling, in the value of the many kinds of narratives found in folklore, and in aspects of Ireland and her culture new to American children. A survey of the essays, reviews and advertisements in the *Horn Book* over the course of Padraic Colum's career, along with a look at any other mention of Irish authors in that period, helps to clarify Colum's position in children's literature and as a representative of Ireland in the US.

The *Horn Book* sought to review the best books and those deemed worthy because of their literary and educational value. While there was an inherent idealism and a tendency to promote books reflecting values of liberal education

---

14 Gordon Henderson and Zack Bowen, 'Introduction', *A Journal of Irish Literature*, 2:1 (1973), 3. 15 '100 favourite Irish poems', Weekend Supplement, *Irish Times*, 31 Dec. 1999, p. 4. 16 Padraic Colum, 'Ninety years in retrospect: excerpts from an Interview with Zack Bowen', *A Journal of Irish Literature*, 2:1 (1973), 25–6. 17 Zack Bowen, *Padraic Colum: a bio-critical introduction* (1970), p. 135.

in the selection process, the reviews were widely read and the reviewed books found their way to school and library bookshelves. By the 1920s children's departments were already established in the libraries of many American cities; publishing houses, beginning with Macmillan in 1918, were establishing children's book departments, and the Newbery Medal, an annual award for a children's book, was first awarded in 1922. From this time on, Americans were increasingly aware of the Irish Literary Revival. Synge's plays appear in the lists of recommended books for older children in various issues of the *Horn Book*, allusions to Yeats abound ('the greatest of all living poets' is a description in the *Horn Book* of January 1934), and 'Carrowmore', a poem by Æ, is reprinted in the *Horn Book* of May, 1928.

The very first issue of the *Horn Book* includes a short review of Colum's *The Island of the Mighty, Being the Hero Stories of Celtic Britain Retold from the Mabinogion* (1924). At this point his published works include *The King of Ireland's Son* (1916), *The Boy Apprenticed to an Enchanter* (1920), and *The Boy Who Knew What the Birds Said* (1918).[18] These works are not mentioned, though. Rather, the reviewer credits *The Island of the Mighty* as 'Padraic Colum's fourth important contribution to the literature of childhood, the earlier three being: '*The Children's Homer – The Adventures of Odysseus and the Tale of Troy*', '*The Golden Fleece – The Heroes Who Came Before Achilles* [sic]'; and '*The Children of Odin*.'[19] Perhaps this selectivity is based on a critical reading of Colum's work, but it is also possible that it was not yet acceptable to discuss Irish storytelling in the same breath as the great classics.

This assessment is fairly consistent with the fame enjoyed by Padraic Colum's children's books in general. His Norse and Greek books remained standard reading through several generations, evidenced by the frequent re-issues in paperback, including Aladdin editions of 2004.[20] Colum's *The Golden Fleece* is one of sixty-three selected titles, for example, in Perry Nodelman's proposed canon of children's literature.[21] The very range of countries from which Colum's books are drawn, however, sends a message: rather than considering only certain cultures to have worthy literature, stories belong to all cultures; art and craft, magic and humanity, are to be found in the literature of every people. In his heroic stories, heroes are driven by pride, enthusiasm and need, all described so that the child reader can empathize. Jason, for example, in the 1922 Newbery

18 Padraic Colum, *The King of Ireland's Son* (New York: Macmillan, 1916); Padraic Colum, *The Boy Apprenticed to an Enchanter* (New York: Macmillan, 1920); Padraic Colum, *The Boy Who Knew What the Birds Said* (New York: Macmillan, 1918). 19 'The island of the mighty; being the hero stories of Celtic Britain retold from the Mabinogion' (review article), *Horn Book*, 1:1 (1924), 11. 20 Padraic Colum, *The Children of Odin: the Book of Northern Myths* (New York, Macmillan, 1920), re-issued by Aladdin in 2004, and *The Golden Fleece and the Heroes Who Lived Before Achilles* (New York: Macmillan, 1922), reissued also by Aladdin in 2004. 21 Nodelman's project is summarized in Anne Lundin, *Constructing the Canon* (New York, London: Routledge,

Honor book, *The Golden Fleece and the Heroes Who Lived Before Achilles*, begins his story being manipulated in a way that any child might understand: 'He looked down the hall and he saw faces all friendly to him; he felt as a king might feel, secure and triumphant.'[22] Although Colum uses language and syntax that convey some of the elevated and formal style of the original, his characters remain within reach of the readers. While bringing the more prestigious literatures of the world closer, Colum at the same time raised the status of Irish folklore by his presentation of collections of Irish folklore and literature organized within a framing story. The common theme of storytelling, the storyteller and the listener, draws all his books together. In the *Golden Fleece*, Orpheus, the minstrel, has an important role among the Argonauts. He is the storyteller who brings various stories into the frame of Colum's composition, telling stories at various times to various audiences. Orpheus' importance in this book is exemplary of Colum's style, in that the storyteller is both part of the story and integral to the story's framework.

The King of Ireland's Son (1916) is characterized by some of the elements of story that Colum later uses for literature of other cultures. That is, the stories are organized in a narrative that communicates a sense of the tradition from which they come, but with an overall form closer to that of the novel.[23] This novel-length book is framed by a wonder tale in which the king's son wins and loses Fedelma and must go on a quest to win her again. Having been sent on a quest for the unique story, his own story becomes intertwined with that of Flann, or Gilly of the Goatskin. A wide range of stories are interspersed, all related, which complement and add richness as the two wonder tales progress towards their resolution. While this book, and a 1918 book, *The Boy Who Knew What the Birds Said*, did not receive the critical acclaim of the Greek and Norse works, they clearly prepare readers for appreciating the role and importance of the storyteller, and for seeing narratives in a context rather than in isolation.[24]

Storytelling and its place in the community are central to a later book, *The Big Tree of Bunlahy* (1933), the only one of Colum's Irish stories to be a Newberry Honor book.[25] (This was a Newbery Honor book in 1934; the other books to be recognized thus were *The Golden Fleece and the Heroes Who Lived Before Achilles*, 1922, and *The Voyagers, Being Legends and Romances of Atlantic Discovery*, 1926.)[26] The publisher's advertisement for the *Big Tree* states the following: 'Tales of this famous story-teller's own countryside in Ireland, folk and fairy stories. Other important works: The Children's Homer, Children of Odin, The Children Who Followed the Piper.'[27]

2004). 22 Colum, *The Golden Fleece*, p. 19. 23 Colum, *The King of Ireland's Son*. 24 Colum, *The Boy Who Knew*. 25 Padraic Colum, *The Big Tree of Bunlahy* (New York: Macmillan, 1933). 26 A complete list of Newbery Medal and Newbery Honor books is on the American Library Association's website: http://www.ala.org/ala/mgrps/divs/alsc/awardsgrants/book media/newberymedal/newberyhonors/newberymedal.cfm. 27 [Macmillan publisher's

Again, it is notable that only Colum's earlier non-Irish writing is cited. However, this book is highly praised in a review article written by Bertha Mahony in 1934. Beginning her review with an appreciative discussion of Lord Dunsany's *The Curse of the Wise Woman*, Mahony continues with enthusiastic praise for *The Big Tree of Bunlahy*. In explaining which stories are 'Colum's own invention' and which are retold from 'Irish legend and folk lore by this master story-teller', Mahony identifies variant tellings, stating, for example 'how that King Iubdaun was ransomed from Fergus the King of Ireland has been told by Norreys O'Conor in the books "There was Magic in Those Days".' Mahony ends her review with the enthusiastic recommendation that the book should be read 'not once but many times' and the commendation that it is a 'beautifully made book with pen and ink drawings and one water color by Jack Yeats'.[28]

The Big Tree of Bunlahy was published in 1933. The narrator of the framing story, a young boy in the village of Bunlahy, frequently sits under the tree which is the daytime gathering place for passers-by, and where many stories are told. Bunlahy has a big house and a number of interesting characters who pique the curiosity of the reader but retain an air of mystery. Simon the Huntsman, the first storyteller, belonged to the big house, Baron's Hall. We are told that Baron's Hall is deserted; we are introduced to it and to its peacocks in the introductory chapter, but we learn the history of the peacocks much later in the book. The stories include local legends, wonder tales, Colum's animal stories, and stories from the Fiannaíocht and the King Cycles of Irish Tales. Part of the craft of this book is the context that knits the stories into a believable whole – the event or throwaway comment that prompts the cobbler to tell the story of a girl who needed shoes for her confirmation, or the found object that prompts the scholar to relate the story of the leprachauns.

As did Bertha Mahony's review, many reviews of Irish writings show appreciation for the art of the storyteller, and the storytelling tradition in Ireland during these early years of the *Horn Book*'s publication. Over its first few years, from 1924 to 1937, there are about forty-eight items, between reviews, short listings and advertisements, featuring the works of Irish writers (or those identified as Irish). Of these listings, ten items feature Colum's books. In addition there are essays by Colum himself, including one called 'Storytelling in Ireland'.[29] The idea of a particular style being associated with Irish writers is first mentioned in the Horn Book in an article that begins with an appreciation of W.G. Dowsley's *The Travelling Men* and continues with a review of Monica Shannon's *California Fairy Tales*. The article segues between the two by explaining that Monica Shannon's parents were Irish, and this accounts for the

advertisement], *Horn Book* (1934), 59.   28 Bertha E. Mahony, 'Tir-nan-Oge and Tir Tairngire', *Horn Book*, 10:1 (1934), 31–6.   29 Padraic Colum, 'Story-telling in Ireland', *Horn Book*, 10:3 (1934), 190–4.

fact that 'there's many a place in the book that reads with the same rhythm heard in "Travelling Men"'.[30]

The first real appreciation of Irish folklore and storytelling, however, comes in 1927, in two articles about Ella Young and her work. In 'Ella Young: How she came to know the Fairies', Jane Verne Terrill bemoans the outcome of education in Ireland:

> Little Irish children learned many modern things, but they forgot the Celtic language which their ancestors had guarded jealously in the face of foreign invasion. Not one of them would admit that he knew a ghost or had seen a *pookah* at his tricks. When their mothers and fathers repeated stories that were like an Irish Iliad, handed down from story-teller to story-teller, word for word for perhaps a thousand years, the children would laugh and call it superstition. So the remnant of ancient Celtic culture lay only with an ageing people, neglected by the young.[31]

Later in the same year, a review of *The Wonder Smith and His Son*, enthusiastic rather than critical, states: 'One who attempts to write of it must be forgiven for using direct phrases from it, for they echo through one's mind and it is impossible to disregard them, or forget them.'[32]

The next time the *Horn Book* discusses Irish storytelling it is in the context of Anne Casserley's (1881–1961) work, in particular her *Michael of Ireland*. The write-up in a list of 'outstanding books for fall 1927' states: 'These stories have the flavor of the old folk tales and should be read and re-read for their simplicity, spontaneity, and humor.'[33] Casserley's account of the home of her storytelling was written for the *Horn Book* in Glasnevin, Dublin. It is apparent in it that she, like Ruth Sawyer and Ella Young before her, finds her storytelling art not in her own family (her mother is described as reading or doing needlework) but among the families of other children her age, who live in mountain cottages. 'Here you sit round the blazing turf fire and listen to stories,' she writes, 'which you more than half disbelieve, of how every bunch of heather in the glen hides a fairy – Joe O'Donnell saw one with his own eyes – "a wee woman happed in a red cloak" – the speaker will vouch for the truth of it!'[34] Another instance in 1930 of the storytelling inherent in Irish life coming to the fore may be found in the work of Arthur Mason. Writing about the inspiration for his story, *The Wee Men* or *The Wee Men of Ballywooden*, he describes his mother's familiarity with 'wee men' and her delight in telling stories about them.[35]

30 'Adventures among new books', *Horn Book*, 2:4 (1926), 22–8.   31 Jane Verne Terrill, 'Ella Young: how she came to know the fairies', *Horn Book*, 3:2 (1927), 3–9.   32 Elinor Whitney, 'A draught from the Sacred Well', *Horn Book*, 3:2 (1927), 6.   33 'Twenty-five outstanding books for the fall and spring', *Horn Book*, 3:4 (1927), 9–10.   34 Anne Casserley, 'The home of 'Michael of Ireland', *Horn Book*, 3:4 (1927), 29.   35 Arthur Mason, 'The Wee Men', *Horn Book*, 6:4 (1930), 337–8.

Ella Young's books are highly praised, but rather than dwelling on her rich cultural heritage, this appreciation concentrates on the art she brings to her books. *The Unicorn with Silver Shoes* is, according to a 1932 review, 'a book so rarely imaginative that it reminds one of that height of creativeness – musical composition'.[36] A 1933 article claims that Ella Young is in close harmony with some bygone days: 'More truly than any one else who has rewritten Irish folklore, Ella Young has gone back in spirit and understanding to those ancient days when gods and heroes walked in windy, starlit spaces, when the white horses of Faeryland might trample outside a king's doorway, when the Hidden Folk rode out of the green raths and there was laughter in the heart of the hills.'[37]

The same article includes an assumption that Ireland alone has a culture in which the gods and heroes of ancient myth live on in ordinary life: 'Only in Ireland does the talk of the country people, with its "images of magnificence", echo the speech of the ancient gods and heroes. Characteristically Irish, too, is the sudden humorous turn, the contrast between high heroic deeds and more homely matters.'[38]

While Ella Young and Padraic Colum's interpretations of Irish folklore were setting the standard and moulding the American taste for Irish children's literature, other writers becoming popular in Ireland were not receiving the same critical acclaim. In a 1935 list of new books, for example, Patricia Lynch's *The Turfcutter's Donkey* is described as a 'rather long drawn out fanciful Irish tale which has charm but not the flavor of those of Padraic Colum, Ella Young, or Anne Casserly'.[39] Americans now had views on what a good Irish children's story should be like, and expectations regarding both charm and flavour.

In the early 1930s, Irish folklore was in high esteem among the reviewers of children's literature. Poems by W.B. Yeats are mentioned from time to time during these years, and Æ's poem, 'Carrowmore', is printed in one issue, and quoted elsewhere.[40] These writers lend scholarly and literary authority to such fantasy literature. We must remember that it is only a few short generations since Lydia Maria Child was writing for American parents about the dangers of fantasy and fairytale, and the wisdom of setting children reading the moral stories of Maria Edgeworth.[41] The late nineteenth century encouraged realist fiction, including some that was quite sentimental, and the turn to folklore and fantasy in the twentieth century has therefore to be defended, implicitly if not loudly, with a more recent understanding that the child's exposure to literature of the imagination helps to develop a well-rounded person.

A measure of the influence of Padraic Colum's storytelling is the respect given

36 'New books for the fall, 1932: picture books and stories with a foreign flavor', *Horn Book*, 8:4 (1932), 254.   37 Anne T. Eaton, 'Ella Young's unicorns and kyelins', *Horn Book*, 8:5 (1933), p. 116.   38 Ibid., 120.   39 'Books of the summer and early fall', *Horn Book* (1935), 295.   40 AE, 'Carrowmore, by AE, from his collected verse, the Macmillan Company', *Horn Book*, 4:2 (1928), 1.   41 Lydia Maria Child, *The Mother's Book*, pp 86–97.

to his essay, 'Story Telling, New and Old', initially published in the story collection, *The Fountain of Youth* (1927), twice reproduced in the *Horn Book*, and later published as a book (1961).[42] In addition to the *Horn Book*'s reviewers, a highly influential person in early twentieth-century children's literature was Anne Carroll Moore (1871–1961), head of the Children's Department of New York Public Library, and author of the 'Three Owls' literary review articles, published in the *New York Herald Tribune*. A compilation of reviews, *The Three Owls* (1931), includes three articles on Padraic Colum and his work, just one instance in the number of references to Colum's stories which occur in Anne Carroll Moore's writings.

As mentioned above, Colum had three books recognized as Newbery Honor books, making him the first Irish writer so honoured, and one of very few, up to this day. In 1922, the first year of the Newbery Medal (the first children's book award in the world), *The Golden Fleece* was one of the five honour books. His next, in 1926, was *The Voyagers*, and the next Irish honour book was Ella Young's *The Wonder Smith and His Son* in 1928. During these years, the award-winning and honour titles include a number of books that cast light on different cultures, suggesting that children's literature professionals were enthusiastic about broadening the horizons of American children through literature. A further mark of respect for Colum's work is the Regina Medal, the annual award of the Catholic Library Association, for 'continued, distinguished contribution to the field of children's literature.'[43] In 1961, Colum became the third recipient of this award.

While Padraic Colum's children's stories are unevenly received, they contribute greatly to the emerging understanding among twentieth-century educators of the role of stories and storytelling in our lives. His *Story Telling, New and Old* explains some of his own childhood relationship with stories, and describes the art of the storyteller, thus demonstrating what he and other storytellers are trying to convey when they commit Irish oral stories to the written page.[44] American perceptions of the Irish, and of Irish literature, had changed by the 1920s, and it is apparent from the reviewing literature that the regard for Irish literature was influenced by Colum's writing. It is by viewing the reviews, not only of Colum's work, but also of other Irish writers that we understand how Padraic Colum's storyteller's craft, applied to Greek, Welsh, Irish and other literatures, along with his other writing and his presence in the United States, elevated the Irish in American children's literature.

42 Colum, *Story Telling, New and Old* (New York: Macmillan, 1961).   43 http://www.cathla. org/awards.php.   44 Colum, *Story Telling, New and Old*.

Gulliver travels in the lands of childhood

MARY SHINE THOMPSON

INTRODUCTION

Gulliver's Travels plays a crucially important role in the history of children's books, especially in Ireland, where a history of Irish childhood has yet to be written. What we know of childhood's history therefore remains incomplete, contested, coloured by preconception and conventional thinking. So the life of a book that has remained a firm favourite of young readers since the early eighteenth century deserves serious consideration in any assessment of the evolution of attitudes to children. The problem of the decentering of children goes deeper than literary and nationalist canon makers forgetting or merely excluding children's writers of the stature of, say, Eilís Dillon or Patricia Lynch, as happened in *The Field Day Anthology of Irish Writing*.[1] For example, Flann O'Brien's fertile mind conjured the character of Orlick Trellis, son of Dermot Trellis, in his novel, *At Swim-Two-Birds* (1939), as a fully grown, wholly developed adult, thus dispensing entirely with the need to take account of childhood in his plot. With one literary and metonymic device, O'Brien excised childhood; Laurence Sterne's *Tristram Shandy* (1759–67) adopts another to the same end. The novel begins with the moment of conception of its protagonist, but we reach volume four before he is even born. Its hilarity is met in equal measure by its parody and satire, and by repeated images of disconnection and human isolation. Resistance to and absence of childhood is as much a feature of Irish literature as is its manipulation.

Parallel to the partial erasure and amnesia are Ireland's adoption and adaptation of constructions of childhood primarily from its imperial neighbour, along with a British juvenile literary canon. That canon began to take its recognizable shape in the last half of the eighteenth century, when ideas of childhood primarily derived from John Locke and Jean-Jacques Rousseau. 'Children's fiction,' Jacqueline Rose writes, 'has never completely severed its links with a philosophy which sets up the child as a pure point of origin in relation to language, sexuality, and the state'.[2] There is considerable evidence to support Rose's claim in the Irish historical context. Much of the actual historical detail that might have contradicted her assertion that the generic [Irish] child and

---

1 Seamus Deane (gen. ed.), *The Field Day Anthology of Irish Writing* (Derry: Field Day, 1991).
2 Jacqueline Rose, *The Case of Peter Pan; or, the impossibility of children's fiction* (Basingstoke: Macmillan, 1994), p. 8.

childhood embody linguistic, sexual and sovereign origins has been erased or silenced, but piecemeal revelations of recent decades on hidden childhoods hint at a complex, often distressingly cruel, tale.

However, her assertion that children's literature has always assumed the world is 'knowable in a direct and unmediated way' is debatable,[3] especially if weighed against certain texts written *before* Romantic notions of childhood took hold, and especially texts that circulated in an early modern (early eighteenth-century) Ireland riven with violence, poverty, political upheaval and linguistic change. *Gulliver's Travels* is such a text: read by adults, it is a satirical allegory that recounts Jonathan Swift's experience of politics in Queen Anne's England. It interrogates Enlightenment logic through its main protagonist, a man who rejects humanity because it fails to live up to its ideal of reason. Its narrative veers from low scatological farce to the near-tragic psychological breakdown of what Clive Probyn calls a 'representative Englishman'.[4] Yet versions of *Gulliver's Travels* enjoy both the status of a classic and of a living book, in that it is repeatedly re-edited for scholars and rewritten for children, and has entered the international public imagination: in 1988, for example, a 25-metre Gulliver was 'washed up' on a Dublin beach to mark the city's millennial celebrations. Romanian and Czech puppet theatres adapted the tale as a vehicle for indoctrinating the young in Communist ideology.[5] In Germany *Gulliver* has been so integrated into the domain of childhood that 1999 saw the publication of *Gulliver's Travels into the Country of Orthodontic Braces: an adventure story for children and parents in search of successful orthodontic treatment*! Sabine Baltes does not exaggerate when she claims that *Gulliver's Travels* is recognized as one of the most popular books of all time.[6] Indeed, many scholars see the need to rescue it from the realm of childhood. In 1988, for example, Spanish critic Inaki Mendoza has lamented the fact that the book's status within the literary canon is reduced by virtue of its having been adapted as a children's book.[7] Yet Swift, and *Gulliver* in particular, notwithstanding – or because of – their unstable complex tone, their satire, irony, and passion, both offer some insight into how childhood has been perceived.

As this essay will show, evidence suggests that immediately *Gulliver's Travels,* the sophisticated but swingeing political satire – on Tories and Whigs, on the state of Ireland, on misanthropy – was published in 1726, it found its way into the hands of children, and has never left them. It will also demonstrate that

---

3 Ibid., p. 9.   4 Clive Probyn, 'Swift, Jonathan (1667–1745)', *Oxford Dictionary of National Biography* (Oxford UP, 2004), http://www.oxforddnb.com/view/article/26833, accessed 22 Oct. 2008. In this essay, *Gulliver* (italicized) is an abbreviation of the title of Swift's book. 'Gulliver' in roman type refers to the character.   5 Hermann J. Real (ed.), *The Reception of Jonathan Swift in Europe* (London, New York: Thoemmes, 2005), pp 266–7.   6 Sabine Baltes, 'Swiftian Material Culture', in Real (ed.), *Reception of Swift in Europe*, p. 275; Real also comments in his 'Introduction' that *Gulliver's Travels* is one of the most popular children's books of all time, p. 1.
7 Ibid., p. 67.

generations of earnest bourgeois parents directed their children to a book suffused with 'an excremental vision', and yet saw it as a suitable vehicle of instruction. What are the implications of the modes of transmission of *Gulliver* to children? The editing, rewriting, abridging, illustration? The acts of canonization? Its absorption into curricula? The complex textual status and the complex reception history of Swift and *Gulliver* challenge Rose's claim that the world they relate to is 'knowable in a direct and unmediated way'.

From its earliest days, commentators on *Gulliver* remarked on the fact that it drew to it a diverse audience, that it was seen as belonging to the realist/fantasy/travel genres, that its style was marked by the accretion of minute detail and the mediation of an apparently (and appearances prove to be misleading) reliable first-person narrator, well educated, middle-class, added to its plausibility. That it was full of topical and political allusion added to its zest; that the travel genre had been popularized by Daniel Defoe's *Robinson Crusoe* published in 1719, a mere seven years earlier, gave it the aura of the exotic-familiar. Its linguistic instability and its parody added to its playfulness.

THE EARLY DAYS

Gulliver was scarcely published in November 1726 when poet and dramatist John Gay (1685–1732) announced: 'About ten days ago a Book was publish'd here of the Travels of one Gulliver, which hath been the conversation of the whole town ever since … From the highest to the lowest, it is universally read, from the Cabinet-Council to the Nursery … It has pass'd Lords and Commons, *nemine contradicente:* and the whole town, men, women, and children are quite full of it.'[8] Already in its first days in public circulation, therefore, its attractions for children are apparent. Swift's friend and fellow member of the Scriblerus Club, the polymath John Arbuthnot (1667–1735), wrote to Swift also that November to say that it had reached the children of the highest echelons of society. He found both the Princess and her little daughter: 'Reading *Gulliver* … *Gulliver* is in every body's Hands.'[9] Whether or not Arbuthnot's claim is literally true is less important than the indication the comment gives of the enthusiastic reception of the book among the young.

A half-century later, Dr Johnson was able to look back and say that 'it was read by high and low, the learned and illiterate'.[10] Almost immediately, then, it was

8 Extract from a letter from John Gay to Swift, 16 Nov. 1726, in 'The reception of *Gulliver's Travels*', Kathleen Williams (ed.), *Swift: the critical heritage* (London: Routledge & Kegan Paul 1970), p. 62.   9 Extract from a letter from John Arbuthnot to Swift, 5 Nov. 1726, 'The reception of *Gulliver's Travels*', in Williams, p. 61. The ironic tone of much of the correspondence between Artbuthnot and Swift should caution us against taking the message too literally but the point here, that it finds its way into children's hands, is clear.   10 Samuel Johnson, *The Lives of the*

clear that the first two books of the four that comprise the novel were most attractive to a young readership (the tales of Lilliput and Brobdingnag), and abridged versions may have appeared as early as 1740. The earliest Gulliver chapbook I have traced is in the Bodleian Library. Somewhere between 1740 and 1790 a 12° (duodecimo) adapted, abridged chapbook version with woodcuts is published whose title shows it pitched at the young: *The Travels and Adventures of Capt. Lemuel Gulliver: Shewing how he was cast upon an unknown land, where the inhabitants wer but six inches high, the customs of the country, court, king, &c. and the author's exploits, and surprizing return.*[11] The British Library holds one chapbook *Gulliver* dated 1750[?], and another dated 1809.[12] However, Zohar Shavit claims that chapbook editions of *Gulliver* were in print much earlier.[13] Illustration became a central feature of the book from the earliest editions, making it more attractive to a younger audience. A second edition of *Gulliver* published in Dublin in 1727 contains 'cuts and maps of the author's travels', and an illustration of the projectors' language-crunching machine.[14] However, it is clear that Swift did not foresee that his audience would include the young. Benjamin Motte, the publisher, discussed an illustrated edition with Swift, but their correspondence reveals that their agenda was misanthropic, misogynistic and scatalogical, and related more to the fourth book (the one least edited for children), than to any other:

> The Country of Horses, I think, would furnish many [occasions for illustration]. Gulliver brought to be compared with the Yahoos; the family at dinner and he waiting; the grand council of horses, assembled, sitting, one of them standing with a hoof extended, as if he were speaking; the she-Yahoo embracing Gulliver in the river, who turns away his head in disgust; the Yahoos got into a tree, to infest him under it; the Yahoos drawing carriages, and driven by a horse with a whip on his hoof. I can think of no more, but Mr Gay will advise you.[15]

Poets, 2 vols (London: Everyman, 1925, 1st pub. 1779–81), vol. 2, p. 261, in Williams, p. 202. 11 The British Library Integrated Catalogue further reads 'London, 1740–1790 An abridgement and adaptation of the work by J. Swift. Woodcuts on the title page and in text.' 12 Jonathan Swift, *The Travels and Adventures of Capt. L. G. Abridged from the work of Swift. A chapbook* (London, 1750?) 12°, listed on the British Library Integrated Catalogue, Humanities; T.1854.(2.); *The Adventures of Captain Gulliver, in a Voyage to the Lilliputian Country, etc. A chapbook*, p. 16 (Lancaster: C. Clark, 1809). 12° British Library Integrated Catalogue, Humanities; 12331.de. 5.(4.). 13 Zohar Shavit, *Poetics of Children's Literature* (Athens and London: Uni. Georgia P., 1986), p. 115. 14 Jonathan Swift, *Travels into Several Remote Nations of the Earth … with cuts and maps of the author's travels* (Dublin: printed by S. P. for G. Risk, G. Ewing, and W. Smith, 1727). 15 Quoted in John F. Ross, 'The final comedy of Lemuel Gulliver', in Richard Gravil (ed.), *Swift: Gulliver's Travels: a casebook* (Basingstoke: Macmillan, 1974), p. 113.

Nonetheless, editions of the book were now being prepared for child readers. By 1776, Francis Newbery was selling a lavish, 128-page version of the story adorned with cuts,[16] and a well-regarded children's publisher, Benjamin Tabart, mentions chapbook editions from about 1804. Among other early editions for children is one by Falkirk, who publishes an abridged chapbook edition, *The Adventures of Captain Gulliver, in a Voyage to the Lilliputian Country*, in 1808. The title of C. Clark's 1809 chapbook with a woodcut suggests that it is designed to appeal to the young: *The Adventures of Captain Gulliver, in a Voyage to the Lilliputian country: where the inhabitants are only about six inches high*. In Glasgow *The Adventures of Captain Gulliver in a Voyage to Lilliput* was published by Lumsden in a high-quality edition characterized by the multi-coloured type and reversible heads with engraving that have been attributed to Thomas Bewick.[17] By the turn of the nineteenth century, then, numerous children's editions of the book are already in circulation.

LIBRARIES

Matthew Grenby has examined the catalogues of over fifty circulating libraries from this period to establish to what degree they catered for children, and found versions of *Gulliver's Travels* in over half of them, in addition to fairy tales. *Gulliver's Travels* is a crossover book, a book whose appeal is as strong to adults as to children. While crossover texts appear relatively frequently, children's books *per se* constitute only a negligible number of the books recorded in the catalogues.[18] Lowndes' Circulating Library, for example, which was catalogued in about 1766, contained a copy of *Gulliver's Travels* for children, as did Hookham's Bond Street Circulating Library, catalogued in 1820. Grenby is at pains not to overstate the role of libraries in the provision of children's reading matter, but he does note that *Gulliver* is well represented. In the catalogue of Brighton Circulating Library of 1817[19] is listed *Gulliver Revived; or, The Vice of Lying Properly Exposed by Baron Munchausen*. Grenby calls it, 'a frivolous fusion of Swift and Rudolf Erich Raspe'.[20]

16 Jonathan Swift, *The Adventures of Captain Gulliver, in a Voyage to the Islands of Lilliput and Brobdingnag. Abridged from the works of … Dean Swift. Adorned with cuts.* (London: Newbery, 1776). 17 Jonathan Swift, *The Adventures of Captain Gulliver in a Voyage to Lilliput* (Glasgow: Lumsden, 1815) The Hockliffe Project, http://www.cts.dmu.ac.uk/AnaServer?hockliffe+7811+ hoccview.anv (22 October 2008) 18 Matthew Grenby notes that: 'Of more than fifty catalogues of separate circulating libraries, dating from 1748 to 1848, that were consulted, only a very few include more than a handful of children's books. As a rule, the catalogues contain less than one percent children's literature', in 'Adults Only? Children and children's books in British circu- lating libraries, 1748–1848', *Book History*, 5 (2002), 19–38, at p. 19. 19 *Catalogue of Donaldson's Extensive and Increasing Circulating Library, on the Steyne, Brighton* (London: C. H. Reynell, n.d. [1817?]), cited in Grenby, 'Adults only?', p. 35. 20 Ibid., p. 20. 21 Jonathan Swift, *Travels*

GULLIVERIANA

By the mid-eighteenth century, the lands of Gulliver were firmly associated with the young, and gave rise to a child-centred Gulliveriana industry. By 1751 or 1752, Newbery, the first bookseller to take the publishing of juvenile books seriously, has launched *The Lilliputian Magazine; or, The Young Gentleman and Lady's Golden Library*. Although it may only have run for two or three issues, at most for a year, it was published in several editions. Despite its limited run, what it suggests is that Lilliput is now firmly fixed in the imagination as a domain of childhood. Another publisher, David Willison, publishes a two-volume edition in Edinburgh in 1770.²¹ In 1779–80, 'Lilliputius Gulliver' (a pseudonym for Richard Johnson [1734–93]) edited into ten volumes (published in two volumes, at 5s.) *The Lilliputian Library; or Gulliver's Museum: Containing, lectures on morality, historical pieces, interesting fables, diverting tales, miraculous voyages, surprising adventures, remarkable lives, poetical pieces, comical jokes, useful letters. The whole forming a complete system of juvenile knowledge, for the amusement and improvement of all little masters and misses, whether in summer or winter, morning, noon, or evening*. Lilliputius Gulliver claimed to be a 'citizen of Utopia, and knight of the most noble order of human prudence'.²² The volumes are organized as follows, to contain the elements of an earnest yet attractive literary education for the young: Gulliver's lectures; A curious collection of voyages; Fables of the wise Aesop; Gulliver's tales: containing The renowned history of the white cat; The Lilliputian letter-writer; The poetical flower-basket; The merry companion; The Lilliputian biographer; The entertaining medley; and Lilliputian fragments.

Despite *Gulliver*'s popularity, not everyone was persuaded of its appropriateness for the young. By the early eighteenth century, puritan sentiment had turned against fiction. This is evident in that *Gulliver* finds its way into cautionary tales, among them W.F. Sullivan's *The Young Liar!!! A tale of truth and caution; for the benefit of the rising generation* (1817).²³ The book's hero, Wilfred Storey, turns out to be a liar because his nursemaid, Nurse Fibwell, inculcates untruths into him in the form of fairy stories. The case is not helped because Wilfred's 'children's library' included not only the 'Fairy Tales of the Countess D'Anois [D'Aulnoy], Persian Tales, Valentine and Orson, Arabian

---

into Several Remote Regions of the World. By Lemuel Gulliver etc. Abridged. (Edinburgh: printed by David Willison, 1770).   **22** Richard Johnson, *aka* Lilliputius Gulliver, *The Lilliputian Library; or Gulliver's Museum: Containing, lectures on morality, historical pieces, interesting fables, diverting tales, miraculous voyages, surprising adventures, remarkable lives, poetical pieces, comical jokes, useful letters. The whole forming a complete system of juvenile knowledge, for the amusement and improvement of all little masters and misses, whether in summer or winter, morning, noon, or evening* (London: printed for W. Domville, under the Royal Exchange, and Byfield and Hawkesworth, Charing Cross, 1779–80).   **23** London: Dean and Munday, 1817.

Nights', but also *Gulliver's Travels* and Daniel Defoe's *Robinson Crusoe*. The narrator observes that 'all, save perhaps the latter, were "either too frivolous, improper, or incomprehensible, for children".'[24]

CRITICS

Many critics acknowledge children as readers of *Gulliver*, and in the process, they betray their assumptions and prejudices about childhood, thereby highlighting some contemporary concepts of childhood. James Beattie (1735–1803), a professor of moral philosophy, recognized that *Gulliver* was a crossover text in 1783:

> *Gulliver's Travels* are a sort of allegory: but rather Satirical and Political, than Moral. The work is in everybody's hands ... Gulliver has something in him to hit everybody's takes. The statesman and, the philosopher, and the critick, will admire his keeness of satire, energy of description, and vivacity of language: the vulgar, and even children, who cannot enter these refinements, will find their account in the story, and be highly amused by it.[25]

Beattie's comments are a measure of the dismissive attitude to children's capacity as meaning makers, and he was not alone in this. Others are less disapproving of the crossover phenomenon, among them William Hazlitt (1778–1839), who notes that Swift: 'enlarges or diminishes the scale ... in a manner that comes equally home to the understanding of the man and the child, [that] does not take away from the merit of the work or the genius of the author.'[26] In contrast, Henry Craik writing in 1882, during the glory days of children's writing, can note the parts of the book most attractive to children without any disparaging overtones: 'If it is the voyages to Lilliput and to Brobdingnag, in which no thought of the satire they contain mingles with the interest of the story, that have proved most attractive to children, it is the voyage to the Houyhnhmnms which is likely to excite most interest amongst men.'[27]

---

24 M.O. Grenby, 'Tame fairies make good teachers: the popularity of early British fairy tales', *The Lion and the Unicorn*, 30:1 (2006), 1–24, pp 6, 19. 25 James Beattie, 'On fable and romance', *Dissertations Moral and Critical* (1873), pp 514–18, in Williams, p. 196. 26 William Hazlitt, *Lectures on the English Poets*, pp 217–24, in Williams, p. 328. 27 Henry Craik (ed.), *Jonathan Swift: selections from his works*, 2 vols (Oxford: Clarendon Press, 1892–3), vol. 2, p. 125.

GULLIVER: A FAIRY TALE?

The early reception of *Gulliver* in many cases categorizes it as fairy tale as well as satire. Jonathan Smedley (1689–1729), dean of Clogher and pro-Whig arch-enemy of Swift, denigrates the seriousness of Swift's book with a sustained attack on its childish and fantastical content, its capacity to corrupt young children, and by implication its author's dissolute character:

> For persons who do not appear to be perfectly stupid, To be led away by Tom Thumbs in a Thimble and a Fairy Giant in a Cowslip Cup, which the dean has invented for their Entertainment, without Humour and Allegory, is the most monstrous things that ever happen'd in the bookish World ... It is no jesting thing to see Boys and Girls lose their play-time to divert themselves with the pious Divine's Lilliputians, Brobdingnagians Houyhnhnms &c, and fill their heads with an old Man's Dreams. A thought he doubtless took from the School-Boys spelling the Word *Drunk, double dd double rr* &c. If one considers the Matter ever so little, will it not appear, I do not say Idle only, but Wicked, for a Man whose Vocation it is to preach the Holy Gospel, to spend so much Time purely to tempt Youth to mispend it? ... This pious Author seems to have taken his Hint, if not from the celebrated history of Tom Thumb, from the Author who a few Years ago obliged the World with the Travels of *Robinson Crusoe*. I would ask the Dean's greatest Admirers, whether they believe that the Boys and Girls, or the more elderly sort of People in the *Bookish* World, who judge like Boys and Girls, were ever taken with any Thing in the Doctor's Fables, but the Impertinence, or ever had the least sense of any M*oral* in his Fable?[28]

Deane Swift (1707–83), cousin of the writer, is moved to respond to this tirade by stressing the morality of his cousin Swift's stance. His strategy is to exhort people to teach Swift's values to their children, thereby suggesting that they are impeachable: 'Inscribe; engrave [the political principles of Dr SWIFT] on the tablet of your hearts; teach them unto your children's children.'[29] John Aiken (1747–1822), a critic who found Swift's poetry 'perplexing', finds the tale works at two levels, in that it is 'wonderfully amusing, even to childish readers, whilst the keen satire with which it abounds may gratify the most splenetic misanthropist'.[30] It is notable that Aiken does not admit to any conflict between these two readerships, adult and young.

However, there were also those whose objections went beyond scoring points,

28 Jonathan Smedley, *Gulliveriana: or, a Fourth Volume of Miscellanies. Being a sequel of the three volumes, published by Pope and Swift*, 1728, in Williams, pp 90–1. **29** Deane Swift, *Essay upon the Life, Writings and Character of Dr. Jonathan Swift* (London, 1755). **30** John Aiken, *Letters to a Young Lady on a Course of English Poetry* (1804), pp 62–76, in Williams, p. 271.

who saw the genre of fairytale itself, as well as its main body of readers (that is, children), as insignificant, and believed the book devalued by the elements familiar from fairy tales. Voltaire (1694–1778), who read an early French version of the book and was much taken with it (it was translated first in 1727 by the Abbé Desfontaines), nonetheless complained that 'That continued series of new fangles, folies of fairytales, of wild inventions pall at last upon our taste.'[31] Not all readers, however, disapproved of its readability. One unnamed critic inserts it into a diverse field of good yarns: 'If our Judgement of Books was to be determin'd by their Success, *Gulliver's Travels* is certainly the best Piece that ever was written, except *Pilgrim's Progress*, and *Seven Champions* [*of Christendom*], *Jack the Giant-Killer* and a few more.'[32] Generally, however, commentators who wanted to dismiss *Gulliver* or Swift found a handy weapon in their links to common and child-friendly narrative forms. Translator Abbé Desfontaines, on the other hand, distinguishes the *Travels* from fairy tales, of which he disapproves, because Gulliver's tales have an inherent moral: 'The [voyages] are not fairy tales, which commonly contain no moral conclusions and which in that case are good only to amuse children: indeed we ought to prevent even children from reading them for fear of familiarizing their minds with frivolous things', he writes.[33]

Desfontaines' point about *Gulliver* is well taken. It seems that commentators have not distinguished between folktale and fairy, which is more literary. Whether the *Gulliver* narrative – or narratives – can be termed fairy tale at all is indeed highly debatable. Jack Zipes' 'authoritative'[34] *The Oxford Companion to Fairy Tales*[35] does not include mention of Swift or *Gulliver*. During the eighteenth century, at around the time of *Gulliver*'s publication, fairy tales began to gain a solid foothold in English culture, and, equally, to be resisted, especially by Puritans, who saw them as vehicles for ignorant superstitions and devoid of moral content. *Gulliver* is inserted into this conflicted literary site. According to

31 Voltaire, letter to M. Theiriot (March 1727), *Oeuvres Completes*, 52 vols (1880), vol. 33, p. 167, in Williams p. 74. 32 Unidentified author, quoted in Kathleen Williams, 'Introduction', in Williams, p. 9; *The Seven Champions'* full title includes mention of giants: 'The heroicall aduentures of the knight of the sea : comprised in the most famous and renowned historie of the illustrious & excellently accomplished Prince Oceander, grand-sonne to the mightie and magnanimous Claranax, Emperour of Constantinople, and the Empresse Basilia; and sonne vnto the incomparable Olbiocles Prince of Grecia, by the beautious Princesse Almidiana, daughter vnto the puissant King Rubaldo of Hungaria. Wherin is described … his owne losse, strange preseruing, education, and fostering (by Kanyra Q. of Carthage) his knighthood, admirable exploytes, and vnmatchable atchieuementes, graced with the most glorious conquestes ouer knights, gyants, monsters, enchauntments, realmes, and dominions; with his … combating, affecting, and pursuites in his loue towards the rarely embellished princesse and lady-knight Phianora, daughter vnto the inuinicible Argamont King of England. 1600.' 33 Abbé Desfontaines, 'Preface du Traducteur', *Voyage de Gulliver* (1727), vol. 1, pp v–xxviii, in Williams, p. 82. 34 The term is Iona Opie's, on the book's cover. 35 Jack Zipes (gen. ed.), *The Oxford Companion to Fairy Tales* (New York and Oxford: OUP, 2000).

Sarah Trimmer (1741–1814), *Cinderella* and other such tales 'were in fashion' back in the mid-eighteenth century, and, writing at the turn of the nineteenth century, she admitted to enjoying them in her own childhood. Looking back on them as an adult, however, she opposes them. 'A moment's consideration will surely be sufficient', she writes, 'to convince people of the impropriety of putting such books as these into the hands of little children.'[36] Andrew Becket notes in 1788 that 'it is with much satisfaction ... that we find [fairy tales] gradually giving way to publications of a far more interesting kind, in which instruction and entertainment are judiciously blended, without the intermixture of the marvellous, the absurd, and things totally out of nature.'[37]

Benjamin Tabart, the innovating bookseller, published *Gulliver*, now associated in the public's mind with the fairy-tale genre, as one of his 174 children's books - fairy tales, bibles and poetry books - between 1801 and 1818. Tabart's publications usually consisted of about thirty-four printed pages and three copper-plate engravings, and cost sixpence. It is perhaps an indication of *Gulliver*'s popularity and high standing that it exceptionally ran to four volumes (*The Voyages of Sinbad the Sailor*, also an exception, ran to two).[38] Maria Edgeworth and other instructionalists opposed adventure stories such as *Robinson Crusoe* and *Gulliver's Travels*. Edgeworth warned that: 'the taste for adventure is absolutely incompatible with the sober perseverance necessary to success' and that these books would only be useful to boys intending to take up seafaring or an army career.[39]

Andrew Lang's inclusion of *Gulliver* (May Kendall's version) in the *Blue Fairy Book* in 1889 was controversial. Bjorn Sundmark writes that it 'has puzzled critics. It drew Tolkien's ire (it belongs to "the class of traveller's tales" and "it has no business in this place"), while Lancelyn Green called it "inexplicable" and "alien to anything in any of the fairy books" (81) while Eleanor de Selms calls it an "aberration" (138).'[40] Nonetheless, there is a surface comparison between the Lilliputians and the Brobdingnagians and Tom Thumb or Jack the Giant-Killer:

36 *Guardian of Education*, quoted in Marjorie Moon, *Benjamin Tabart's Juvenile Library: a bibliography of books for children published, written, edited and sold by Mr Tabart, 1801–1820* (Winchester: St Paul's Bibliographies, 1990), p. 6. 37 Quotation attributed to Becket by Benjamin Christie Nangle, *The Monthly Review. First Series. 1749–1789. Indexes of contributors and articles* (Oxford: Clarendon, 1934), p. 253. Quoted in Grenby, 'Tame fairies make good teacher's, 3. 38 See details in Moon, *Benjamin Tabart's Juvenile Library*. 39 Maria Edgeworth, *Practical Education* (London: J. Johnson: 1798), vol. i, p. 336. Sharon Murphy discusses this point both in relation to *Practical Education* and to Edgeworth's *Essays on Professional Education*, in *Maria Edgeworth and Romance* (Dublin: Four Courts, 2004), pp 32–3, 73–4 (and passim). 40 Eleanor de Selms Langstaff, *Andrew Lang* (Boston: Twayne, 1978), p. 138; J.R.R. Tolkien, 'On fairy-stories' *Tree and Leaf* (London: Unwin, 1964), pp 11–70, p. 18; Roger Lancelyn Green, *Andrew Lang: a critical biography* (Leicester: Ward, 1946), p. 81; in Bjorn Sundmark, 'Andrew Lang and the Colour Fairy Books', http://dspace.mah.se:8080/bitstream/handle/2043/8228/Lang%20present.pdf?sequence=1 ; Accessed 12 June 2008.

the latter was first written down (and subsequently lost) in the decades before the publication of *Gulliver*. Tom Thumb enjoyed enormous popularity in the eighteenth century, and according to Carpenter and Pritchard, it is one of a number of classic giant incidents that were put together in the late seventeenth century.[41] Henry Fielding's play, *Tom Thumb: a tragedy*, appeared in Dublin in 1730 and 1731, that is, in the years immediately following the publication of *Gulliver*. Stories of giants and little people therefore had a contemporary resonance for readers of Swift's tale. While the lawyer Francis Jeffrey points out much later, in 1816, *Gulliver*'s 'touches of satire and observation [without which] the work would have appeared childish and preposterous', he also draws parallels with the tale of Sinbad the sailor:

> A considerable part of the pleasure we derive from the voyages of Gulliver, in short, is of the same description with that which we receive from those of Sinbad the sailor, and is chiefly heightened, we believe, by the greater brevity and minuteness of the story. [42]

It is noteworthy that the exploits of Gulliver in particular but also of Swift himself became firmly embedded in folklore in Ireland, even during his lifetime. Gulliver's iconic status within folklore may have contributed to his appropriation in the nineteenth century as a model of popular nationalism,[43] and simultaneously, to the significant role he plays in textbooks, as is noted later in this essay. It may be that the intelligentsia then undervalued the capacity of fairy tale to review issues – especially as they relate to perspective and power – a capacity that critics Jack Zipes and Maria Tatar[44] have explored in recent decades.

RECEPTION IN THE NINETEENTH CENTURY

As the nineteenth century rolled on, critical opinion of *Gulliver's Travels* as it relates to childhood may be seen to fall into several categories. One, outlined above, sees it as a trivial tale that gives pleasure to an inconsequential audience, and which attracts varying level of disapproval. The century opens with Richard

41 Humphrey Carpenter and Mari Pritchard, 'Jack the Giant Killer', *The Oxford Companion to Children's Literature*, p. 277.   **42** Francis Jeffrey, *The Edinburgh Review*, 27 (Sept. 1816), 1–58, in Williams, p. 319.   **43** See Mackie L. Jarrell, '"Jack and the Dane": Swift traditions in Ireland', in *Fair Liberty Was All His Cry: a tercentenary tribute to Jonathan Swift*, ed. A. Norman Jeffares (London, 1967), pp 311–41; and Daithi Ó hÓgain, *The Hero in Irish Folk History* (Dublin, 1985), esp. pp 87–99.   **44** See for example the following indicative texts: Maria Tatar, *Off with Their Heads! Fairy tales and the culture of childhood* (Princeton: Princeton UP, 1992); *The Hard Facts of the Grimms' Fairy Tales* (Princeton: Princeton UP, 1987); Jack Zipes, *When Dreams Came True: classical fairy tales and their tradition* (London, New York: Routledge, 1992); *The Enchanted Screen: the unknown history of fairy-tale films* (London, New York: Routledge, 2011).

Payne Knight's (1751–1824) attack on *Gulliver* as a text likely to impede moral education of the young.

> We have a work, in our own language, in which the most extravagant and improbable fictions are rendered ... sufficiently plausible to interest ... those who do not perceive the moral or meaning of the stories ... I have known ignorant and very young persons, who read them without even suspecting the satire, more really entertained and delighted, than learned or scientific readers, who perceived the intent from the beginning, have ever been.[45]

A darker view is summarized in William Makepeace Thackeray's (1811–63) famous condemnation of Gulliver in Book 4 – more often than not omitted from children's editions – as 'a monster gibbering shrieks, and gnashing imprecations against mankind – tearing down all shred of modesty, past all sense of madness and shame; filthy in word, filthy in thought, furious, raging, obscene.' Thackeray believes that the book, like the *Drapier's Letters*, is the product of 'one always alone, – alone and gnashing in the darkness.'[46] Thackeray represented a growing body of writers whose objections to Swift's work was such as to question his suitability as a model of childhood for a middle-class child readership. Alexander Andrews was another such, writing in 1859 that Swift was 'one of those beings ... blighting all they pass, poisoning all they come in contact with, withering all that clings to them ... In death he was a wretched Yahoo of his race, as in life he has been a base forgery of the image of his creator.'

Still others – such as William Hazlitt and Walter Scott – were praising Swift's formal excellence, thereby stressing his suitability as a literary model. And some from very diverse backgrounds commented on his formative role, how he had shaped them intellectually: William Cobbett (1763–1835), the radical politician, for example, recalled in a public address in 1820 that *A Tale of a Tub* delighted him in his boyhood and 'produced what I have always considered a sort of birth of intellect'.[47] When sixteen-year-old William Rooney (in 1900 he would go on to co-found Cumann na nGaedheal, whose aim was to advance Irish separatist and nationalist policies, and would also co-edit *The United Irishman*) addressed the Irish Fireside Club in 1889, he complained that few people had studied the beauties of Swift.[48]

45 Richard Payne Knight, *An Analytical Inquiry into the Principles of Taste* (2nd ed. 1805), p. 285, in Williams, p. 272.   46 William M. Thackeray, *The English Humourists of the Eighteenth Century* (London: Smith, Elder, 1853), p. 40. In Robert Mahony, *Jonathan Swift: an Irish identity* (New Haven, London: Yale UP, 1995), p. 103.   47 William Cobbett, electoral address, 5 Feb. 1828, quoted in *The Life of William Cobbett*, 2nd ed. (London: Mason, 1835), p. 235, in Mahony, p. 82.   48 William Rooney, 'Illustrious Irishmen', in Philip Bradley, 'Introduction', Rooney's *Poems and Ballads* (Dublin: Gill, [1901]), p. xviii, in Mahony, p. 191.

GULLIVER, SWIFT AND EDUCATIONAL TEXTS

During the nineteenth century, Swift gained some favour among Irish speakers and nationalists who had strong and well articulated policies about the importance of education, and who devoted considerable energy to educating the young. By 1815 it is recorded that Irish-language poet Risteárd Bairéad admired Swift 'with rapture'. A parliamentary report in the First Report of the Commissioners of Education in Ireland in 1825 indicates that the *Drapier's Letters* formed part of the curriculum of hedge schools,[49] where anti-imperial values often held sway. Two decades later the journal of the Young Ireland movement, *The Nation*, annexed Swift to its cause of educating the Irish people, crediting him with rescuing 'our popular poetry ... and [giving] it a vigour and concentration which it has never wholly lost. During his lifetime it became a power in the country; the obscure precurser of a free press.'[50] Denis Florence McCarthy (1817–1882) sees Swift as a father-figure for rhetorical boldness,[51] and rhetoric was an important feature of a nationalist education.

Swift's appearance on official school curricula and in school textbooks from the mid-nineteenth century on is evidence that he has been elevated to canonical status and put to the task of the formation of imperial and national-colonial identity. He featured, for example, in books prepared for use in national schools, among them *Biographical Sketches of Eminent British Poets ... Intended for Teachers, and the higher Classes in Primary Schools*. The book places Swift unequivocally on the side of the establishment: he was, according to Robert Mahony, 'an inveterate opponent of the claims of Catholics and Dissenters to an equality of political power. The important services he rendered to Ireland at a very critical period of her history, are admitted by Irishmen of every party and every creed.' Mahony further suggests that 'the 1849 schoolbook addressed the question of his modern relevance, ultimately implying that his historical function possessed an enduring potential.'[52] By contrast, a text produced by the Christian Brothers in 1859, *Historical Class-book*, changes the emphasis, and, in one of the earliest of Victorian school histories designed specifically for Irish Catholic pupils, briefly notes the success of the *Drapier's Letters* in the face of English corruption. The Christian Brothers' *Irish History Reader* of 1905,[53] however, cautiously and noncommittally notes that Swift was a 'remarkable' eighteenth-century man who 'wrote very able books and pamphlets'. Martin

---

49 *First Report of the Commissioners on Education in Ireland, House of Commons Papers 1825*, xii, app. No. 221, p. 555; P.J. Dowling, *The Hedge Schools of Ireland* (Dublin: Talbot Press, 1935), p. 156; Dáithí Ó hÓgáin, *The Hero in Irish Folk History* (Dublin: Gill and Macmillan, 1985), p. 96. In Mahony, p. 185. **50** *The Nation*, 2 Aug. 1845, p. 698. **51** Mahony, p. 98. **52** Ibid., p. 100 **53** Christian Brothers, *Historical Class-book: comprising outlines of ancient and modern history, adbridged from Dr. Fredet, with outlines of English and Irish history* (Dublin: Powell, 1859). Christian Brothers, *Irish History Reader* (Dublin: Gill, 1905).

Haverty's popular Irish history of 1860 is laudatory, in that it asserts that Swift 'practically separated' himself from his own people and 'employed his great powers as a writer to uphold the interests of Ireland against the hostile influence of the British cabinet', thereby achieving unprecedented popularity.[54] After the foundation of the Irish state, Timothy Corcoran, the professor of education at University College Dublin whose influence at all levels of education was overwhelming, unequivocally condemned Swift as 'this foul brute and callous bigot'.[55] Aodh De Blacam throws up his hands in his 1934 school history: Swift is 'incomprehensible – a sceptic who was a cynic ... a hater of injustice, yet a cynic, often obscene - a genius who dies mad'.[56] Yet two decades later James Carty's *A Class-book of Irish History* approves a version of Swift's Irishness based on his social observations and economic exhortations.[57]

As its experience both as a popular book and within educational texts in Ireland shows, unlike many other 'classics', which, when abridged for children, lose their status as adult books or become reclassified as canonical texts, *Gulliver's Travels* has continued to lead parallel lives. It survives as a living, ever-evolving children's story, reinterpreted and reinvented regularly in multiple media (edited/abridged text, interactive text, textbook, film, television drama, DVD, etc.), and an academic text with particular historical, social and political resonance, especially for Irish scholars, such that it transcends its status either as classic or classroom resource.

EDITORIAL INTERVENTION

Pruning and bowdlerizing have been the price of this success with younger readers. As the views expressed by the commentators reviewed above suggest, Swift's satire was deemed either beyond or unsuitable for children, and the complex semantics it created were the first to go in the majority of texts. More to the point was the abhorrence by the genteel juvenile book-buying public of the physicality that is so marked a feature and a theme of the book. Noel Perrin identifies five categories of expurgation. The first is the practice of reducing the book to tales of Lilliput and Brobdingnag, or in many cases, just to Lilliput. This bypasses the difficult issue of how to treat the apparent misanthropy of Book 4, and the repulsiveness of the Yahoos. The second category is a bland retelling: Perrin credits Padraic Colum (1917) and Alfred Blaisdell (1886) with such

54 Martin Haverty, *History of Ireland: ancient and modern* ([Dublin], 1860, 1861, 1865, 1875). **55** [Timothy Corcoran] 'Donal MacEgan', 'Stephen Gwynn on Jonathan Swift', *Catholic Bulletin*, 23 (Dec. 1933), 1004, in Mahony, p. 152. **56** Aodh de Blacam, *A First Book of Irish Literature: Hiberno-Latin, Gaelic, Anglo-Irish, from the earliest times to the present day* (Dublin: Talbot Press, 1934), in Mahony, p. 153. **57** James Carty, *A Class-book of Irish History* (London: Macmillan, 1956), pp 43, 55.

versions. Then there are the elaborate illustrated editions, which he sees as appealing to adolescence: those illustrated by Arthur Rackham and John Hassall are good examples; fourth are schools' editions, such as Routledge's new edition in 1868, 'Carefully edited by a Clergyman' (J.L., that is, James Lupton) or '*Gulliver's Travels* ... Abridged ... With introduction, notes, glossary, questions, and subjects for essays, by G.C. Earle ... With illustrations by Charles E. Brock' (1909); and, finally, expurgated editions for a general audience. Of these Harriet Beecher Stowe's edition of 1873, as part of *A Library of Famous Fiction Embracing the Nine Standard Masterpieces of Imaginative Literature* is probably best known. She writes that 'Swift's genius commands our admiration, but his works should never be introduced into the home-circle save in such revised and cleanly editions as the present one'.[58]

CHILDREN'S GULLIVER IN EUROPE

In many cases, the earliest translations of *Gulliver's Travels* are geared towards children, with the result that critics regularly state the need to reclaim the book for adults, and display dismissive attitudes towards children. Filipina Filipova baldly states that 'For most Bulgarians ... Gulliver ... [is] a memorable freak who never quite makes it into the adult world.'[59] In the early decades of the century, Italian publishers and readers, writes Flavio Gregori, 'mutilated and maimed (... "castrato", literally "gelded") it into a thin booklet'. Writing as recently as 2005 about the Italian situation, Gregori comments that 'the majority of [the] abridgements confirm that *Gulliver's Travels* was downgraded to mere children's literature, "along with the Fairy Tales and the Robinsons".'[60] Michael Düring cites thirty different children's versions in Russian, published between 1844 and 1990,[61] many of which replace the first-person narrator with an omniscient narrator, and at least one revises the ending so that Gulliver is a philanthropist.[62] A Romanian critic, Mihaela Mudure, suggests that the priorities of nation-building may be behind some receptions. In her view, 'a national culture ... still in its infancy [such as the Romanian]' may not be comfortable with *Gulliver's* misanthropy, and as a result found 'an infant's Swift' easier to swallow.[63]

58 Harriet Beecher Stowe, 'Introduction', *A Library of Famous Fiction Embracing the Nine Standard Masterpieces of Imaginative Literature* (New York: Ford, 1873), p. 16. 59 Filipina Filipova, 'Swift's reception in Bulgaria', in Real (ed.), *Reception of Swift in Europe*, p. 238. 60 Flavio Gregori, 'The Italian reception of Swift', in Real (ed.), *Reception of Swift in Europe*, p. 37. Gregori quotes Luigi Di Marchi from the introduction to the 1892 edition, *Viaggi de Gulliver in Alcune Remote Regioni del mondo* (Milan: Hoepli, 1892), p. xii, in Real (ed.), *Reception of Swift in Europe*, p. 37. 61 Michael Düring, 'From Russian "Sviftovedenie" to the Soviet school of Swift criticism: the Dean's fate in Russia', in Real (ed.), *Reception of Swift in Europe*, pp 170–213, p. 206. 62 Ibid., p. 206. 63 Mudure, in Real (ed.), *Reception of Swift in Europe*, p. 249.

A more positive outcome of the diverse history of translation is that the book becomes a children's classic throughout Europe: all the editions that appeared in Italy during the high period of children's literature between 1864 and 1899, for example, were for children, resulting in the book being established as a children's classic.[64] Some 200 children's editions of *Gulliver* have been identified in Germany.[65]

Gulliver arrives in European translation mainly in the nineteenth century, but there are exceptions. In 1727, almost as soon as it appeared in English, Pierre-Francois Guyot, Abbé Desfontaines, translated it into French where it enjoyed considerable success as a philosophical, satirical and allegorical text. Over a hundred different versions subsequently appeared in France between 1815 and 1898, including numerous abridged, revised and bowdlerized versions.[66] Indeed, Desfontaines took considerable liberties while translating the first edition, and his preface draws attention to a long list of weaknesses he perceives in Swift's text, which he claims to put right. Among these are some that indicate his dismissive attitude to the young; he disapproves of details that are, he writes, 'puerile' (*'des détails puerils [et] des réfléxions triviales'*).[67] According to one critic, Benoit Léger, editors and publishers of the various translations in the nineteenth century sought to infantilize Gulliver and to efface his essence.[68] In 1838 a highly successful version containing 206 illustrations by Jean Ignace Isidore Gérard, known as Grandville, was published for children; it displays his keen observations of character combined with a fantastic imagination. Another of the earliest countries to produce a children's version was Denmark, where the Lilliput episode was published in 1768. The first version to appear in Norwegian was for children, in 1869.[69]

One critic, the Sterne scholar Giovanni Rabizzani, writing in 1913 in Italy, highlights the book's pessimism and warns that children should stay clear of it,[70] so echoing sentiment expressed in the Anglophone world of the nineteenth century. In the 1930s, edited extracts from the book found their way into Italian school texts. Once its 'immodest and unruly' aspects are brought to heel, it is found to be an appropriate vehicle for teaching English.[71] In Spain, the first children's edition appears in 1841 and there, as elsewhere, the first two books are the most often adapted.[72] In the 1920s it is included in a Spanish series of The

---

64 Gregori, in Real (ed.), *Reception of Swift in Europe*, p. 37.   65 Real (ed.), *Reception of Swift in Europe*, p. 3.   66 http://ccfr.bnf.fr/portailccfr/servlet/LoginServlet.   67 P.F.G. Desfontaines, *Voyages de Gulliver* (Paris: Guérin, 1727), vol. 1, p. xv.   68 Benoit Léger, 'Nouvelles Aventures de Gulliver a Blefescu: traductions, retraductions et rééditions des *Voyages de Gulliver* sous la monarchie de Juillet', *Meta*, 49:3 (2004), 526–43, p 526.   69 Nils Hartmann, 'Swiftian presence in Scandinavia: Denmark, Norway, Sweden', in Real (ed.), *Reception of Swift in Europe*, pp 142–55, p. 145.   70 Gregori, in Real (ed.), *Reception of Swift in Europe*, p. 43.   71 Ibid., p. 45.   72 José Louis Chamosa González, 'Swift's horses in the Land of the Caballeros', in Real (ed.), *Reception of Swift in Europe*, pp 57–78, p. 59.

Best 100 Works of Children's Literature, and the anonymous introductory essay, apparently unaware of its racial prejudice, comments that: 'The sharp-tongued book is so imaginatively and pleasantly composed that for two centuries all white children have amused themselves with this account of voyages to the lands of the dwarfs and the giants, without suspecting the dark background from which it arose.'[73] Portuguese versions for children began appearing in 1864, and follow the well-established pattern of excision of scatological elements and simplification of narrative approach.

A version adapted by Leyguarda Ferreira in 1945 takes a strongly patriotic line: the Lilliput episode, for example, refers to the strengths of small countries – such as Portugal. A 1955 edition was commissioned by the Portuguese government, while a 1966 version, prepared as part of a series of classics designated for either boys or girls, is included in the girls' category, along with Charles Perrault, E.T.A. Hoffmann, Hans Christian Andersen and Jacob and Wilhelm Grimm. This version unexpectedly retains the episode in which Gulliver urinates to extinguish a fire in Lilliput.[74] *Gulliver* first came to Polish children in 1893 and thereafter in several editions. During the period of dogmatic social realism beginning in 1949 (and continuing to 1956) an 1892 Polish children's edition was reissued and reprinted several times.[75] The first versions to appear in the Czech language were for children, and date from 1875. Czech modernism led to some several editions for children in the first decade of the twentieth century.[76] Adaptation for children began to appear in Hungarian from 1865 and according to Gabriella Hartvig, it is now 'one of the favourite books for children and young adults'.[77]

ILLUSTRATION

Given that Swift's 1727 version of *Gulliver's Travels* contained maps and illustrations, and given the book's focus on fantastical subject matter and the very visual theme of perspective, it is not surprising that its visual potential appealed to publishers who doubtless saw its commercial possibilities. The legend of an early, undated chapbook edition published in Glasgow indicates that it is 'embellished with beautiful coloured plates'. Newbery announces its children's version contains 'cuts' (woodcuts). An edition printed in London for printers P. Osborne, T. Griffin and J. Mozley in 1785 (entitled *The Adventures of Captain Gulliver, in a Voyage to the Islands of Lilliput and Brobdingnag*, 'from the works of

73 Ibid., p. 62.   74 Jorge Bastos da Silva, 'A Lusitanian dish: Swift to Portuguese taste', in Real (ed.), *Reception of Swift in Europe*, pp 79-92, p. 85.   75 Michael Düring, 'No Swift beyond Gulliver: notes on the Polish reception', in Real (ed.), *Reception of Swift in Europe*, pp 156-69. 76 Michael Düring, 'Detecting Swift in the Czech lands', pp 214-23.   77 Gabriella Hartvig, 'The dean in Hungary', in Real (ed.), *Reception of Swift in Europe*, pp 224-37, p. 225.

the celebrated Dean Swift') is also 'adorned with cuts'. Early children's versions were likely to have been hand coloured. In France, Grandville, a predecessor of the surrealist movement, did a series of engravings in an 1838 version that established it firmly within French children's literature. Other French artists to meet its challenges included Hippolyte Chevalier, alias Gavarni (1862); Adolphe Lalauze (1875); Albert Robida (1904); and J-M-G Onfray de Breville ('Job') (*c.*1900). Willy Planck's 1907 version, *Gulliver Reisen*,[78] is probably the best-known German illustrated edition.

Among the British illustrators to respond to *Gulliver* are Charles Edmund Brock (1894); Gordon Browne (1886); and possibly best known, Arthur Rackham (1900). Rackham's sinister quality, which was evident in his water-colour images of Grimms' tales, is again used to good effect, as are his unsettling perspectival shifts. Possibly one of the most controversial illustrated editions is Thomas Morten's from 1865, which substantially plagiarized John Gordon Thompson's edition (1864) but amplified and enhanced it. Paul Golden has judged Morten's 'fine line and disconcerting whimsy' memorable.[79] The influence of Art Nouveau is evident in the highly successful edition John Hassal did for Blackie's in 1910. His use of bold colour, lack of clutter and absence of shadow, combined with a small person's perspective, serves to empower his little readers. Savile Lumley uses a similar palette but with more conventional results.[80] In 1917 Willie Pogány, the Hungarian-born artist who worked in the United States, executed a series of fluid line drawings, endpapers and exotic and extravagant coloured tip-in colour plates for Padraic Colum's Macmillan version for the American market. In the majority of the representations cited, Gulliver is depicted as an affluent, solid citizen, a suitable model for middle-class children.

Not all illustrations of *Gulliver* likely to appeal to children may be found in children's editions. Cavan County Library commissioned the artist P.J. Lynch to paint murals in its new library buildings depicting Swift's links with Cavan, and details of the local landscape are rescaled as both Lilliput and Brobdingnag. (The new library was completed in 2006.) In general, children's versions of Gulliver's voyage to Lilliput are more likely to be depicted than his other voyages. It is noteworthy that images intended for an adult audience often situate him in Brobdingnag. One such representation is James Gillray's cartoon etching of 1803 entitled *The King of Brobdingnag & Gulliver*, which shows the king staring intently at Gulliver through a magnifying glass. An oil painting of Richard Redgrave's (1804–88) *Gulliver's Travels* is at the Victoria and Albert Museum, London.

78 Jonathan Swift, *Gullivers Reisen ins Land der Zwerge und Riesen und auf die schwebende Insel. Translated and adapted for the Young by F. Klein.* Illus. Willy Planck (Stuttgart: Weise, 1907). **79** DNB http://www.oxforddnb.com/view/article/19340?_fromAuth=1   **80** Savile Lumley (illus.), *Gulliver's Travels* (London: Gawthorn, 1950).

More recent French illustrators of children's *Gullivers* include Jean Reschofsky (1973), Kelek (1996) and Marthe Seguin-Fontes (1994). Among Italian illustrators are Aleardo Terzi and Attillio Mussino. Swiss illustrator Joseline Pache did an edition in 1978. One recent text that engages with the satirical intent of the original is Martin Jenkins and Chris Riddell's Kate Greenaway-prizewinning *Jonathan Swift's Gulliver*. Riddell is a political cartoonist and here he caricatures Tony Blair and directs his barbs at New Labour. A linguistics scholar who is having his ear tweaked bears a distinct resemblance to the former Prime Minister: a neat topical parallel to the carica-turing of Walpole as Flimflam, prime minister of Lilliput, in Swift's original. This is proof, if needed, that children's editions need not be drained of the original's satirical impact.[81]

Film versions run the gamut from irony through instructionalism to cutesiness, and are geared primarily towards child-viewers. The first film of *Gulliver* was made in France in 1902 (and released in the US in 1903), and is entitled *Le Voyage de Gulliver à Lilliput et chez les géants*. It was adapted and directed by Georges Méliès. The Russian Aleksander Ptushko, with A. Vanichkin, directed the next, entitled *The New Gulliver* (1935), and Ptushko wrote the script with Grigori Rosha. This film is as notable for its sophisticated puppetry as for its communist ideology. Hollywood's Fleischer Studios and Paramount Pictures responded to the success of Disney's *Snow White and the Seven Dwarfs* with *Gulliver's Travels* (1939), directed by David Fleischer.[82] Jack Sher uses Ray Harryhausen's 'Superdynamation' photographic process when he directed *The Three Worlds of Gulliver* (1960). Although Peter Hunt's 1977 attempt, with Richard Harris as Gulliver, combines live action with animation, it makes few demands on its viewers. The tale attracted Cruz Delgado who made a Spanish animation, *Los Viajes de Gulliver*, in 1983. Among the television mini-series is *Gulliver in Lilliput* (1982) starring Frank Finlay and Elisabeth Sladen, produced in the Britain by the BBC, and scripted and directed by Barry Letts. *Gulliver's Travels* (1992) was an animated television series starring the voice of Terrence Scammell. Charles Sturridge's 1996 version starring Ted Danson as Gulliver urinating on the flames in Lilliput and John Gielgud as the Lagadon scientist extracting sunlight from cucumbers shows the tale retaining its satiric edge despite the compression and the limitation of narrative strands that screen conventions demands.

Such success as *Gulliver's Travels* enjoyed since 1726 was bought at the price of expurgations, excision, elision and erasure. Censors focused mostly on bodies, or more precisely, torsos, and especially sexual organs; body odours; and bodily

---

81 See Valerie Coghlan, in Máire Kennedy (ed.), *Reading Gulliver: Essays in celebration of Jonathan Swift's classic* (Dublin: D. City Pub. Libraries, 2008), pp 66–92.   82 This film has entered the public domain, and can be downloaded at no charge from the Prelinger Archive at http://www.archive.org/details/prelinger.

functions, such as urination and defecation. Even eating may be problematic. Perrin cites one edition of the book, the Rand-McNally from 1912, which omits 200 passages instead of the hundred or so deletions that he considers common-place. Perrin calls on an unidentified source to explain this: Swift's name, he quotes, 'echoes through history ... as the clerical exposer of human frailties in a manner to call forth only innocent mirth.' Perrin simplifies: 'innocent mirth' is far from Swift's mind.

CONCLUSION

From the moment of its publication, *Gulliver's Travels* 'cracked the mould of secure mental boundaries'[83] and crossed class, age, gender and geographical barriers. It became a children's book before the category was invented, as Zohar Shavit has noted,[84] through circulation in chapbook form, which was widely read by children, and it was popular from the beginning of the nineteenth century in editions marketed specifically for children. It has been perceived as an appro-priate formative influence on the young by instructionalists, and by imperialist, religious and nationalist educators, and it has raised the hackles of at least as many more. In time, it became an instrument of empire-building in the British Isles in the nineteenth century and in Communist Eastern Europe in the twentieth - and of anti-imperialist nation-building, especially in nineteenth- and twentieth-century Ireland. It was formalized into school curricula in the second half of the nineteenth century. By then it had been recognized as a children's classic, and widely translated. Translations in particular tended to erase much of the satire, as it reinvented the tale within a particular genre – fantasy, or adventure, for example. Nonetheless, the text rarely remains monogeneric.[85]

Gulliver's Travels also formed part of the leisure reading among all classes, for very young children and for those in the young adult category, and enjoyed wide popularity throughout Europe. The price of the success was at best severe pruning, more often down to the first two books of the original, and in many cases to the Lilliput episode. At worst editing was characterized by crude reduc-tionism. Despite the book's widespread popularity, as the nineteenth century wore on, its perceived misanthropy was met with animosity and repulsion. That it is often categorized as a fairy tale may be seen as an attempt by its critics to denigrate or disarm it. The manner in which it is dismissed as 'childish' offers some insight into then current dismissive attitudes to children. Illustration became an integral part of many editions as the tale was adapted to trends that

83 Andrew Carpenter, 'Jonathan Swift (1667–1745)', in Seamus Deane (gen. ed.), *The Field Day Anthology of Irish Writing*, vol. 1 (Derry: Field Day, 1991), pp 327–30, p. 329. 84 Zohar Shavit, 'Translation of children's literature as a function of its position in the literary polysystem', *Poetics Today*, 2:4 (1981), 171–9, p. 173. 85 Ibid.

included the aesthetic movement and later the popular market. However, illustration retained the possibility of additional complex strands of meaning.

One question central to this essay but with implications that go beyond it is how to assess the book's impact on its young readers. As Michael De Certeau suggests: 'We must first analyze [a text's] manipulation by users who are not its makers. Only then can we gauge the difference or similarity between the production of the image and the secondary production hidden in the process of its utilization.'[86] *Gulliver's Travels* refuses to allow itself to be the normative literary event of a political, cultural or literary elite or a means of instruction for children: it disrupts and exacerbates the logic of enlightenment rationality. Its transmission within multiple reading domains has underlined the manner in which it is more and other than a 'scriptural' text[87] (the term is De Certeau's), monopolized by authoritative interpreters such as teachers, intellectuals, academics, critics and parents. Its history underlines the impact of 'great books',[88] confirming Jonathan Rose's thesis that they have been more influential than popular literature on literate members of non-elite classes. It is also evidence that reading was disseminated not in a hierarchical way but 'through a web of cultural institutions and personal networks that were often created and controlled by common readers.'[89]

Latterday critics can only speculate as to what happened when young readers encountered versions of *Gulliver's Travels*, since we have limited evidence of their reaction and few specimens of their books survive (the more youngsters read them, the more likely they were to perish). Official meaning makers such as educators (including designers of curricula), scholars and parents strove to monopolize interpretation and used *Gulliver* as a 'cultural weapon'.[90] However, children, in common with other readers across social classes, also engage in what De Certeau calls 'the silent, transgressive, ironic or poetic activity of readers … who maintain their reserve in private and without the knowledge of the "masters".'[91] The impact of reading is not confined to the agenda of instructors. De Certeau sees it as consisting of 'drifts across the page, metamorphoses and anamorphoses of the text produced by the travelling eye, imaginary or meditative flights taking off from a few words, overlapping of spaces on the militarily organized surfaces of the text, and ephemeral dances'.[92] In other words, it can be a subversive process, a voyage through an emancipatory space, a site of transgressive, disruptive power.

The *content* of *Gulliver* – a fantastic traveller's tale – encourages what De

86 Michel de Certeau, *The Practice of Everyday Life*, tr. Steven Rendall (Berkeley, CA, 1988), pp viii–xi. 87 Ibid., p. 169. 88 Jonathan Rose, 'Rereading the English common reader: a preface to the history of audiences', *Journal of the History of Ideas*, 53 (1992), 47–70, p. 57. 89 William J. Gilmore, *Reading Becomes a Necessity of Life: material and cultural life in rural New England, 1780–1835* (Knoxville: Uni. Tennessee P., 1989), p. 55. 90 De Certeau, *Practice of Everyday Life*, pp 171, 176. 91 Ibid., p. 172. 92 Ibid., p. 165.

Certeau terms deterritorialization. More than any other body of readers, children, as marginal members of literate society, 'move across lands [metaphorical and real] belonging to someone else'. De Certeau's argument continues with a simile that underlines both the pleasure and freedom that come with being outside the power structure: unauthorized readers resemble 'nomads poaching their way across fields they did not write, despoiling the wealth of Egypt to enjoy it themselves'.93 Ellen Gruber Garvey refines De Certeau's argument by replacing 'poaching' with 'gleaning'.94 Gleaners gather the remnants of the crop from the field in the wake of the more orderly and mechanical process of harvesting. Children both glean and filch authorized and transgressive meanings on the basis of a collection of signs that the (reinvented/abridged) text presents. Within that semantic process a child-reader 'deterritorializes himself [sic], oscillating in a nowhere between what he invents and what changes him ... to read is to be elsewhere ... to constitute a secret scene, a place one can enter and leave when one wishes.'95 What possibilities emerge from the free play of the trope of the voyage and the voyaging self, between the tale and the social context in which it is read, between Gulliver's voyage and other popular odysseys the child reader has encountered?96 This free flow of meaning-making not only has implications for the formation of personal identity, but, combined with the adaptations to Swift's original text that are a feature of children's editions, ownership, a matter fundamental to the structure of society since the eighteenth century, is called into question. And yet, the children's *Gullivers* are exemplary consumer products; and consumerism is the foundational concept on which property ownership is built. Produced as children's texts the various versions of *Gulliver's Travels* are necessarily adapted to appeal to consumers. That very act of adaptation also interrogates traditional hierarchical readings: semantic power is now in the hands of the consumer of the product. Reading is then predicated upon, and promotes, an erotics of reading, to borrow Susan Sontag's concept.97 In summary, young people's readings of *Gulliver's Travels* have the potential to be complex and contradictory.

Notwithstanding the bowdlerization, the excisions, and the attempts to restore stability to the narrative voice that are features of children's versions of a very adult satire, one fundamental element remains unchanged. The issue of proportion is the subject matter of the book, regardless of the adaptation, and it exposes the folly of what is considered to be the ideal relationship between 'rational man', the pinnacle of creation, and the world he believes he has shaped. Parables of incomprehension and partial vision abound in *Gulliver's Travels*. It

93 Ibid., p. 174.   94 Ellen Gruber Garvey, 'Scissorizing and Scrapbooks: nineteenth-century reading, remaking and recirculating', in Lisa Gitelman and Geoffrey B. Pingree (eds), *New Media, 1740–1915* (Cambridge, MA: MIT Press, 2003), pp 207–28.   95 De Certeau, *Practice of Everyday Life*, p. 170.   96 See ibid., pp 173–4.   97 Susan Sontag, 'In place of hermeneutics we need an erotics of art', *A Susan Sontag Reader* (New York: Vintage, 1983), p. 95, p. 104.

seems that vantage point is crucial to defining what is preposterous and what is momentous. What is enormous and important can seem tiny and insignificant, depending on the survey point. Walter Scott noticed in 1814 that 'by assimilating our ideas of proportion to those of his dwarfs and giants, [...] Swift renders lively and consistent a fable, which, in other hands, would only have seemed monstrous and childish.'[98] For Scott, Swift's retention of 'ideal' concepts of proportion is what prevents implausibility. Monstrosity and childishness are, after all, distortions of the idealized adult vantage point.

One might consider the issue of the ideal proportion also as it pertains to the relationship between rationality and physicality, and this too is the subject of the unexpurgated (rather than the sanitized children's) text of *Gulliver's Travels*. Although Gulliver is suffused with disgust and repulsion at humanity by the end of the story, the *book* is less judgmental. The very details that some sought to erase from children's books – the defecation, the urination, the breasts – are stated plainly, and in the kind of detail that has created a narrative admired for its plausibility by critics as diverse as Walter Scott and Payne Knight. Gulliver's disgust may be interpreted at one level – as Seamus Deane has done[99] – as a satire on the growing materialism of Swift's age in which the bourgeoisie was well established, on the sense that the spiritual had become debased. In Book 4 reason, since it has cut adrift from morality and humanity, has gone mad, as it has for the speaker in 'A Modest Proposal'. When intelligence is elevated into a virtue while moral discrimination becomes a vice, the world has become a mad place, and the perspective that has allowed this to happen is skewed. When a satire such as *Gulliver's Travels* is put in the hands of small, younger readers, a new perspective – a proto-Lilliputian perspective, within which the structures of Enlightenment rationality play a more modest part – is brought to bear on the world of *Gulliver*. With that alternative perspective of the young and less powerful come alternative proportions, since it is in the eye of the beholder that the proportion is perceived.[100] So put in the hands of the young, *Gulliver's Travels'* satirical exposé of the limitations of Enlightenment rationality is carried a step further.

---

98 Walter Scott, *The Works of Jonathan Swift, DD, Dean of St Patrick's*, Dublin 19 vols, 2nd ed. (Dublin, 1814), in Williams, p. 311. 99 Seamus Deane, lecture delivered at the Keough-Notre Dame Irish Seminar, Dublin, July, 2003. Deane's comments on perspective have substantially informed this paragraph. 100 How childhood is constructed in Swift's work is further examined in M. Shine Thompson, 'Jonathan Swift's childhoods', *Éire-Ireland* 44 (1 and 2), Earrach-Samhradh/ Spring-Summer (2009), 10–36.

Contributors

JOY ALEXANDER was a secondary school English teacher for twenty years before taking up her present position in 1995 as a lecturer in education in the School of Education at Queen's University Belfast, where she has responsibility for the training of prospective English teachers. She has published a number of articles on matters relating to English teaching and on children's literature.

AEDÍN CLEMENTS is the Irish Studies Librarian at the Hesburgh Libraries, University of Notre Dame, Indiana. She has worked as a librarian in Ireland, the Gambia and the United States. She is completing a dissertation on poets and the Irish language, under the patient supervision of Western Michigan University's English Department.

VALERIE COGHLAN, librarian at Church of Ireland College of Education, Dublin, is co-editor of *Irish Children's Literature: new perspectives on contemporary writing* (Routledge, 2011). She co-edited *Bookbird: an International Journal of Children's Literature* (2005–2009) and is a former review editor of *Inis*. A founder member of the Irish Society for the Study of Children's Literature (ISSCL) and of Children's Books Ireland, she served as board member of the International Research Society for Children's Literature and is a past president of IBBY Ireland.

CORALLINE DUPUY wrote her PhD on nineteenth-century Gothic fiction. Her research interests include the Gothic, children's fiction, detective novels and translation (French-English). She now works in the National University of Ireland Galway where she teaches literature and the French language at under-graduate level.

MICHAEL FLANAGAN is a lecturer in Popular Media Studies in All Hallows College (DCU). He has an interest in the influence of popular culture on children and his publications in this field include 'Republic of virtue – *Our Boys*, the campaign against evil literature and the assertion of Catholic moral authority in Free State Ireland', in Linda King and Elaine Sisson (eds), *Ireland, Design and Visual Culture: negotiating modernity, 1922–1992* (Cork: Cork UP, 2011).

MARNIE HAY lectures in Irish history at University College Dublin and Trinity College Dublin. She is the author of *Bulmer Hobson and the Nationalist Movement in Twentieth-Century Ireland* (Manchester: Manchester UP, 2009).

ANNE MARIE HERRON is an An Foras Feasa Fellow at St Patrick's College Drumcondra, and is supported by the Irish Research Council for Humanities and Social Sciences. She is currently completing an interdisciplinary doctorate that addresses the role of memory in the work of Eilis Dillon and includes a related digital resource. She is the author of an English-language programme for primary schools and stories for emergent readers.

ANNE MARKEY teaches in the School of English at Trinity College Dublin. Her research focuses on the intersections between Gaelic traditions and Irish writing in English and on the representation of childhood in literary texts. Reflecting these interests, her recent publications include *Patrick Pearse: short stories* (Dublin: UCD Press, 2009); *Children's Fiction, 1765–1808* (Dublin: Four Courts Press, 2011) and *Oscar Wilde's Fairy Tales: origins and contexts* (Dublin: Irish Academic, 2011).

SHARON MURPHY is an assistant lecturer in the English Department, St Patrick's College, Drumcondra, where she contributes to the teaching of the MA programme in Children's Literature. Her monograph on the works of Maria Edgeworth was published by Four Courts Press in 2004. She is currently working on a study of the official provision of libraries to nineteenth-century British soldiers, and has published a number of articles on this subject in journals and essay collections.

CIARA NÍ BHROIN lectures in English in Coláiste Mhuire, Marino Institute of Education, Dublin. She is interested in identity and ideology in Irish children's literature and has published on the works of Maria Edgeworth, Lady Gregory, Eilís Dillon, Elizabeth O'Hara and Siobhán Parkinson. She is a founder member and former president of the Irish Society for the Study of Children's Literature and an IBBY (Ireland) committee member.

JANE O'HANLON is education officer with Poetry Ireland/Éigse Éireann. She is undertaking a Doctorate in Education with St Patrick's College, Drumcondra (DCU). She has an MA in Children's Literature from St Patrick's College, Drumcondra (2003) and an MA in Women's Studies from University College Dublin (1997). Her current research interests are in the area of arts and education.

EMER O'SULLIVAN is Professor of English Literature at Leuphana University in Lüneburg, Germany. She has published widely in both German and English on comparative literature, image studies, children's literature and translation. *Kinderliterarische Komparatistik* (Winter 2000) won the International Research Society for Children's Literature Award for outstanding research. An English language version, *Comparative Children's Literature* (London: Routledge, 2005), won the Children's Literature Association Book Award. *Historical Dictionary of Children's Literature* (Lanham MD: Scarecrow Press) came out in 2010. She is currently co-writing a book on children's literature in foreign language teaching.

MARY SHINE THOMPSON has co-edited three previous volumes in the Studies in Children's Literature series. She was a founder member of the Irish Society for the Study of Children's Literature and former chair of Poetry Ireland. She has contributed to the MA programme in Children's Literature at St Patrick's College, Drumcondra (DCU). Her publications are mainly on children's literature and Irish studies.

Index